HOMOCORE

HOMOCORE

THE LOUD AND RAUCOUS RISE OF QUEER ROCK

DAVID CIMINELLI AND KEN KNOX

alyson books
los angeles
Celebrating Twenty-Five Years

MANUFACTURED IN THE UNITED STATES OF AMERICA.

THIS TRADE PAPERBACK ORIGINAL IS PUBLISHED BY ALYSON BOOKS,
P.O. BOX 4371, LOS ANGELES, CALIFORNIA 90078-4371.
DISTRIBUTION IN THE UNITED KINGDOM BY TURNAROUND PUBLISHER SERVICES LTD.,
UNIT 3, OLYMPIA TRADING ESTATE, COBURG ROAD, WOOD GREEN,
LONDON N22 6TZ ENGLAND.

FIRST EDITION: AUGUST 2005

05 06 07 08 09 **a** 10 9 8 7 6 5 4 3 2 1

ISBN 1-55583-855-3

COVER DESIGN BY MATT SAMS.

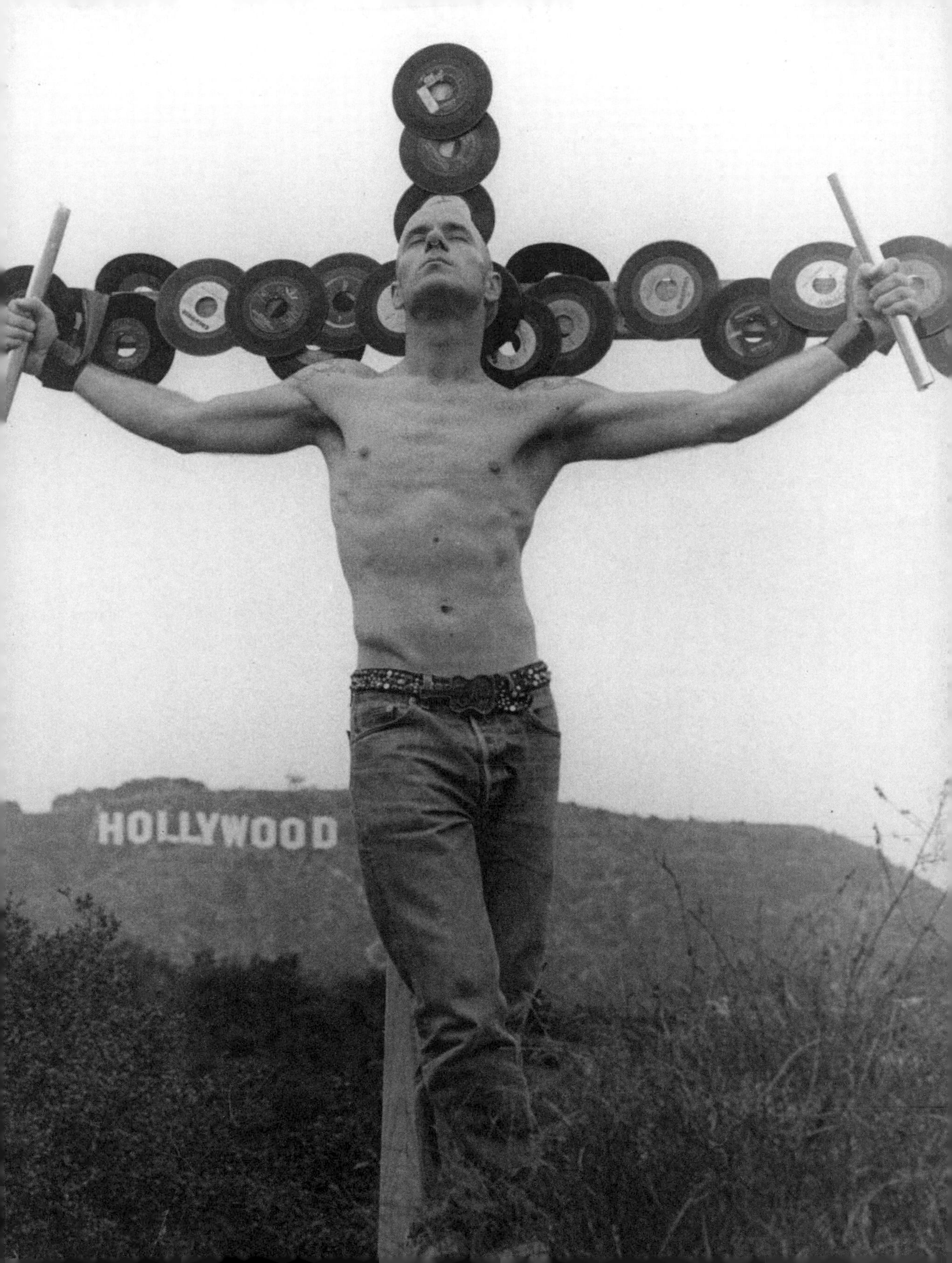
HOLLYWOOD

CONTENTS

PROLOGUE

SUMMER 1996, LOS ANGELES: WHEN THE SUN GOES DOWN AND LOS ANGELES'S UBIQUITOUS NEON SIGNS CAST THEIR LIVELY GLOW OVER SUNSET BOULEVARD IN WEST HOLLYWOOD, THE SCENE CHANGES FASTER THAN THE Z-3S AND HUMMERS ZIPPING DOWN THE FAMOUS THOROUGHFARE. THE THRONGS OF CELL PHONE-CLUTCHING INDUSTRY TYPES HAVE ABANDONED THE SIDEWALK CAFES THAT DOT THE BOULEVARD TO HEAD TOWARD THEIR HOMES IN THE HOLLYWOOD HILLS.

Tonight the Strip is alive with a crowd of young and restless rock fans who are milling about in front of the Viper Room. Cliques of trendy 20-somethings lean against the front wall of the nightclub and practice their best James Dean poses. They drag on Marlboro Lights while they wait for the next act on tonight's multiband lineup to set up and start rocking.

An eclectic roster of some of L.A.'s more popular local bands promises a packed house. Included on the bill is the homocore group Extra Fancy, an uncompromising, hard-rocking quartet composed of three straight guys—bassist D.A. Foster, guitarist Mike Hateley, drummer Derek O'Brien—and an out and outspoken, edgy queer front man and songwriter, Brian Grillo. The band has amassed a cult-like following with its mercilessly melodic hard rock tunes that expertly fuse elements of punk, pop, and rock. Grillo's lyrics unapologetically address topics such as S/M and gay leather sex ("Yes, Sir"), and he has composed a searing rock ballad about confronting a lover after becoming infected with HIV ("Seven Years Ago").

On the sidewalk in front of the club, a cheap bouquet of flowers and a stray candle sit to the right of the front door. They have been left by a fan to remember River Phoenix, whose shining star crashed on this very spot on Halloween night, 1993, after he attended a Red Hot Chili Peppers concert where he loaded up on a lethal mix of hard drugs.

Ironically, Extra Fancy (a band that coincidentally first hit the Hollywood scene in 1993) kicks off its set with its antidrug crunch-rock anthem, "Benzedrine Shuffle." The packed-to-capacity room is energized with a sweaty, sexy energy emitting from a crowd composed primarily of hard-edged queer rocker boys and a few tough-looking lesbians with varicolored hair—some sporting pink triangle tattoos and multiple piercings.

When the band kicks into the next song, "What I Have," a sonic assault about same-sex attraction, fists are raised and pump to the beat as the crowd chants the anthemic chorus. When lead singer Brian Grillo gets to the line "I won't tell my man I love him…somebody might be listening. They kill the ones they fear…" a jarhead jock standing a few feet from the stage begins heckling him. Apparently the jock's a curious straggler left over from the earlier crowd who came to see the first band, a forgettable frat-rock trio.

Most of the crowd is too immersed in Extra Fancy's raucous rock spectacle (complete with a blond Bettie Page-type go-go girl gyrating atop one of the amps) to even notice the jeers from the jock, who seems to think it's important to let Grillo know he's not a fan. Things get ugly quickly after the jarhead yells out the word "fag" one time too many while flipping the bird to Grillo.

Without warning, midway through "Yes, Sir," the band's front man slams his mike to the floor and leaps off the stage in the direction of the heckling homophobe. The other band members are perplexed but don't miss a beat as they stretch the song into an impromptu jam session, providing an adrenaline-pumped soundtrack to a chase scene that has Grillo racing through the crowd toward the heckler, who hurriedly makes his way toward the exit. Grillo, who's shirtless and clad in only tight leather pants and boots, chases the coward out of the club and down Sunset Boulevard.

A few moments later, Grillo returns with sweat from the chase dripping off his shaved head and onto his chest. He saunters back to his place on the stage as the band ends its jam session. He laughs coolly and announces, "Couldn't catch him." Then, looking like an alterna-rock general, Grillo waves his arm and signals the band to charge into the next song. The crowd goes wild. But it's hard to tell if they're cheering because they recognize the opening chords of the band's hook-laden signature song, "You Look Like a Movie Star, Honey" or to give props to homocore rock's sweaty, shining hero. The self-confident smile on Grillo's face proves that he doesn't care why the crowd is cheering. He's just glad most of the people in the room are on his side.

That was the summer of 1996. Much has changed in the world of queer-oriented rock and roll since that night at the Viper Room. Although Extra Fancy has since disbanded and Brian Grillo has embarked on a solo career, the band—along with other brave pioneering queer-oriented bands from New York to San Francisco like Tribe 8, Team Dresch and Pansy Division—has left an indelible mark on mainstream music. Along the way, these bands have not only inspired a new generation of politically charged queer rockers but also given birth to homo-core, a fiercely independent music genre that embraces pride, passion, and power chords and that continues to blaze a path of liberation through the often stodgy institutions of rock and roll.

CHAPTER 1

Music for the Masses

EMINEM IS A PARADOX. THE MORE HE RAPS ABOUT THE PAINS AND FRUSTRATIONS OF BEING INFAMOUS, THE MORE INFAMOUS HE BECOMES. HE HAS BUILT A MUSIC EMPIRE WITH HIS RHYTHMIC RANTS ABOUT HOW TOUGH LIFE IS FOR A STREET-SMART PUNK FROM DETROIT WHO MANAGED TO MUSCLE HIS WAY INTO HOLLYWOOD AND POP MUSIC WHILE STRUGGLING TO MAINTAIN STREET CREDIBILITY AND INTEGRITY AS HIS WALLET GETS FATTER BY THE BEAT. AND HE SEEMS TO THRIVE ON CONTROVERSY. NOT SINCE AXL ROSE HAS A MUSICIAN CAUSED SUCH A FUROR AMONG GAYS AND LESBIANS BY PEDDLING INSENSITIVE AND CONFRONTATION-AL MATERIAL TO THE MAINSTREAM MASSES, ESPECIALLY TO THE EYES AND EARS OF IMPRES-SIONABLE TEENS.

"What really bugs me about Eminem is that I think he's smart enough to know better," says Jon Ginoli, front man for the all-gay rock band Pansy Division. "He identifies himself as the underdog, the one who was picked on. But does that give him compassion? No—he turns around and bullies people who are lower than him in the pecking order. The way he uses the word 'faggot' is very calculated—in hip-hop code he's 'keeping it real.'"

While maintaining that he is merely fronting a loosely autobiographical but essentially fictional character named Slim Shady (a jaded street-smart trailer-trash tough guy who was raised in a soulless urban society), Eminem has been publicly protested by gays. He has managed to provoke a heated response from both fellow pop stars and the media watchdogs at the Gay and Lesbian Alliance Against Defamation. And as unpleasant as it is to admit, gays have helped Eminem acquire mass media exposure merely by reacting so vocally to his caustic music (which proves, once again, that even bad press is good press).

On the other hand, we really had no option but to protest and publicly denounce the rap star. It's nearly impossible not to get heated and take things personally after hearing a statement like "My words are like a dagger with a jagged edge that'll stab you in the head whether you're a fag or lez… Hate fags? The answer's 'Yes,'" which is rapped in rhythm over an arresting loop in Eminem's "Criminal" from his multiplatinum 2000 disc *The Marshall Mathers LP.* The hip-hopper even has the gall to respond to the homophobia controversy surrounding him by stating in the same song: "Homophobic? Nah. You're just heterophobic."

"From the day Eminem's *The Marshall Mathers LP* was released, GLAAD has worked toward a singular goal: to increase public awareness by initiating a high-profile national dialogue about the impact of hate lyrics and the continued glorification of violence against lesbian, gay, bisexual and transgender people," said GLAAD news media director Cathy Renna in a public statement. "Our campaign and public dialogue is not, nor has it ever been, about restricting or curtailing anyone's speech. If anything, this has been about more speech, not less. It's been about injecting the reality of prejudice, hate, and violence against our community into the mainstream consciousness, showing firsthand the powerful role popular culture plays in shaping attitudes and beliefs toward lesbian and gay people."

When the National Academy of Recording Arts and Sciences honored Eminem's music with four Grammy nominations later that year—and when gay icon Elton John decided to perform with the controversial hip-hop star at the ceremony's worldwide telecast in 2001—GLAAD and nearly a dozen other activist groups staged a protest outside the 43rd Annual Grammy Awards ceremony in Los Angeles. GLAAD had organized a similar demonstration the previous year when the raucous rapper performed at the MTV Video Music Awards in New York.

"We're always concerned when either women's organizations or civil rights groups or groups that represent gays and lesbians are upset by anything our organization does," said then-NARAS president Michael Greene to RollingStone.com in response to the public backlash against Eminem. "But I think you have to take a look at the role of art in this society. Part of what it's supposed to do is provoke…. We certainly don't condone the message, but it is a curious situation when probably the most repugnant recording is also, in some ways, the most remarkable," Greene said of *The Marshall Mathers LP*, which won a golden gramophone for Best Rap Album of 2000. The outcome, of course, elated Eminem's fans and further stoked the ire of GLAAD and of gays and lesbians in general.

As gay men, avid music fans who dig Eminem's music, and as the authors of this book, we were emotionally caught somewhere in the middle regarding this controversy.

"Ironically enough, the first time I heard 'Criminal' I was on Santa Monica Boulevard in the heart of L.A.'s gay ghetto of West Hollywood, listening to my Discman while walking home from purchasing *The Marshall Mathers LP* at Virgin Records," says *Homocore* coauthor David Ciminelli. "When I heard the line about brutalizing a 'fag or lez,' I quite literally stopped dead in my tracks. Then as if to deflect a sucker punch to the senses, I hit the stop button on my Discman and stood there dazed and con-

fused for a few seconds as his words raced through my head. I was dumbfounded and angry that I had just spent nearly $20 to have an artist I admired boast that for no apparent reason he condones or even encourages viciously attacking another person because of his or her sexual orientation.

"The visceral reaction prompted by 'Criminal' is the same response I, and I imagine most gay rock fans, had after hearing the controversial Guns N' Roses song 'One in a Million' from the band's 1988 sophomore release, *Lies*," Ciminelli continues. "When Axl Rose got to the line 'Immigrants and faggots, they make no sense to me. They come to our country and think they'll do as they please, like start some mini-Iran or spread some fucking disease,' I slammed my hand down on the stop button of the stereo.

"After both bouts with musical homophobia I seriously considered marching back to the record store where I purchased the discs to ask for a refund. I never made it that far either time. Instead I replayed the tracks, listened more intently to each artist's lyrics from the beginning of the song and then, though still cringing, tried to understand their viewpoints. After playing the songs over a few times, surprisingly, I started to appreciate the quality of song craft and the raw honesty of the lyrics. Both songs were hard to ignore. In fact, I quickly grew to appreciate the unabashed delivery of emotion of the artists and now consider 'One in a Million' and 'Criminal' to be among the best work in the respective careers of Guns N' Roses and Eminem."

It was somewhat easier to comprehend where Eminem's and Rose's rather ignorant, redneck viewpoints about gays were coming from because both preface their controversial statements with brief but telling autobiographical lyrics. In "One in a Million," Indiana-born Rose, who later famously moved to Hollywood and became a superstar, confesses that his limited views of big city life originate from a guy who at heart is still just a naive "small-town white boy." Like ground-breaking hardcore rap groups N.W.A. and Public Enemy, which gave voice to oppressed minority groups around the same time that "One in a Million" was causing a stir, Rose was addressing the sociopolitical and cultural issues that were most personal to him. In that, he spoke for a particular segment of a blue-collar youth generation that had felt voiceless until the rise of a band like Guns N' Roses. The same phenomenon is true with Eminem.

"Eminem's antics are nothing more than putting a voice and a face to the worst American youth attributes possible—the 'bad kid next door' routine," says Pansy Division bassist Chris Freeman. "It's just button-pushing for shock value to sell records, but I like him. I have all of his records and I think he's an exceptional talent and truly gifted.

"We all have to lighten up and be able to take a joke, even when it doesn't seem like one to us," continues Freeman. "If we're truly going to have equality, we can't keep being so overly sensitive. People are going to have their own opinions regardless of any politically correct restrictions. It's up to us how we take it. If you make a fuss, it just lets them know that they got to you. And that you let them get to you. By calling yourself a 'fag,' or whatever, it disarms them. 'Yeah, I'm a fag. So?' What's the worst thing they could say after that? If there's actual physical danger involved, then that's a whole other story."

"I do think music can influence hate," adds Alicia Warrington, out drummer with the Kelly Osbourne Band. "There are so many testosterone-fueled bands these days that only talk about their hate and anger. It gets annoying after a while. There is only so much of that type of music that you can take without getting angry yourself. If I am having a bad day, or if I am in a bad mood and listen to angry music, it only fuels the fire.

"I think that a lot of artists forget that there are a lot of impressionable people listening to their music," Warrington goes on.

"There are a lot of kids and teenage boys who might not be able to distinguish between someone rapping to make money and their reality. But it's not just rap either.

"On the flip side," says the Saginaw, Mich.-born musician, "I also think that a band like Pansy Division can create a more tolerable environment in rock circles. It took a lot of courage for Pansy Division to stand in front of Green Day crowds [as a support act on Green Day's 1994 tour], singing songs about being a 'Bad Boyfriend' and songs from [the gay-oriented album] *More Lovin' From Our Oven.*

"Some people may get angry and not want to hear about it, but at least they now realize that there are gay musicians, and hey! there are gay musicians that are going to sing gay-themed songs. Not all gay professionals, including myself, wear their pride flag on their sleeve, but we're still here. We're not backing down and we're not hiding our lifestyles anymore. People are afraid of what they aren't exposed to on a regular basis.

"With openly gay professionals, it makes people think, *Wow, I really liked Rosie O'Donnell before I found out the she's a homo. Maybe I should still support her, like I have since she first came onto the scene.* The same with Ellen DeGeneres, Melissa Etheridge, and countless other professionals.

"In this day and age, we just can't have people feeling afraid to be open about their sexuality. Things need to change."

Regardless of whether it's sometimes abused, freedom of speech is a basic American right that gives all of us an opportunity to understand the motives and mindset of people who piss us off. It also nurtures a fast-growing subculture of musical artists like Pansy Division who are countering the homophobia of some mainstream artists, note for note. As MTV and popular radio continue to chart career paths for the likes of controversial superstars like Eminem, a brash and brave cohort of pioneering out bands is rocking the roofs off of clubs around the world. They hope that one day their viewpoints and unique brand of music—respectfully dubbed "homocore"—will be just as eagerly embraced by mainstream audiences. Queer identity and lifestyle issues make gay musicians distinct from their straight colleagues, and it's precisely this feeling of "otherness" that many of these artists want to freely express. At the same time, they want to earn the respect of their peers—gay and straight alike—not as a "gay novelty bands" but as serious, talented musicians.

Until homocore music is as commonplace on the radio as a U2 hit, there will be artists like New York's Triple Creme, Los

Angeles's IamLoved, and Chicago's Three Dollar Bill who will be pulling into clubs, cranking up their amps, and rocking just as hard as their hetero contemporaries. They are the pioneers who are creating an environment that is safe for bands and band members to be out, proud, and really (sometimes *really*) loud.

CHAPTER 2

From the Page to the Stage

THE TERM "HOMOCORE" WAS FIRST BANDIED ABOUT IN THE MID 1980S IN MUSIC CIRCLES FROM TORONTO TO LOS ANGELES AND SAN FRANCISCO AFTER POPULAR CANADIAN UNDERGROUND FILMMAKER AND PHOTOGRAPHER BRUCE LABRUCE AND G.B. JONES (DRUMMER AND VOCALIST FOR THE DYKECORE BAND FIFTH COLUMN) COINED THE TERM AS A JOKING REFERENCE TO A QUEER ROCK COMMUNITY THAT DIDN'T EVEN EXIST AT THE TIME.

"In the mid '80s I started a fanzine called *J.D.s* with G.B.," says LaBruce. "We pretended that there was a movement of gay punks in full swing in the city of Toronto—where we lived—creating havoc and stirring things up. Actually, it was just me, G.B., and my friend Candy, who had a fanzine of her own called *Dr. Smith*. 'Homocore' was the name of this fictitious movement of gay punks that we created to make ourselves seem more exciting than we actually were."

LaBruce and Jones published their first issue of *J.D.s* in 1986. The queer punk zine would exist for nine issues over the next five years. The imaginary homocore scene depicted in *J.D.s* was an imaginative, exciting mix of sex, porn stars, nonconformity, and punk rock—with music taking precedence over gay issues.

"We were tired of the gay scene, which even in the '80s was starting to get assimilationist and conformist, so we turned to punk rock because it seemed more glamorous and political and aesthetically pleasing," says LaBruce. "But we quickly discovered that the punk scene had become sexually conventional and boring, betraying its early roots. The original punk movement, like the early gay movement, was about embracing all sorts of nonconformist behavior. Early punks experimented with homosexuality, bisexuality, transsexuality, and trisexuality—they'd try *anything*. But by the mid '80s, with the advent of hardcore and the mosh pit, a new era of machismo and heterosexual rigidity was ushered in. It was like being back in high school, with the sissies and the wallflowers standing on the side while the jocks took center stage. We started *J.D.s* as a reaction against the increasing sexual conformity of both the gay and punk movements."

While LaBruce and his colleagues were challenging the conformity of punk rock and the assimilation of gays, the term "homocore" was becoming the choice catchphrase in the mainstream gay media. It soon came to define a bold rock movement that, unlike LaBruce and Jones's confabulation,

did actually begin to flourish in the late '80s and early '90s. The movement was kick-started by loud, reputable, and rockin' gay- and lesbian-identified bands that were tired of having their creative expression stifled by the archaic dynamics of rock and roll, where it seemed virtually every other rock song was about a horny guy trying to seduce a young girl.

In the early '90s, the changing music culture in the Pacific Northwest was beginning to produce a new brand of music, and Southern California's club scene—which was still reeling from the recent death of heavy metal—was also giving way to new trends in music, including the burgeoning homocore scene. While Seattle was experiencing musical nirvana and tending its own sound garden to spawn one superstar grunge band after another, Los Angeles's hip alterna-rock-centric Silver Lake neighborhood was welcoming to its club stages raucous rockers like Extra Fancy, Glue, Black Fag, and Slojack. These were hard rock bands with an unabashed pro-gay attitude and at least one pivotal band member who was out and outspoken.

Longtime Hollywood scenester Brian Grillo was the sole gay member of rock quartet Extra Fancy, but as he was the band's key songwriter and front man, his viewpoints shaped the lyrical expressions of the band.

Regardless of whether everyone in the predominantly straight group identified with the term, Extra Fancy became one of Los Angeles's most popular "homocore" acts.

By the mid '90s, Extra Fancy was fielding offers from indie and major record labels, and at least a dozen other gay- or lesbian-identified bands had sprung from the shadows to take part in the homocore movements centered in Silver Lake. The Eastside arts scene welcomed out rock bands to the stages of neighborhood leather bars like the Faultline, which hosted the gay rock event HARD on Saturday nights. Even trendy straight clubs got in on the act. Promoters at the Garage launched Sucker, a popular weekly queer punk-rock beer bust hosted by outrageous art-rock musician and drag vamp Vaginal Crème Davis. Every Sunday the Garage was packed with punk kids wearing pride pins on their Team Dresch and Pansy Division T-shirts.

Soon a network of like-minded gay and lesbian artists began to form. While the sounds of homocore bands like Extra Fancy and Superfiends blared on the Los Angeles music and club scene, Pansy Division and lesbian quartet Tribe 8 carried the homocore flame in San Francisco. These Bay Area bands struck a chord with local fans like Tom Jennings and Deke Motif Nihilson, who spread the message of out punk and

rock bands in their popular zine *Homocore*—a term Jennings admits he lifted from LaBruce.

"Deke and I kind of engineered and messed with a queer-punk hybrid thing, based upon anarchist principles, discordant silliness, distaste for de facto separatist gay culture, and a burning desire to get laid," says Jennings with a laugh. The enterprising rock fan was spurred on after visiting Toronto to attend the 1988 Anarchist Survival Gathering, a culturally diverse, queer-positive gathering of activists and artists where he rubbed elbows with fellow fringe artists like Nihilson and Bruce LaBruce. After Nihilson relocated from Kansas City to San Francisco, he met up again with Jennings and the two men launched *Homocore*. They developed their concept from *MaximumRocknRoll*, a popular underground, gay-inclusive but predominantly straight punk zine that they felt wasn't giving enough attention to gay rock musicians.

"A major impetus for *Homocore* was *MaximumRocknRoll*, the ponderous nightmare of all punk zines," recalls Jennings. "It had an incredibly active letters column, and queer punks wrote in, but they were usually marginalized. Though to *MaximumRocknRoll*'s credit, they were not actively discouraged; there was no fag bashing from the staff. This was a major good thing, though it sounds slight."

From September 1988 until the pair decided to fold the zine in February 1991, *Homocore* grew from a Xeroxed Bay Area curiosity into a widely distributed periodical that was helping to chart the history of the gay-oriented rock scene. The new networking possibilities and cross-pollination of ideas spawned artist collectives from San Francisco to Vancouver, Canada.

"We were both getting burned out and decided to make it a pretty corpse and quit while we were ahead," Jennings says of the decision to fold *Homocore* after three years. "I think the timing was good. When we started there was virtually nothing queer-punk in the way of zines. By our last issue, there were many."

In the do-it-yourself world of punk, there were plenty of other young activist-artists like Jennings and Nihilson who wanted to get their voices heard and show their support for homocore music by producing their own indie periodicals. Toronto's homocore fans had two hugely popular zines to choose from: LaBruce and G.B. Jones's *J.D.s* and *Bimbox*, a showcase of progressive prose for riot grrrls. The Chicago-based *Thing* kept Midwestern kids in the queer rock loop. And in Silver Lake, Vaginal Crème Davis waxed poetic in her offbeat and hard-to-resist punk zine *Fertile*

LaToya Jackson, which became an underground sensation in Los Angeles's queer club scene.

Along the way, these punk pioneers assembled a coterie of like-minded writers and musicians who supported and promoted each other's work and who began collectively hosting queercore concerts and events. As the visibility of homocore artists increased, they began to earn recognition and support from local chapters of national gay activist groups like ACT UP and Queer Nation.

By 1991 the growing influence of gay punk zines was hard to ignore. On May 25 of that year, the Randolph Street Gallery in Chicago hosted Spew: The Queer Punk Convention, the first-ever national gathering focusing on gay punk zines. Chicago's chapters of ACT UP and Queer Nation were both involved with Spew and staffed information tables alongside display areas hawking zines, gay-themed books, music, and T-shirts from queer bands.

Music fans weren't the only ones covering the queer scene with their various zines; musicians themselves were getting into the act too. Queer rocker Kim Kinakin divided his time between fronting various bands and acting as editor-in-chief and creative mastermind behind *Faggo*, a lauded zine that he launched in 1999 from his home base of

Vancouver, Canada. *Faggo* featured an international roster of contributors (and the fact that its creation was inspired by a stroke magazine couldn't have been any more rock and roll in spirit).

"A friend of mine exposed me to old *In Touch* porn magazines," Kinakin says of the impetus for *Faggo*. "This was the late '70s and early '80s, and *In Touch* had a lot of rock and roll references—mostly punk, thanks to editor Jim Yousling—and I just felt that there needed to be a continuation of that mix of punk and queer. *Teen Fag, Positron,* and *Kill The Robot* were some of the other queer zines that inspired me. I was also very inspired by Mike Bullshit, who wrote an editorial column in *MaximumRocknRoll* in the late '80s. He was the first gay hardcore kid I ever read about and related to."

A true Renaissance man, Kinakin abandoned desktop publishing for cut-and-paste production and laced his queer punk periodical with sharp humor, keen observations of the homocore scene, and first-person accounts of how rock and queer culture shaped his formative years. Included in the debut issue of *Faggo* was the essay "Rob and Me," Kinakin's personal account of attending his first-ever rock concert—an eye-opening, life-changing Judas Priest show—at age 13. Ironically enough, nearly two decades later,

Judas Priest front man Rob Halford came out publicly on MTV.

"Rob and Me"

It was the spring of grade 7—it stuck out with such an impression that it's hard to find the right words to describe it now. I was only 13. I had to leave my softball game early—it might have been a game to some sort of mini-playoffs or something that important, I dunno. I didn't care. I know my teammates felt let down that I ditched them for a rock concert. They didn't understand how I could sacrifice a game of good 'ol baseball for an evening of maniacal metal. And they didn't know how much this rock concert would change my life. Neither did I.

I wasn't prepared for the concert that would lead me not just into a world of underground musical mayhem but also into a world of underground sensual sex.

Rob Halford made me into the fag I am today!!!

And I can't thank him nearly enough. You see, the first concert of my life wasn't just any concert. It was Judas Priest, a band led by a (closeted) faggot front man—Rob Halford. Destiny was in effect and I was wrapped so tightly around its finger that I

11

was unaware of its powerful and long-term impact for years yet to come.

Everyone at elementary school was quite flabbergasted that my parents even let me go. This wasn't just any rock band, this was a heavy metal band, and not just any heavy metal band but Judas Priest. I mean really, the toughest, loudest, and most brutal band at that time. Everyone heard the rumors of the bikers that went to Judas Priest shows—the fights, the drugs, and of course, the leather!

I can still remember being scared shitless as I walked into the Pacific Coliseum with my best friend, Danny—the mood was so-o-o strong. I didn't even look at anyone for fear of what might happen if I looked at someone the wrong way. And yes, the bikers were there in full effect, the biggest, toughest motherfuckers I'd ever seen. Hordes of young head-bangers like myself filled what seats the biker-dudes and babes had left for us to sit in.

When the lights dimmed, the crowd cheered, and slowly the smell of pot filled the coliseum. It was so thick that even I felt stoned. Within a few minutes a dull drone began echoing through the stacks upon stacks upon stacks of amplifiers—it was the

eerie intro to the song "Love Bites." Upon recognizing it, the crowd instantly became quiet, their attention focused, locked in anticipation and suspense. Then, with a blast of light and a burst of sound, the riff-raging metal sliced mercilessly through the air and into our ears. The crowd screamed louder than ever before. I was in complete awe.

Judas Priest had taken the stage, and the man of all men, Mr. Halford, in full leather gear and studs, was the front man, screaming so tough that even the meanest of the biker boys paid attention. Oh yes, I remember still—how could I forget? The world of metal and S/M had just entered my life. Song after song of macho and metal, denim and leather, sex and satisfaction, Rob was force-feeding heavy metal to the audience with a subliminal sexual twist—it was tough, it was raw, it was heavy—and he was gay. Later he drove out onto the stage on a Harley Davidson motorcycle with sweat glistening from his muscular chest and arms. Was I the only closeted fag screaming when he revved the engine? I think not.

The day I actually read a quote from Rob Halford declaring his faggotry on MTV, I was on cloud nine. To know I had subconsciously followed his footsteps into the delights and merriments of man-love was a moment of blissful enlightenment—I felt complete. My two worlds of man-sex and metal had finally collided!

Rob, thank you. Outing yourself to a world of metal was exactly what was needed—not all fags listen to Madonna or sing to George Michael. You dared to go where most wouldn't even consider; I hold so much respect for you.

Judas Priest—the leather, the studs, the Harley Davidson, the short-cropped hair, the muscle, the hairy chest—I can still sing the lyrics that now hold even more meaning than before.

"Then I descend, close to your lips. Across you I bend. You smile as I sip. Softly you stir. Gently you moan. Lust's in the air. Wake as I groan. In the dead of night, love bites."

You know, for years I never understood why I was called to an early teenage world of heavy metal, what purpose it had in making me who I am today. Now it is in focus; it all seems so clear…

Heavy metal made me gay and I am proud!!!

CHAPTER 3

Outpunk'd!

"I DIDN'T REALLY FIND ANYBODY WHO UNDERSTOOD WHAT I WANTED TO DO, SO I DID IT MYSELF," SAYS MATT WOBENSMITH, FOUNDER AND EDITOR OF THE SEMINALLY INFLUENTIAL *OUTPUNK* ZINE—AS WELL AS ITS SISTER EFFORT, OUTPUNK RECORDS, BOTH OF WHICH EMERGED FROM WOBENSMITH'S ASSOCIATION WITH TOM JENNINGS'S EQUALLY IMPORTANT ZINE, *HOMOCORE.*

A newcomer to San Francisco in 1991, 21-year-old Wobensmith was still getting his bearings in the Bay Area when he fell in with Jennings and began to learn the terms "queer-core" and "homocore." Inspired by Jennings's dedication to the burgeoning scene, Wobensmith gladly accepted his invitation to help out with keeping the *Homocore* zine alive. Sadly, by the time he hopped on board, *Homocore* was at the end of its run, and its editors decided to fold the periodical to pursue other creative interests. Wobensmith, however, was already hatching a project of his own—one that would more accurately reflect the community that he wanted to be a part of.

"*Homocore* was great, and Tom managed to make a dent with it, but the people at the zine were older," he says. "I was happy to find a community, but also a bit upset to find out that it really wasn't what I felt reflected me. I was 21, and I wanted something more youth-relevant and approachable."

So in 1992, Wobensmith, who had already been releasing recordings by a few local bands under various indie monikers, started not only his own zine but a record label to go along with it. "When you do a zine, the natural extension is to put out records," he says of the joint venture. "The original fanzines were created to cover bands. I wanted to do more."

Wobensmith initially wrote the zine "like a personal diary gone public," he says. "It started out to be a way of finding other people, and then I decided that I wanted to make it more of a news zine to cover all kinds of stuff." Moving beyond stories on queercore bands, he branched off into more incendiary topics. "It became an attempt to define what the whole queercore scene was politically," he notes. "It's one thing to be known for the music, but then it's also like, 'What is the political platform that this movement rides on?' So I tried to articulate some of the views and politics of the time."

Meanwhile, with the record label, Wobensmith reveled in the opportunity to release the music from the bands that were beginning to shape the movement. He put out several seven-inch singles and albums by Pansy Division, Tribe 8, God Is My Co-Pilot, Fifth Column, Sister George, Stay-Pressed, Cypher in the Snow, the Mukilteo Fairies, and, later, Team Dresch. For Wobensmith, these musical acts represented what he felt to be the heart of the movement's artistic form. "Some people tell you that [queercore] was just about reappropriating music and putting identity politics back into it," he says. "And that was certainly a part of it, but what I realized early on was that if this

movement was going to be any better than that, it had to challenge a lot of artistic philosophies as well." Citing God Is My Co-Pilot as a strong example, he adds, "That's where the musical experimentation came into it."

Running the label was also a way for him to bridge the gap to gay youths in need of a support network. "The biggest accomplishment was getting gay stuff into avenues where you couldn't see it before," he says. "A young person in the mid '90s wasn't going to go to a gay bookstore, so the achievement was getting something into Tower Records so people could buy something based on the musical context but could also get information for themselves about being gay."

An employee in an hour-photo mart where he was making about $7 an hour, Wobensmith says he had to "beg, borrow, and steal" to find the money to put the records out, but that it was something he felt very strongly about. "I had to do it," he declares. Noting that he was also trying to overcome an alcohol abuse problem, he adds, "Being a teenager and trying to find a community of people that mirrored what was inside my head or the way I saw myself—and trying to stay sober, trying to make sense of my life—I needed to be involved in something culturally made up of people to fall in with."

During the next five years, Outpunk would come to be regarded as a definitive and instrumental part of the homocore scene—though, toward the end of its run, Wobensmith found that he was beginning to feel like something of a hypocrite. "Achieving a certain level of visibility and success in the punk and rock scenes was great, but it also felt like a cop-out," he admits. "I felt like, once I got there, it would be very easy to sit 'on the throne,' but I felt that we had to keep pushing boundaries.

"It wasn't enough just being accepted," he continues, adding that he felt the queercore scene was beginning to become far too homogeneous and derivative for his tastes. "Early on I saw that some of the same thought processes and politics of the punk scene that I'd always had a problem with were just being painted in a gay way, and that to me wasn't really much of an achievement. I really wanted to break down more barriers with musical purity, and also break down a lot of these artificial walls that get between [us] because people are stuck on one artistic media versus another."

So in 1998, Wobensmith "ditched the whole punk thing" and decided to focus his energy on backing openly gay artists who were performing electronic and hip-hop music. Under the moniker QueerCorps, he released a few albums (by electronic artist

Cyryus, for example). But, as Wobensmith notes, his new venture proved to be a lot more challenging to sell than he had hoped. "I had a very difficult time bringing my old audience that used to follow *Outpunk* into hip-hop music," he recalls. So, after a few failed attempts to get people interested in his new passion, he decided to take a break from music altogether—though he would soon return more determined than ever to realize his goal of "[throwing] out all the rules and just making gay stuff everywhere to break down racial and cultural and class and stylistic barriers."

As he had done with Outpunk, Wobensmith established a new queer label, a.c.r.o.n.y.m., and began seeking bands and signing acts whose work excited him, including—but not limited to—dance, rock, electronic, punk music, and hip-hop (affectionately coined "homo-hop"). Citing acts like Deep Dickollective, Tori Fixx, Johnny Dangerous, Cazwell and his own Deadlee (whose CD *Assault With a Deadlee Weapon* was released by a.c.r.o.n.y.m. in 2004) as examples of the sensibility he was after, Wobensmith says that the burgeoning homo-hop scene "very closely mirrors the origins and the energy of the queercore movement."

Though he is now employed on a comfortable salary with a software development company in San Francisco (which means he no longer has to beg, borrow, or steal to release the music), Wobensmith is still committed to working hard to provide openly gay artists with the resources they need to be heard. And though he says he doesn't do it for the accolades, he does concede that it's nice to get them just the same. "I meet people through work or out and about who tell me, 'I think I know you. You used to do *Outpunk*. I loved *Outpunk,*'" he says. "That happens a lot, and it's always nice." Would it be nice for the same thing to happen with his latest endeavor? With a smile and a chuckle, Wobensmith says, "I wouldn't mind."

CHAPTER 4

Fancy Dancer: The Long and Winding Road of Brian Grillo

"Self made and single.
Saint on ice, real evil.
Brand new god, spit to shine.
I'm sucking, soul sublime.
Hold my head... This trade is rough.
Self made, his bomb is timed.
Under his, under mine.
Rough trade saint, demands in blood.
Well, hey, am I worthy yet?"
—"Self Made," Extra Fancy

"The queercore movement doesn't really mean anything to me," former Extra Fancy front man Brian Grillo boldly declares over a cup of joe at the Coffee Table, a trendy café and eatery smack-dab in the middle of the funky, arty Silver

LAKE SECTION OF LOS ANGELES. "NOT TO
PUT IT DOWN, BUT I NEVER FELT LIKE I WAS
PART OF ANY MOVEMENT. I THINK IT'S GREAT
THAT [GAY BANDS] HAVE PEOPLE THEY CAN
HANG OUT WITH THAT ARE ALL GAY, BUT FOR
ME, I DON'T LIKE TO ONLY PUT MYSELF IN
CERTAIN KINDS OF CATEGORIES.

"I think they're all doing great stuff," he
adds, "but I don't really know that much
about the movement…it doesn't really mean
anything to me. I'm not immersed in it. I
never was."

These are scandalous words from the
mouth of the man who was once the driving force behind a band whose members
were touted as the messiahs of the queercore movement. Extra Fancy was the one
band that actually "broke through" the bar-
rier and landed a major-label record deal
even though its lead singer was an in-your-
face, out and proud, loudmouthed gay man
with an imposing physical presence (and
who also happened to be HIV-positive). But
talk to Brian Grillo today and it's clear that
he never had a desire to be anything other
than a performer who rocked—regardless
of his sexual orientation. "With being gay,
it's either you are or you aren't," he says.
"And either the music is good or it sucks.
It's all basics. You're either good or you're

not. If you suck, you can be gay and you
can still suck really bad. And if you're
straight, you can suck really bad too. It
doesn't matter."

Extra Fancy has left an indelible mark on
the history of homocore—though not for
the reasons the band might have hoped. In
1996, after several heated skirmishes with its
label—Atlantic Records—over content that
was deemed too controversial in the video
for its single "Sinnerman," Extra Fancy was
dropped from the Atlantic roster. The label
officially cited poor record sales as the primary reason for its decision—though the
band's debut album had been out only a
brief few weeks. Extra Fancy's rough han-
dling at Atlantic would become a cautionary
tale told to other gay bands hoping for some
kind of mainstream success.

For Grillo, however, being a "pioneer" of
the homocore movement was never something he was after in the first place. "I never
wanted to be 'the gay rock singer' or anything like that," he says. "That was never part
of my agenda. I just wanted to get out on
the stage and sing my songs."

So one wonders, then, how a man so
unwilling to allow himself to be categorized by his sexual orientation came to
stand at the helm of the queer rock movement. As Grillo explains, it's a very long
and winding road.

"I'm not about making myself invisible.
Target me for trouble, in the places
that I go.
I went down to the water, and I took
off all my clothes.
Skinheads showed up there; they're
all about breaking bones.
I never seen their girlfriends.
I guess real men run in packs.
Cops wouldn't save me; now I swim
with a baseball bat."
—"Yes Sir," Extra Fancy

Brian Grillo was born in Harbor City, Calif., and raised in Torrance, a small beach community on the southern edge of Los Angeles. From a very early age, he was drawn to performance, appearing in community theater productions of musicals and cutting the plastic records off the backs of cereal boxes. He loved the Archies, Rufus, and Chaka Khan and longed to be a member of the Partridge Family. "As a kid, that was what exciting to me," he says of pop music in the 1970s. "All those pop bands—I pretty much always wanted to do that."

Music wasn't the only thing that caught his interest. Grillo recalls being attracted to other guys at a very early age, and his sexuality eventually played a large role in the teenage rebellion that would get him tossed out of his home—twice. His parents had divorced when he was 7, and he'd remained

with his mother. Their relatively warm early relationship was strained, however, when Grillo reached his teenage years. It wasn't uncommon for Brian and his mother—who was trying to raise two other children (Grillo's siblings, sister Dominique and brother Paul, who is also gay)—to get into emotionally explosive fights around Brian's budding sexuality. "She kinda knew," he says. "I'm sure everybody figured like, with the way that I was dressing in school, that I was really different from everybody else.

"One time we were in the back yard and we got into a big fight, and she started calling me a 'fucking faggot,'" he recounts. "And this time, I'd just had enough, and I said, 'Yeah, that's right. I am.' And her mouth just dropped open and she picked up a stick and started beating me with it. And I just stood there, thinking, *You can't hurt me anymore.*"

He found it hard to stay in his mother's house after that. His sexuality and his continuing rebelliousness—as well as his growing fondness for marijuana—were too much for his mother to handle. Eventually she forced Brian to go live with his father and stepmother in Hermosa Beach. His penchant for "being different from everybody else" was reflected in the music he listened to (punk) and the fashions he wore (black goth clothes, flaming pink bowling shirts, and eyeliner). Naturally he fell in with fellow outsiders, including the guys from the legendary punk band Black Flag, whom he met through a mutual friend. The band members were renting an old 1900s church that they had converted into a rehearsal and recording space, and they had invited several of their other friends to come and live there as well. Grillo, who was ecstatic at finding others who were outsiders as well, often hung with the band members and their crew.

Grillo's desire to be different soon led to more trouble at school, with other neighborhood kids, and at home. He recalls several incidents in school where he was cornered and taunted because of his sexuality, and he eventually learned the art of fighting back as a means for survival—something that would prove useful in later years as an out rock singer. "Every night I would walk home from the church and these surfers would chase me down the street," he recalls. "And one night I took a brick and threw it through the window of their car, so they were after me and it turned into this big fight. And later my dad was like, 'Well, if you wanna look that way, then you should expect to be treated that way.' And I was like, 'Fuck you.'"

Homeless for a second time after his dad kicked him out, Grillo found himself moving in with the crowd at the church. "There were like 15 to 20 of us there, and a few other gay kids," he recalls. It was among those creative, wayward teenagers that Grillo had his first real taste of the rock and roll life. Other up-and-coming rock bands, including Redd Kross and the Disposals, would stop by to hang out with the guys from Black Flag, and eventually they took a liking to Grillo. "I just started playing music with them, and they were teaching me how to play instruments," he says. "They didn't care that I was gay."

Grillo and his pals began hitchhiking into Hollywood to take in rock shows on the Sunset Strip. "We would ditch school, hang out in Hollywood until nightfall, then we'd go see bands like Led Zeppelin or Suzi Quatro or the Runaways," he says. Before long, Grillo incorporated other activities into his trips to Hollywood, including sex with tricks and older men. He discovered a permissive and sometimes seedy new world that would eventually inspire some of his most personal music.

"When I was 16 I used to hitchhike all the way to Hollywood,
and I'd give it away to the first person who said,
'Hey come here. I love you. I wanna take you home.'

Because back then anywhere was
better than my home.
It's a goddamn beautiful world!"
—"Goddamn Beautiful World,"
Extra Fancy

In his early teenage years Grillo met
plenty of guys who wanted to get it on with
him. Sometimes he took them up on their
offers because he wanted to get laid—other
times he just wanted a place to sleep. Then,
one night, after showing up at Los Angeles's
Hong Kong Café to check out a show, Grillo
met Tomata DuPlenty, singer for the
buzzed-about rock band the Screamers. "It
was kismet," Grillo recalls. "He looked at me,
I looked at him. The next thing I knew we
were walking around in the rain in a court-
yard in Chinatown, and we kissed each
other. Two weeks later I quit my job at
Shakey's Pizza and moved to Hollywood to
be closer to him."

Eventually, Grillo's relationship with
DuPlenty started to lose its luster, and the
two men broke it off. Brian fell in with a
Hollywood punk-rocking soul band called
Ella and the Blacks. The band members
asked him to join their ranks after they
found out he had a clarinet. "I actually took
clarinet lessons in the eighth grade, and
somehow I had ended up with a clarinet,
but I didn't even really remember how to

play it," he says with a chuckle. "I was just
making noise." (His ability to lie, he notes,
would eventually lead to most of his big
breaks in music.)

Grillo joined Ella and the Blacks and
eventually wound up playing with several
other bands until, inspired by the art-house
cinemas of the time, he put together a
troupe of ragtag "street urchins" that he
dubbed the Grillo Follies. "I wanted to do a
sort of cabaret show," he says. "I used to love
the old Ziegfeld Follies movies and the old
musicals from the '30s and '40s, so I wanted
to do something like that." He began writing
a lot of music on his own, and calling on his
love of dance, he choreographed the shows
as well. The troupe performed at the Olio
Theatre on Hollywood Boulevard (now
called the Tantra), where, impressed by what
he saw, the theater's owner let Grillo and his
posse have the run of the place. After a
while, the shows started to attract
Hollywood trendsters and fellow rockers
(the Red Hot Chili Peppers and Tom Waits
were regular attendees), and Grillo reveled
in the attention. "It got my name out there,
and it got my ego built up to the point that I
actually believed I was a good songwriter
and a good performer," he says. "It took me
a few years to get it together to where I was
like, 'OK, I'm getting good at this.'"

Shortly after debuting the Grillo Follies,

Brian landed a job choreographing a music video for Luther Vandross after producers read an article about the Grillo Follies in the *L.A. Weekly* that made it sound as if Grillo was an accomplished dancer. When they contacted him, Grillo laughingly recalls, he said, "Sure, I'm a professional dancer," and the job was his. "Once again, I was bullshitting my way into something. I mean, how many punk rockers get to choreograph a video for Luther Vandross?"

Grillo made about $2,000 from the gig, and after deciding he needed a break from the West Coast to see other parts of the world, he moved to New York City, where he was lured by the creative energy. But once his funds were depleted and his landlord came calling, Grillo realized it was time for "drastic measures." So he ended up doing what many other attractive young gay boys do when they lack other means of support and they're in need of money—he used his body to earn income. He auditioned at the Gaiety Theatre, a notorious Times Square adult entertainment complex and strip joint for gay men, and immediately got a job go-go dancing. Grillo recalls that the experience was daunting at first, but, as he recounts, it opened him up to the idea of incorporating his sexuality into his music—something that would later become his defining trait in his role as front man for Extra Fancy. "I was

cute and young, and once I got past the fact that I was taking my clothes off in front of old men, the whole experience made me start to think, *Oh, this sex thing kinda works mixed with the rock and roll thing.*"

That job—and a desperate need for rent money—led him to explore other avenues for acquiring cash, and eventually he found himself turning tricks. "It was like, 'This guy is offering me hard cash to go to a bathhouse with him and fuck him,' so I did it because I didn't have any other options," he says. "I didn't really get off on it. And it didn't seem like that big a deal." Still, dropping trou for strangers was not his idea of an ideal job, and after saving up enough money to buy a new guitar, he stopped dancing and hustling to focus on his music.

By chance, he ran into a Los Angeles acquaintance, Margot Olivera, who had just been ousted as the original bass player for the Go-Go's and was about to go on tour with her new band, Brian Brain—if the band could find a guitarist. "And I'm like, 'I can play,'" Grillo laughs, "even though I'd only been playing for two weeks. I got the audition and made the band."

Brian Brain did tour, but, having gotten used to being the leader in his other groups, Grillo found it hard to blend in as part of an ensemble, and the tension soon began to take a toll on the band's cohesion. "I was

23

more of a front man, and it got to the point where I was upstaging them," he says. "It was sort of this mutual thing where I was like, 'I don't want to do this anymore,' and they were like, 'Well, we don't *want* you to do this anymore.' I was really unhappy." So, Grillo packed his belongings and headed back out west, where once again he landed in Los Angeles with an idea for a brand new band, one that would be a hybrid of all the musical styles that he'd grown up with and had been inspired by. The band would provide him with his first taste of mainstream success.

"Don't take it personally if I make restless faces
when they say the way I live my life is gonna take me to the wrong places.
See, I just wanna rock and do what I wanna do.
And I'm gonna fight the repression that I see starting to brew."
—"Nothing New," Lock Up

Back in Los Angeles, Grillo took the occasional odd job, including a stint working for a nude-housecleaning company. Determined to get his new music project off the ground, he took out ads in the local trades and began auditioning potential band mates.

The lineup for his new band Lock Up included Chris Bebe on bass, Vince Ostertadj on drums, and guitarist Tom Morello, who would later go on to bigger fame in Rage Against the Machine. Grillo and his band mates managed to lure Morello away from a "really horrifying heavy metal act" by having Bebe's girlfriend call Morello's band and pretend to be a groupie so she could get Tom's phone number. "It was a really insidious thing to do," Grillo laughs, "but he was a really excellent guitar player."

With Morello on board, the lineup really gelled. Brian and Tom did most of the writing. "He was sort of my nemesis in a way, really prodding me and encouraging me to go for the broader, more political-type stuff," says Grillo of Morello. "We were two guys who were very politically aware. Tom wanted to take on the world, and I basically decided to focus my energy on what was going on in the gay and lesbian community and be the protester for that scene." For Grillo, the desire to "speak out" was a natural extension of his childhood: "I think it had a lot to do with my mom always playing Joan Baez and Bob Dylan and all this great protest music around the house."

Lock Up's sound was different from anything Grillo had been a part of before, mixing elements of funk, punk, soul, and rap into a coherent whole.

After performing all over the L.A. scene for several years in the mid to late '80s, Lock Up finally snagged the attention of Geffen Records founder David Geffen, who signed the band to a deal in 1989 after one of his talent scouts caught it playing in Hollywood. Lock Up's new label immediately sent the band out on tour. "We just toured, toured, toured," Grillo recalls, "and played hundreds and hundreds of shows."

During this time, just before Lock Up's record was about to be released, Grillo learned that he was HIV-positive. "It was terrifying," he remembers. "Especially at that time, because there weren't the kinds of medications and drugs that they have now that are able to sustain life."

Grillo remembers the day he learned the news. "I had to go into the Gay and Lesbian Center, and the guy that was going to give me my results was sitting in this room with a poster of [notoriously non-famous Los Angeles personality] Angelyne behind his head where she's lying on her pink Corvette, and he's like, 'You've tested positive.' And all I remember is just walking out on the street and I had to take the bus home because I didn't have a car, and I just broke down and started crying."

Though Grillo says he has a "pretty good idea" who infected him ("There was this guy who used to be one of Madonna's backup singers before she got famous, who had told me his boyfriend died of a drug overdose, but had really died of AIDS," he says), he admits that he is not certain. "There were a lot of times in my life that I was really indiscriminate about who I would fuck or who I would let fuck me," he confesses. Part of that, he says, had to do with self-esteem issues he was struggling with, though a good bit of it can also be attributed to financially motivated behavior. "There were certain times where I really needed a place to stay, especially when I lived in New York, where it was like, 'Well, if I let this guy fuck me tonight, then I can sleep there and have a roof over my head.'"

Grillo's way of dealing with the news, after telling his band mates ("They were great about it," he says. "Real supportive.") was to simply forget about it. He opted not to take antiretroviral meds ("I don't believe in the American Medical Association," he would later tell Poz magazine. "I don't want to have a bunch of pills in my cabinet."), choosing instead to commit to a health-conscious, vegan diet (which he largely credits for keeping him alive to this day), and to focus all his energy on doing promotion for the band. "The record was coming out, and we had to keep touring," he says. "It was really hard, though, because we would be on the road for three months at a time and then we'd come home for a week and go out for three months again, and it wasn't easy to come by vegan food in small rural towns."

Meanwhile, back at Geffen, the label was doing what it could to sell its new band, but it had a hard time developing a marketing plan for Lock Up. The record, *Something Bitchin' This Way Comes,* had been released to little fanfare—and the absence of ripples was soon felt among the band's members. "It was the beginning of that time where [labels] stopped developing bands," Grillo says. "If you didn't make money right away, you were a liability. We came out at the time of [Geffen label mate] Guns N' Roses, so they didn't really know what to make of us. And to top it off, Hi! We had the gay singer!"

Having suffered through problems with previous bands because of his sexual orientation, Grillo had decided from the get-go that he was going to be as "out" as possible with Lock Up—though his decision didn't sit well with the label. "I remember David Geffen said to us, 'I think you should change the name of the band because it sounds like a gay leather bar,'" Grillo says. "I had to fight to keep the name of the band. I fought with them through everything.

"I remember our manager called me up one time and said, 'What are we going to do with you?'" he adds, "and I remember being

really pissed off, like, 'What does it fucking matter?' We did tours through the South, through Ku Klux Klan country, and people had more of a problem with Tom than they did with me. He couldn't get served in the clubs sometimes because he's black. It was never a problem with my sexuality, but the record label was so paranoid about it. And it was so ironic, because here's David Geffen running the whole show. But we were always a little ahead of our time, and they didn't really know how to market us.

"If you have a great label behind you, they could sell snake oil to the public," he continues. "But it was too risky for Geffen. I can understand. It was uncomfortable with me being gay. They were like, 'This is not something we want to deal with.' It was like, 'We're just going to act like it doesn't exist. We all know, we're all aware of it, and everyone loves Brian, but that's not something we're going to make a selling point of this band because it will destroy them.'"

The label didn't make a point of Grillo's sexuality at all. In fact, it didn't make much of a point of anything. A year after signing Lock Up, Geffen dropped the band from its roster, and it wasn't long before things within the group became unbearable. Creative differences between Grillo and Morello over the band's future soon began to fester. "Tom's style at the time was different from mine," Grillo says. "I wanted to do something more arty, and he was way into the metal thing." Before long, Brian decided to call it quits. "It was kind of like two brothers," Grillo recalls of his rift with Morello. "Like, 'OK, it's time to go out on your own now.'" He maintains, however, that Morello was very supportive of his decision to leave the band: "Tom was always a hundred percent behind me, because he could relate to [my struggle being gay] because of his own experience in the band."

Though the experience—and his newly acquired health issues—left Grillo feeling drained, it wouldn't be long before he would once again show up on the scene. And even he was surprised to discover what was in store for him at that point.

"Red eyes searching the TV, surfing the vultures.
Everything I see's a crime sewn up and censored.
Sell me 1990s, yeah, so sweet, same old.
I get no validation anywhere I go."
—"C'mon Louie," Extra Fancy

By 1995 the homocore movement had gained some momentum. Bay Area bands like Team Dresch were rocking music halls all across America on DIY tours, and Pansy Division had introduced homocore music to unsuspecting hetero kids in nearly every pocket of the country as part of Green Day's tour the previous year. The queercore "scene" was no longer relegated to the West Coast alone, and the bigwigs in the music industry were starting to take notice. It seemed like the perfect time for a gaycentric rock and roll band to finally break through with a major-label record deal. Extra Fancy was that band.

Formed in 1993, Extra Fancy was not "a gay band." It was, however, a band with three straight dudes fronted by an out gay singer whose intimidating appearance as a hard-bodied hard rocker and openness about his sexuality defined the band's music and politics—and eventually caught the ear of execs over at Atlantic Records. Having realized the potential in tapping into the gay market, Atlantic had established a gay music division and was looking for up-and-coming bands to sign to the label.

"Extra Fancy was a reaction to the whole [experience with Geffen Records and Lock Up]," Grillo explains, "all the anger over what had happened [with me being gay]. I wasn't as fully out in Lock Up, so I wanted to be in a band where the music was speaking about my experience as a gay man." The band's name was also a reaction of sorts, as it had been one of the "500 or so" names tossed around for Lock Up—only to be shot down by the other guys for being "too gay." "That was one of those 'I'll show them' moments," Grillo laughs.

There were other reasons for starting a new band, he says. "In the late '80s, I'd started losing a lot of friends to AIDS. It was a reaction to that, like my political stance. Like, 'Fuck you; all my friends are dying of AIDS and I'm pissed off and the way that I'm going to express it is through this band and get out there and rock and shatter stereotypes through the music.'"

To that end, Grillo's appearance reflected his new creative vision (though he initially chose to remain silent about his HIV status). Sporting several tattoos, a newly buff body, and a freshly shaved head, he was the perfect front man for a band out to break down expectations of what gay men looked and acted like. "I wanted to take more of a straight guy's stance on being gay, rather than just perpetuating the humorous stereotypes that everybody laughed at and that are very nonthreatening," he says. "I wanted to bring up some issues and scare the shit out of people, basically. Make them think."

Having recruited D.A. Foster (a former roommate of an ex-boyfriend of Grillo's, Foster had originally wanted to be part of Lock Up), Brian went in search of two other members to round out his new musical endeavor. He came across drummer Derek

O'Brien's ad in *The Recycler* and set up a meeting with him. "I did have to say, 'I have to tell you that I'm gay,'" Grillo recalls of their first meeting. "Foster didn't give a fuck at all, but Derek was coming out of the Orange County hardcore scene, and he was a little weird about it. But he knew I was really good at what I did and he knew I didn't fuck around—that this is what I really wanted to do.

"Besides, once you start playing music with people, everything else goes away," he continues. "It's like you become brothers after a while, and it doesn't matter at all."

After the band went through three different guitar players (including a lesbian named Beth), Mike Hateley—a friend of O'Brien's who, Grillo says, "really wanted to be in the band"—came on board to complete the foursome. It was simply by chance that Grillo was the only gay member, though it didn't bother him at all. "Luckily, I had three straight guys in my band who were totally down with whatever you wanted to say or whatever you wanted to talk about," he says with a chuckle. "And it was a cool time. It was very political. It seemed like the right time for that kind of band."

Grillo had already started writing songs—angry, emotional tirades and missives reflecting on his experiences as an openly gay man who had seen far too much death in his short life. With Foster, O'Brien, and Hateley all cowriting the music, Grillo put everything he had into the songs that would make up Extra Fancy's first record—and made no bones about his disenchantment with society's attitude toward gays. He tackled the alienation that gays and lesbians feel living in a predominantly hetero-defined society in the self-righteous "C'mon Louie":

"Did your dad's belt rule you the
same way it ruled me?
And in the school in the showers, do
you feel like a criminal?
I wanna tell the preacher but I know
I'm gonna lie.
He's got the blood on his hands of a
thousand suicides.
I can't be a good man in your eyes.
Everything you've got to offer don't
feel right.
Attaché...ugly wife...two kids...
long life.
Well I would rather die."

—"C'mon Louie," Extra Fancy

On "Goddamn Beautiful World," Grillo lashed out at the education system and the government for ignoring the AIDS crisis and accused them of profiting from the epidemic:

"So where are all the teachers
and the posters making the
danger clear?
I guess there's a lot more money to
be made off of ignorance and fear."

—"Goddamn Beautiful World,"
Extra Fancy

Meanwhile, the tellingly shame-filled "What I Have" recounts the plight of a man forbidden to express any kind of affection toward his partner. Its jarring rockabilly-cum-punk groove is carried along by its equally powerful lyrics:

"I won't tell my man I love him.
I won't tell my man I care.
Somebody might be listening.
They kill the ones they fear.
We sneak around at night.
We ride that lonesome train.
They shot that kid's hands off,
so he can't hold his man.
What I have.
What you have.
And what you take for granted
is what I never had."

—"What I Have," Extra Fancy

The new songs provided Grillo with a cathartic experience through which he not only purged himself of his pent-up emotions but also gave a voice to the people who were no longer with him in the physical sense. "I felt like I owed it to a lot of people who weren't around anymore," he admits. "Some really excellent, great people who were young—gay musicians that had died and who never got to be heard. I just thought, *I sort of have an obligation to do this,* and it was time. It felt good to sing those songs, but I felt like I was doing it for something bigger."

After several songwriting sessions and rehearsals, the band began performing in and around Los Angeles's Silver Lake neighborhood, earning a loyal group of fans (dubbed the "tribe") who revered Extra Fancy for its aggressive, emotionally driven, and politically oriented music—not to mention its energetic live performances. Grillo soon became known for being "the gay guy with the oil drum" after he incorporated a huge metal oil drum into the band's act—often catapulting himself off of it into the high-energy crowd.

The band eventually snagged the attention of Paul V., the manger for Perry Farrell's post-Jane's Addiction project, Porno for Pyros, who recalls watching Extra Fancy play in a few of those poorly-lit dives and music halls: "I would watch the reaction of the people when [the band] played, and they

would just light up," he says. "There are a lot of great bands that don't have that magic with the audience, but Extra Fancy did. Brian did, and that band did."

Adulation wasn't the only reaction from audiences at shows. Grillo remembers a few instances in which members of the crowd were less than tolerant of the band's message. "Every now and then you would have your idiots who had a problem with what we were doing," he sighs. "One night we were playing the Viper Room, and this guy was taunting me through the whole fucking set, and I just thought, *Here I am; I have my platform.* And I'm not really into fighting, but I just kind of felt that that was the moment I was going to show everybody that this was not a fucking act. I was like, *If this person is going to do this, I might get my ass kicked, but I'm going to go up against him and show him.*"

He continues: "So finally, I was like, *That's it,* and I remember I jumped off the stage and chased him down Sunset Boulevard. And the band was like, *What the fuck?* and just kept playing. And I ran back and got onstage and finished the set." (Grillo adds that he later ran into the same guy at a street festival in Los Angeles and received a sincere apology from him.)

Another time, the singer from a band of punk rock skinheads booked at the same venue attacked Grillo's brother, who was attending the show with a date. "My brother was making out with his boyfriend, and this singer just came up and decked him," Grillo says. "And Foster took a cigarette and flicked it into this guy's face. And I was like, *Let's get the fuck out of here.*" The band members grabbed their equipment and headed out to their van, but they were jumped on the street by the skinheads. "It turned into a free-for-all," Grillo laughs. "It was raining out on Ventura Boulevard, and they punched Foster in the face, and I just went insane. And the next thing I knew my brother is out there fighting the other guys, and then our friend Sean D'Lear [cross-dressing leader of homocore band Glue] was out there in full drag with his purse whacking these skinheads in the face, and we basically beat the shit out of them."

Fights weren't the only kind of physical contact taking place during those early Extra Fancy gigs. Once, the band ended up playing a show during one of the now-infamous O Boys orgy parties, where gay men gathered to have sex in secret locations in and around Los Angeles. As Grillo recalls, "That was pretty out of control. That was early in the day, when we had just gotten started. A friend of Derek's got us that gig, and it was unlike anything you'd ever seen. These guys were fucking all around us, there

was some clandestine drug use going on, and my friend Willy put his head through a wall. It's like, you're mixing booze, rock and roll, and sex." Naturally, Grillo says, "It turned into a riot."

Sex and Extra Fancy shows seemed to go well together. In addition to the O Boys gig, the band played at the Fetish Ball, gay leather bars like Los Angeles's Faultline, and Tom of Finland benefits where tattooed and pierced leathermen were getting tied up, flogged, and tortured in the background. Grillo chuckles, "The cool thing about Extra Fancy is that we did everything from rocking an orgy to playing the Playboy Mansion [for an AIDS Project Los Angeles fund-raiser]. I have a picture of Hugh Hefner and his kids covering their ears during our show."

In the meantime, Paul V. had become the band's manager, and he was hell-bent on getting Extra Fancy another record deal. Once the band had released an independent recording—the aptly titled *Sinnerman* on indie label Diablo Musica—Paul V. began to heavily market the group toward the mainstream press and radio. It paid off: Extra Fancy received write-ups in some of the top national music entertainment magazines, including *Details.* The band managed to raise the money to produce a $15,000 video clip for its underground single "You Look Like a Movie Star, Honey" and sent it to

MTV, where it ran on *120 Minutes*. Using that exposure as leverage, Paul V. sent the band's CD to several record labels, none of which would touch it. Paul V. remembers, "Extra Fancy got a $15,000 video on *120 Minutes* three times. To get a slot on that show was next to impossible. The video aired, and the band did a showcase, but there was not one peep from the record companies. We were handing them this amazing band with their own press and MTV play, and they wouldn't touch it."

The band kept sending the CD to record labels with little success—then Atlantic Records caught wind of it. Having just announced its brand new gay music division, the label was hungry to sign the division's very first act. When Extra Fancy's CD came in, the company jumped at the opportunity to be a pioneer in a relatively untested market—gay entertainment.

"Everybody [at Atlantic] started saying they needed the band so they could look cool so they could launch their gay marketing department," Paul V. remembers. "The only reason we went along with aligning ourselves with that was because we didn't want the gay kids who had supported this band for so long to think that we had turned our backs on that.

"We knew damn well that this was not a band for mainstream straight America," he continues. "It wasn't like, 'Market us with the Pet Shop Boys and everyone's happy.' "

The band did sign with Atlantic and set about rerecording its independent CD for a major-label relaunch. The members called in some of their friends and mentors to help out, scoring guest appearances by X's Exene Cervenka, Nymphs singer Inger Lorre, actress Susan Tyrrell, L7 guitarist Donita Sparks, and Jane's Addiction/Porno for Pyros singer Perry Farrell. Elsewhere, Paul V. fueled the fires of the publicity machine, highlighting Grillo's sexual orientation and getting the band write-ups in just about every gay publication on the stands—to the chagrin of the other three members. Grillo recalls, "They never really had a problem [with me being gay] until Paul V. started putting all the emphasis on my sexuality. They were like, 'Why is this the main focus of what we're doing?' And I can understand why they were like that. It did get kind of cheesy. It got to the point where I couldn't do an interview where it wasn't about my sex life. "I got really sick of it," he continues. "It was like, 'You know, ask me about my music and ask me about my words. I'm sick of talking about my sexiness or my bald head or how it feels to be in a gay rock and roll band. It got really insulting after a while, like, 'Aren't you even listening to the music?'

"I came from a really Okie, industrial,

working-class family and a town where you didn't really make much out of your sexuality. It was all about whether you could work as good and fight as good and fuck as good and drink as good. All this other lofty media-created stuff…it's boring to me. I just wanna rock."

Frustration with the media aside, things were moving quickly for the band. An even stronger buzz swirled around it, buoyed by the ruckus stirred up by Pansy Division's Green Day gig. The remixed, major-label version of *Sinnerman* was released to a flourish of positive reviews. *The San Francisco Bay Times* raved, "Extra Fancy have created the queer-rock hybrid or balance that many have been waiting for decades to happen, and *Sinnerman* is essential for any comprehensive collection," while *Genre* proclaimed, "*Sinnerman* rocks with raw, man-to-man lyrics and an unapologetic, wholly queer sensibility." Not surprisingly, other publications singled out Grillo for his sweaty swagger; "Brian Grillo shatters those confining gay images, striking a traditionally aggressive rock stance— including gritty vocals and an imposing presence," wrote the *Los Angeles Times*. *The Advocate* reported that "Grillo's charisma and ferociousness are impossible to ignore." National entertainment publications were equally generous in their

reviews: *Entertainment Weekly* awarded *Sinnerman* a "B+" in its review, saying, "Extra Fancy play raging, melodic punk garnished with industrial beats and rockabilly rhymes." *Rolling Stone* included the band in its 1996 year-end issue, writing, "Extra Fancy's debut CD was a standout, an inspired meld of Grillo's blistering songwriting and good old-fashioned rock."

Pleased with the critical response, Atlantic ordered a video for what was to be the relaunched *Sinnerman*'s first single, the title track. Inspired by a pre-AIDS era porn film called *Nights in Black Leather*, Grillo worked closely with the video's director, John Reiss (who'd helmed a few Nine Inch Nails videos) to conceptualize a clip that incorporated themes of morality, religion, and sexuality into an explosive three minutes that were unlike anything ever seen on television. "When I showed the porn movie to John, he totally got it," Grillo says. "But he wanted to put his own spin on it as well.

"Coming from the artist in me, I was like, 'Boy, oh, boy, I have this chance to do this tribute to an era that's been buried and devastated over the last decade because of the AIDS virus," Grillo says of his inspiration for the clip. "It was sort of the gay version of all the retro stuff that was going on at the time, but more aggressive and meaningful."

Actor Alexis Arquette, long a staple on the Silver Lake scene as a cross-dressing performance artist and musician, appeared in the clip as a repressed man of God who finds himself tempted by a scrappy, gay punk rocker (played by Grillo). As Grillo and the band chant the melodic chorus ("Oh, Sinnerman, where ya gonna run to?") over and over, Arquette eventually gives into his desire, and he and Grillo lock lips in an erotic kiss that escalates into a hot 'n' heavy make-out session—complete with clothes being ripped off each other's bodies and an "affectionate" punch delivered by Grillo meant to highlight his "bad boy" street cred. (It was Arquette, incidentally, who delivered a copy of the single for "Sinnerman"— which featured an artist's rendering of John Travolta naked with a raging erection—to the *Saturday Night Fever* star himself. Upon seeing it, Travolta urged his lawyers to serve the band with a cease-and-desist order to prevent it from printing any future editions of the single with the same cover. "We knew we were taking a chance [using that artwork]," Grillo admits. "But we put it out because it kind of summed up everything the band was about. The cool thing about it now is that it's a collector's item!")

When the video was completed, the band was elated. "I was really excited about the video," Grillo says. "I love the look of it, and we were all pretty proud of it."

When the clip was delivered to Atlantic, however, things took an unexpected turn. The band was called in to meet with label executives, who, as Grillo tells it, "were totally freaked out by the video. They were like, 'This is two guys making out, and we're supposed to sell this? We're supposed to try to get this on MTV?'"

Grillo's reaction was pure anger. "I was like, 'Fuck you. This is punk rock. This might be really upsetting to people, but it needs to be seen because it exists.' But they just weren't ready for it to be seen."

The video actually did end up on MTV—with the gay kiss intact. (The chest punch, however, was gone from the final edit because it was too extreme.) The band had scored a minor victory with its airing, but the triumph was short-lived. Right around the same time, *Rolling Stone* ran a story on queer-oriented bands and carelessly "outed" Grillo as an HIV-positive man. Grillo was crestfallen. "That was something that I really wanted to keep quiet about," he says. "It was bad enough to have the stigma of being gay that I was trying to hold the torch for, but now [there was] this other thing on top of me, so it was, like, 'Great, now I've got a torch in each hand, basically.'"

Grillo's reluctance to publicly claim his

serostatus, however, didn't last. The day the article came out, he went out for a beer with a longtime friend, Tom of Finland Foundation cofounder Durk Dehner. As Grillo remembers, Dehner told him, " 'Dude, you gotta take it like a man and stand up and use it to your advantage.' And that's when I really decided, 'Maybe I *can* be a role model for people who are terrified of being HIV-positive and show them that it's *not* a death sentence.' "

The media ran with the story, and just as Grillo's sexual orientation had dominated most of the band's press up until that point, his HIV status followed suit. "What can you do?" Grillo laughs. "I learned to be very careful with the gay press. They tend to go for trends."

The fallout from the video and the *Rolling Stone* article—and subsequent stories about Grillo's serostatus—came quickly. Atlantic went on record as supporting Grillo in his health struggles (Atlantic talent scout Darren Higman was quoted in *Poz* magazine: "Grillo's HIV status [is] not a big deal. It shouldn't be used as a marketing tool, but if we can manage to change people's perceptions about HIV and make some money, we'll be thrilled.") But Paul V. was having problems getting anyone at the label to talk with him, and the band was supposed to begin a tour in support of the record. "We

were having troubles," Paul V. says. "We couldn't find a booking agent to work with the band. The label was supposed to help us with that, but all of a sudden nobody would return our calls. It was very strange." So Paul V. booked the tour himself, and the band hit the road to play venues both gay and mainstream across the country.

"That was a really cool time for us," Grillo says. "Being able to play every single night. Being able to play in front of these huge audiences, whether they were gay or straight or whatever. We opened up for everyone from the SugarHill Gang to Evelyn Champagne King. It was unreal—having Bronski Beat show up at one of our shows in Long Beach and saying they were big fans, and Rob Halford from Judas Priest coming up to me and being like, 'I'm a huge fan of yours.' Opening for Iggy Pop and for the Cramps. Going on tour with the Buzzcocks. Like, those are my idols!"

Those gigs provided Grillo the opportunity to convince any skeptics in the audience that he was prepared to rock them silly. "To this day," he says, "the coolest time is when we opened up for the Cramps, and their crowd is pretty hardcore—Orange County skinhead-type people. And people still come up and say, 'You were that guy in Extra Fancy. You were, like, one of the best bands.' Because we got up there and we were, like, 'We're gonna kick ass as hard as this band we're opening up for.' And just in case, I always had that oil drum in front of me and those steel sticks, like, 'If you fuck with me…' "

Paul V. recalls one show in particular, a gig opening for No Doubt at an outdoor music festival sponsored by Philadelphia radio station K-Rock, that defined the band's ability to connect with its fans. "The band played on a side stage at like 2 in the afternoon," he says. "When they started, there were maybe 80 people who happened to be walking by. By the time they were finished, there were three or four hundred kids packed against that fence. And they just blew these kids away. When they were done, there were these 10- and 12-year-old kids clamoring for a sticker. Brian was signing Styrofoam cups, and we sold out of all of our T-shirts and other merchandise.

"We drove away from that thinking, *Wow, this is what it's all about,*" he adds. "It wasn't like, 'Oh, this isn't a gay band' anymore. It was like, 'This is a really fuckin' great rock and roll band.' "

Grillo recalls the show as well. "At first, I was like, 'Fuck, I have to get up in front of these, like, throngs of straight kids and do my songs,' " he says. "It was all these straight hesher boys that looked like they could kick your ass. But once we started playing, we

won them over, and they loved us. It was one of the best shows."

But when Paul V. tried to report this to the record label, the response was less than encouraging. "I got this collective, 'Yeah, so what?' " he says. He tried to get the label to secure coverage in *Rolling Stone* and *Spin,* but he was informed that the magazines weren't biting.

Since he was going to be in New York on business for Porno for Pyros, Paul V. decided to do some Extra Fancy footwork himself. "I figured I would make my presence known, so I was actually calling radio stations myself," he says. What he heard surprised him: "Stations were saying they weren't getting the single, or if they did, it wasn't being worked by the label. Everything at the time was all about [new Atlantic acts] Jewel and Sugar Ray."

Paul V. did encounter a few stations that were privy to Extra Fancy's music. In particular, one station in Colorado had moved the "Sinnerman" single into top-five rotation after getting several listener requests for the song. "So I'm trying to get a hold of the rock guy over at Atlantic, trying to get them to service the song to rock radio, and I was pulling my hair out," Paul V. says. "I was thinking, *Why am I not getting a response on this?*"

The response came two days later when

he received a call from Atlantic: The band was being dropped; the reason attributed to a housecleaning of more than 30 bands that were not making money for the company. The news came only *eight* weeks after Atlantic's release of *Sinnerman*.

"Hey, little babe, won't you come over?
We'll put out our hands on the boulevard.
Street corner prophet, dressed like a warrior.
Your 15 minutes come and go.
Hey, little wild one, don't break up the moment.
All we gotta do is let it go."
—"Just Like That," Brian Grillo

Confusion and anger followed in the wake of Extra Fancy's untimely departure from Atlantic Records. Grillo did an interview with *Poz* magazine in which he boldly declared, "Whether [Atlantic] dropped us because I'm positive doesn't matter. They fucking lied to us."

The band members weren't the only ones who felt let down. Paul V. minces no words when he describes the label's decision to drop Extra Fancy as "performing an abortion on the band—and they didn't even sterilize their wire hanger to do it.

"I don't have many kind words for Atlantic or the people who were there at the time," he says, "because no one ever gave us a tangible, real reason for the band getting dropped. It was like, 'These things happen.' It was eight weeks to the day [after the CD came out] that the band was dropped!" Paul V. exclaims. "Alanis Morissette didn't break in *eight weeks*. There's no way in hell to determine anything about any artist in that amount of time. You could not telescope it and say, 'Oh, well, it's not getting played, so we're going to dump it.' So when that happened it literally pulled the rug out from under us."

"I felt I'd been screwed," Grillo admits, adding that the experience soured him in terms of what to expect from corporate America when it comes to gay culture. "It forced my eyes wide open, because I could see the kind of music that they promote to gays. It has to be some awful house music where they know they'll make a shitload of money off the White Party or whatever. Or it's a lesbian folk-rock artist, which is totally nonthreatening. But you put a guy up there with a bald head who looks like he'll take two steel poles and fuck you up with them if you mess with him, and it's over."

Meanwhile, the blow from Atlantic was generating other repercussions among the band members. "After we were dropped...it does something to bands when you all of a sudden come from here to there," Grillo laments. He says that as time went on, tension began to grow between him, O'Brien, and Hateley. Grillo's band mates were especially critical of the new songs that he brought into rehearsals.

They managed to put their differences aside long enough to record a second album, and they scored a distribution deal with EMI Records. But just as they were about to release their follow-up to *Sinnerman,* Hateley called it quits and left the band following a performance at the Sunset Junction Street Fair in Silver Lake.

Hateley's departure came as a shock to his band mates, and they decided not to release the new record. Instead, they regrouped, recruited Foster's roommate Steve Browne to play in Hateley's place, and recorded a few new songs, which they released on an EP called *No Mercy* for their own Butch Ditties label. (The disc also featured a few songs from the sessions with Hateley.)

The new material represented a slight shift in sound for the band, including the inclusion of keyboards, and a stripped-down, acoustic version of "Son of That Man" that foreshadowed the work to come in Grillo's solo future. While the new release generated some fairly positive reviews ("The music is as charged as ever," wrote Los Angeles's *Buzz Weekly*), something was

amiss in Extra Fancy. The band members' hearts were simply no longer in it (Grillo later referred to the EP as "shit"), and there were financial concerns as well. "All of a sudden you don't have any money and the guys' wives are screaming at them that they're not gonna support them," Grillo says. "I didn't have a problem, because I was always able to get by on nothing. But it did something to us."

So six years after Extra Fancy had been hatched—and only two years after it had been dropped from Atlantic—the band parted ways. Brian Grillo was once again back where he had started—nowhere and with no resources other than his own raw energy.

"Falling down is good for the soul.
Falling down from what I thought
I know.
Falling hard onto the fallacy that all
is safe.
This ride ain't free.
Like a boxer, step into the ring.
If this life has taught me anything,
every time I hear that faithful bell, I
get back up.
I might as well."

—"Falling Down is Good for the Soul"
(written by Brian Grillo, performed by
Mink Stole)

Starting over was something Brian Grillo had grown accustomed to over the years. Following the breakup of Extra Fancy, he attempted to do just that by getting right back on the proverbial horse with a new band. Having maintained a friendship with Foster, Grillo and his buddy hooked up with openly gay bassist William Tutton, who was himself coming off the breakup of his critically praised rockabilly punk band, the Geraldine Fibbers. Silver Lake drummer Bernard Yin (who had worked with fellow queercore artist Micah Barnes) rounded out the new mix. The band members dubbed their new project the Glitter Panthers and set about writing new songs together.

"The music touched on some of the same topics as Extra Fancy, but I started to become conscious of the fact that I had a chance to start breaking free from being the big gay spokesperson," says Grillo. "I realized I could write about much broader issues. I mean, I was proud of the work that I did with Extra Fancy, but I didn't want to be locked into that.

"All the musicians were excellent," he maintains of his new band mates. "I had never worked with such great quality before. It was like being a painter who only worked with finger paints, and then all of a sudden somebody hands you this kit of oil paints, and all of the colors suddenly become 10 times more vibrant. That's what it was like working with those guys.

"They weren't as concerned with being rock stars as some of the other guys I'd worked with," Grillo adds. "They just had this need to make music."

There was another element of the new band that appealed to him as well. "It was great because Bill [Tutton] was gay too," he says. "It was like having a brother in the band—someone who really got it."

The band eventually came up with enough songs for a demo and went into the studio to lay down the tracks. "I think it's one of the best things that I've ever done," Grillo says frankly. Sadly, though, the band would not even last a year. It did some shows, hawked its CD, and tried to build a buzz, to no avail.

Part of the problem, Grillo says, was that audiences were coming to see the band for the wrong reasons. "People would come expecting to hear all the Extra Fancy songs, and it was a completely different thing," he notes, recalling the hecklers who would call out for "Sinnerman" or "You Look Like a Movie Star, Honey."

But there was more to it than disappointed fans. Even though Grillo was very fond of the project, his heart still wasn't in it. "It was kind of like a rebound thing," he explains. "Like where you have a boyfriend who you're totally in love with and then you break up and you get together with the first person that you can because you want to take your mind off the breakup. It was like, 'I have to keep doing music,' but I don't think I was ready to do it yet."

Thus, the Glitter Panthers split up after just six months, and Grillo decided it was time for him to take a break. "I just sort of dropped out of everything for a while," he reports. "Everything in Extra Fancy had been about me being the sexy, aggressive gay singer with HIV. It was like all of a sudden I wasn't a musician anymore. I was just this weird caricature, like 'Here's the gay cartoon character that rocks.' It was like I'd created my own Frankenstein. And one day I just woke up and I was like, 'I don't want to write another fucking gay song.' That's why I just went away and wasn't seen for a while. I just wanted to get back to being *me* for a while."

So he took some time off from music and painted houses instead. He would write the occasional new song if the mood struck him, and he even reunited with the members of Extra Fancy for a few benefit shows here and there ("It was kind of like having sex with your ex," he reports. "It felt like the magic was gone"), but by and large he steered clear of the music biz. At least for a while.

Though he turned in solo musical outings on occasion and collaborated with other Silver Lake performers (including a stint writing songs for Mink Stole, a staple of John Waters movies), Grillo only dabbled in music during the creatively barren years following the breakups of Extra Fancy and the Glitter Panthers. The truth was, he'd stopped having something to look forward to, and the failure on his part to feed his creative soul did nothing to lift his spirits.

Then, in 2000, Grillo's health finally caught up with him.

He'd been working 17-hour days painting houses and scenery backdrops for Hollywood movie studios to make his rent, and the paint toxins were slowly killing him. With his immune system compromised, he developed shingles. He went to the Los Angeles Gay and Lesbian Center (he could not afford health insurance), and was told that his T-cell count was dangerously close to 200—the count that designates an AIDS diagnosis. The doctors urged him to start taking antiretroviral meds, but Grillo was having none of it. "I was like, 'Fuck you, I'm not going on the meds,'" he says.

A short time later, he developed a serious pain in his side, and he ended up in the emergency room, where the doctors told him that he had a cyst in his stomach. When Grillo reported that he was not taking meds for HIV, they were stunned. "They were totally freaked out that I'd been positive that long and I had not died," Grillo relays.

He spent three weeks in the hospital, teetering dangerously close to death as his body and the hospital antibiotics tried to fight off the cyst. Eventually it did go away, but Grillo still refused to go on any meds. He returned to his life of working too hard and just scraping by, but his body once again revolted. A year later he was back in the hospital—the cyst had resurfaced. This time, however, Grillo's doctor from County USC Medical Center paid him a visit and urged him to consider taking medication. As Grillo recalls, "He was like, 'You can make your own decision, but I'm telling you, you've done really good for all these years, but your body can't do it on its own anymore. You need help.' And I said, 'Well, if I get out of here, I'll start.'"

Luckily for Grillo, there was a light at the end of the tunnel, and he eventually found his way to it, albeit 35 pounds lighter. A few weeks after winding up in the emergency room for a second time, he was released—and, true to his word, started taking antiretroviral medications.

He began feeling much better physically, but that didn't matter: Something was missing from his life—the only thing he really cared about: music.

"Fall for it and settle down
on every screen in Sensurround.
And on the radio, the only sound I hear
is just the hollow sound of madness
screaming in my ears.
Once I had a taste of their celebrity,
until I found out how cutthroat that it
could be.
Since then I've been suspended in a
county ward.
What used to seem important isn't
anymore."
—"Shutdown," Brian Grillo

For many people, the experience of knocking on death's door (and surviving the experience) can have a rejuvenating effect. For Grillo, getting close to death—twice, no less—was the wake-up call he needed to refocus his energies on his music. "I just started kicking ass," he trumpets. "I was like, 'I'm going to go to school, I'm going to do another record…'" He started playing the guitar again, teaching himself chords and melody, enrolled in night classes so that he could learn everything he could about computers "from the inside out" (a skill he plans to put to use as a replacement for painting houses), and began to write a brand new batch of songs for himself to perform. To Grillo, the new music was just what he needed to reinvest himself in his life. "I realized that all [my health problems] started happening to me when I stopped doing music," he says. "I was getting by until I stopped having something to live for."

But, unlike his work in his previous musical outings, the new tunes weren't loud, aggressive rock songs at all, but rather a series of quiet, acoustic pieces that Grillo strummed up from deep inside him. Surprisingly, he found he *liked* his music that way—even if the challenge of performing "unplugged" terrified him. "I think the new stuff definitely shows growth," he says. "Before I never would have had the nerve to get up onstage by myself with an acoustic guitar, trying to pull off what I'm pulling off now. But I have to admit, I am afraid.

"It's scary, because now I'm really baring my soul," he adds. "But I'm really proud of the words that I'm writing. I feel like I've kinda come full circle, where it's more or less that I'm writing about things that aren't gonna peg me into being the guy who only writes things about gay issues or whatever. I'm just singing about things that everyone goes through. It's the stuff that Joe Schmoe sitting in Idaho might hear and go, 'Whoa, this is a really good tune. Who is this?'"

Grillo played the new songs for his friend Ryan Revenge, a local musician who had started his own gay-owned and -operated independent record label, Spitshine Records—and who'd gone on record in interviews claiming Grillo as one of his chief influences as an artist (he fronted the homo- core band Best Revenge in the early 2000s before starting his current band Terazzo.). Revenge loved the new tracks and asked Grillo if he would like to release them on an album for Spitshine. For Grillo, there was no question—he immediately said yes. "I'm so happy to be on the Spitshine label," he enthuses, "because they get it. They *are* it. They're punk rock kids that are like, 'Let's go. You do whatever you want to do.'"

Meanwhile, for Revenge, bringing Grillo aboard Spitshine is a dream come true. "When I was in college, he didn't know it, but Brian was changing my life," he gushes by way of explanation. "He was an example to me that the road was wide open for a gay musician. I didn't have to give up on rock and roll just because I'm queer. I didn't have to hand over the keys to the DJs at the gay disco. No, here it was—an out gay man fronting a loud band and pounding on an oil drum! And in his voice there was so much power and sincerity.

"I felt honored to release his solo debut on my own record label," he continues. "The sym- metry of it all isn't lost on me, believe me."

The eventual Spitshine album, appropri- ately titled *Stomping Back on Fire*, was released in late 2004 and contained several of the sparse, very personal songs Grillo had written in the year following his second release from the hospital. From the simple but emotion-packed title track and the outspoken protest song "Democracy" to the heartbreakingly Johnny Cash–like "Sunblind" and the more aggressive "Right Here" (a tune that recalls the hypersexualized urgency of Grillo's work with Extra Fancy), the songs represent the journey of a man who has seen and done it all. Grillo is a hard-rockin' "troublemaker" with a heart of pure passion for life and his art—and he has lived to tell about it. This triumphal spirit shines through the lyrics to the CD's title track:

"Well, his house went up in flames.
Sent all he had right up twisting black and gray.
That took him all away.
A war was raging down below.
Was enough to start more smoke and fire.
Sometimes you gotta make it like a soldier on the mend.
Jump in and fight and kick it up again.
I'm stomping back on fire...
Hey! I never went away.
—"Stomping Back on Fire," Brian Grillo

For Grillo, the new songs represented a chance for him to let go of the past and embrace the present. And embrace *himself*—warts and all. He doesn't worry that fans of his previous efforts will be disappointed with the quieter, gentler Brian Grillo offering, "That's kinda why I'm doing it—to get as far away from [the past] as I can. I think it would be really pathetic right now in my life if I was still jumping on top of an oil drum onstage. Let the other bands do the sexy rock and roll thing."

"I think I was really fucking good at doing that," he adds, "and some day I might like to do it again, though in a different way. But right now I've made a commitment to this new thing. It's a challenge. And I'm really up to the challenge."

"It's another low-down almost-after Sunday afternoon.
My guitar won't play; I broke some strings, can't get myself in tune.
Hear what I'm saying: Won't somebody call?
'Cause I feel so empty, staring at the wall."
—"The Other Ones," Brian Grillo

Fitting in has never been an option for Grillo. "I never even thought about how I might fit into rock music as a gay musician," he professes with confidence. "Before I was defined as a queer artist or homocore or whatever, I was playing in clubs at 16 and 18 years old. There was never a problem with me being who I am. Either your music was good or your music sucked. You knew how to hold yourself in that arena.

"I always looked up to—and wanted to be as good as—the hetero performers I saw growing up because they were the only role models there were back then, you know?" he explains. "I liked Freddie Mercury and Queen, but I wanted to be more like Alice Cooper or Lemmy from Motorhead or John Doe from X. I studied how honest the Clash and the Sex Pistols and the Buzzcocks were…how brutally poetic they were. It never even entered into it for me that they were straight or gay. And so I never measured myself on a scale of how I fit into the hetero world, you know?"

To that end, he doesn't measure himself in terms of how he might fit into the gay world either. Talk to Grillo about his views on such gay staples as *Will & Grace, Queer as Folk,* or *Queer Eye for the Straight Guy,* and you'll likely get an earful. "It's all insulting to me," he spits. "With *Will & Grace,* it's like, 'Boy, we've made it on TV,' but what do we have to show for it? A guy who never gets to fuck anybody and this other guy who is this screaming, nonthreatening queen? And the other shows…I don't even watch them, because I've seen their ads, and I think, *This is the standard of what we are supposed to be?* It's all these stereotypes of what people are.

"I've fucked a lot of guys who were preachers or sailors or Army men," Grillo notes. "But they don't show those people. It's too much of a mind-fuck for America to deal with. But it's lurking right in their neighborhoods and their yards."

Not surprisingly, given his views on pop culture directed at gays and his experience with Lock Up and Extra Fancy, Grillo is also not too fond of being lumped in with other musicians simply because he shares their sexual orientation. "I'm a little uncomfortable with this label 'homocore,'" he says. "It's like, 'Why are you making such a big deal out of it?' I guess it might be fine for some, but if you have ever listened to my music or seen my art, you might notice that there is a lot more to it than just the fact that I'm attracted to guys.

"I started doing what I do way before somebody had come up with a label for it, and I can only hope that anyone who wants to can experience my art—not just one specific group of people," he elaborates. "I think it's important to be honest and not be ashamed about who you are, but in no way do I speak for the gay community only. I guess a lot of it has to do with the fact that I don't limit the way that I look and interact with the world through a gay viewfinder. When I create music I try to convey thoughts and tell stories of my own experiences that anyone—regardless of skin color or sexual preference—might relate to. I try to convey the day-to-day experiences that we all go through."

"I think it's pretty cool, though, that there is a network of people nowadays," he says. "Something must be happening right if all these kids are able to hook up with each other and share their music, have a support system. That's great if you need that. I never felt like I needed it."

"Hang it all up, wait and see what tomorrow brings.
Just one more day we can lose sight of in our dreams.
I've got some choices that I don't want to make.
Somebody dealt me a hand that I don't want to play.
A man can only do so much and then it starts to take its toll.
I'm going to leave it up to luck.
Just say a prayer to send me on my way."
—"Sunblind," Brian Grillo

"I think Brian has moved on from queer-core, to be honest," says Ryan Revenge, though he adds that Grillo's influence on the scene cannot be denied. "Every movement needs deep roots if it's every going to grow into anything. You plant some seeds and

come back later and see what grew there. Brian did that, and what he did with Extra Fancy has had a ripple effect that's still opening doors for people."

Ask Grillo if he feels that he championed the cause, and he shrugs off the suggestion. "I don't take credit for starting anything, because it was already fueled by bands like Team Dresch, Pansy Division, and Tribe 8, and it was fueled by my anger at the time. I just took it upon myself to do my own thing. I had no idea it was gonna go as far as it did."

"I remember those early days back in Hermosa Beach, where it was like, 'I'm the only gay guy here,'" he continues. "There were all these little skinhead punk kids or whatever, and there was that danger element in the air. And that was like church for me. That's what I grew up with. I don't know how to describe it. It does something to me inside my soul that's bigger than…" His voice trails off for a moment as he looks down at his now long-since-cold cup of coffee. "In a way, it's my religion. It's like, some people find it in books, some people find it in God. I find it in music. And it's kept me alive and it's kept me sane and it's helped me through a lot of awful times.

"If I didn't have that guitar and the ability to play music or put on a really good record when I need to, what's the point of living?" he posits. Then, like the grassroots punk rocker that he's always been, he adds, "I don't have any illusions that I'm gonna be able to support myself off of this; it's just something I have to do."

CHAPTER 5

Team Dresch, Grrrl Power, and the Queercore Movement

"I just want a public place
where girls can meet each other's stare.
Sometimes that's what it takes
to know you're alive.
To feel yourself burning just for some girl's stare."
—"Remember Who You Are," Team Dresch

"I WAS ALWAYS IN BANDS, BUT I JUST WASN'T SATISFIED," SAYS SINGER-GUITARIST JODY BLEYLE OF HER PRE-QUEERCORE MUSIC CAREER. "AND THEN, LATER, I KNEW WHAT I NEEDED TO DO: I NEEDED TO BE IN A BAND WITH REALLY GREAT DYKE MUSICIANS."

Bleyle got her wish when she ended up playing in the seminal homocore band Team Dresch along with fellow lesbian musicians Kaia Wilson and indie music wunderkind Donna Dresch. Along with fellow pioneering homocore luminaries Tribe 8 and Fifth Column, Team Dresch would define the burgeoning queercore scene, building a community of out—and loud—gay musicians who aren't afraid to put their music where their mouths are.

For Bleyle, it all started off very small. "In the beginning, there wasn't really a scene," she remembers of the movement's humble origins. "It was just very small—a kind of loose, undefined group of people that shared some ideas and values. You felt like you were the only one in the world, and you had to reach out and find other people like you."

Performing alongside other out lesbians was a dream come true for Bleyle, who says, "It really opened me up. In terms of the music, the other women were great musi-

cians, so I definitely grew in the sense that we could do anything—we could explore anything. And it opened me up emotionally and spiritually as much as it did musically—the lyrics we could write, the ideas that we could think about. It was amazing.

"Starting the band was like going from having no freaky dyke friends to having a little team, and all of a sudden we felt more confident," Bleyle continues. "It gave us the courage to say, 'Hey, we want this thing to exist that doesn't exist. Let's just say that we want it and see if anybody else out there wants to do it too.'"

Of course, others did want it, and in time, the tiny grassroots effort would blossom into a media-endorsed "movement" that would revolutionize the paths of gay musicians in rock music. But in those early days, back before journalists got on board to give the movement exposure, it wasn't always so easy to get gay musicians to come together and form rock groups. Just ask Bleyle.

While attending college, Bleyle started a women's rock collective that used school money to buy amps for women to use. "I was just a kid, and I wanted to hang out with other people that I could relate to. I really just wanted to build a community so I could have friends and dance to their music," she recalls.

Bleyle had played with two bands, the all-girl (but not gay) Lovebutt and the mixed gender Hazel, which released two albums on the popular Seattle-based indie label Sub Pop. It was during her time with Hazel that Bleyle was introduced to the woman who would become not only her girlfriend but her band mate in Team Dresch as well. "Brady [Smith, the bassist in Hazel] said, 'I have to introduce you to this woman that I was friends with when I was living in Olympia. Her name's Donna Dresch,'" Bleyle recounts. As it turns out, Bleyle was already a fan of Dresch's. "I said, 'I know her because she used to play in this band called Dangermouse,' and I had always wanted to meet her," she adds.

"I met her and we started talking about bands," continues Bleyle. "I remember talking about Tribe 8 because I had just put on a show for them in Portland," she says, adding that she was a bit intimidated by Dresch at first. Dresch—who had also been a member of Screaming Trees, Dinosaur, Jr., and Fifth Column (whose song "Donna" was written about Dresch)—was an accomplished musician. Though music was one of the things the two women bonded over, Bleyle says, "I couldn't even imagine the possibility of playing with her."

A few months later, Bleyle met guitarist and singer Kaia Wilson, who was herself coming out of an experience as the only lesbian in her band Adickded ("I was queercore even though they weren't," Wilson says with a laugh). As it happened, Wilson—who was already a friend of Dresch's after discovering her writings in the zine *Homocore* as a 16-year-old living just outside Eugene, Ore.—was also looking to create a dykecentric rock group of some kind. "I sought that out," she says. "I originally sought out other women musicians to play music with, because I knew intuitively that I wanted to play with other women. And that graduated to, 'OK, I want to play with other dykes.'"

"There's something about being in a band with just other girls," Wilson continues. "There's not going to be as much conflict in certain areas of your life. As a gay person, you need to have as little conflict as possible. A band is a very close working relationship; it's like a family, and it can be very challenging."

One night, Wilson approached Bleyle in a club and, as Bleyle recalls, said, "Donna and I are starting a band. Do you want to start it with us?" For Bleyle, the answer was simple—intimidated or not, she was definitely on board.

"My that's a strange costume.
Slip your fingers under my belt.
Put up signs to make up who you are.
Send out signals telling who you are.

Transmit messages about who you are. No matter who you are.
—"Remember Who You Are," Team Dresch

For Jody Bleyle, one major goal had been taken care of—starting a lesbiancentric rock band. With Team Dresch formed (the original line-up included Bleyle, Dresch, and Wilson), the only thing left to do was start playing for queer audiences. "We announced all of our shows as queer shows and put it on the posters specifically," says Bleyle (who also remained a member of Hazel). "Because if we didn't do that, queer people wouldn't come.

"We didn't know anybody," she continues. "There weren't a lot of freaky gay people living in Portland, the way there are now. But there were a few girls that had found each other through fanzines and through letters and through shows. It was a very underground network—kind of like a secret network of people that were trying to bring this to life."

It was that grassroots ideology that really inspired the members of Team Dresch to work hard to establish something meaningful for themselves and their fans. "It was a really exciting time," Bleyle says. "Everybody was making something out of nothing. We wanted to really create our own culture— make music and dress our own way and live our lives in any way that we could imagine without having to think about what we were supposed to do, what our parents wanted us to do, or what society wanted us to do."

They tried hard to have their music heard in gay establishments, but they took gigs anywhere they possibly could. "We played some places that some regular rock bands didn't play," Bleyle concedes. "We played gay bars in little towns. A lot of gay-bar owners would let us put on shows there even though they'd never had a rock band play there before." They also played other venues and had surprisingly few problems convincing booking agents to let an all-lesbian band perform in their clubs. "The other rock clubs didn't mind if we played as long as we were bringing people in or opening for someone who was," Bleyle reports. "It was a really supportive scene, especially in Olympia and Portland and Seattle. There were a lot of promoters who were really into helping bands grow."

But while they faced little opposition from bar owners and promoters, they did come into contact with a few not-so-nice fellow musicians and audience members. "Guys would show up at the shows and scream at us and harass us," Bleyle remembers. "And one time, when I was with Hazel, a band we were playing with harassed me all night because they knew I was in Team

Dresch. They would get right up in my face and scream at me."

Cold stares and name-calling, however, were nothing compared to physical violence. Bleyle and Dresch were gay-bashed after one of the band's very first shows. A man jumped them as they were walking outside the club and punched Jody in the face before Dresch jumped on him and chased him off. Bleyle ended up in the hospital with stitches above her eye, while Dresch escaped with a few bruises. "There was that physical element to carving out a place for yourself in the world, like it or not," Bleyle says. "We really had to look out for each other, and we all would keep an eye on each other."

Wilson remembers the incident as well. "I was so freaked out by that experience," she says. "But as scary as that was, we learned how to watch each other's back and to do as much avoidance as possible. It really sparked us to do something proactive in its wake." Before long, the members of the band began to take self-defense lessons to protect themselves from the dangers of being out. In fact, they took their martial arts teacher on the road for a series of shows they dubbed the Self-Defense Tour, during which self-defense demonstrations were performed prior to each Team Dresch show. (Bleyle later released the double CD *Free to Fight*, which combined rock, hip-hop, spoken

word, and visual art with self-defense instruction, on her own Candy Ass Records.)

In 1994, after putting out a few seven-inch vinyl singles, Team Dresch released its first CD, *Personal Best*. Taking the title from the 1982 film that starred Mariel Hemingway and Patrice Donnelly as Olympic runners who also happened to be lovers, the record was a decidedly crude and raw yet undeniably powerful rock record. It was extremely well-received, cementing the band's status as a staple of the slowly building homocore scene. For the band's members, being part of the movement was both liberating and flattering.

"At the time, I don't think I knew that I was part of something so amazing until I got perspective on it," Wilson says. "I was so young—I was the youngest one in the band. I certainly knew I was a lucky dog, and I knew I was part of something incredible, but I didn't know what it was until I got older and was able to look back on it with perspective.

"I wanted to be in this band for my own selfish reasoning of just being able to relate to these people on this very base, core level," she adds. "Like, 'We all know what it's like to be freaky dykes.' That was our underlying thing, and we had this understanding that felt like a really good foundation."

"It was really exciting when the music and the shows just affected so many people in such a positive way," Bleyle adds. "When we started Team Dresch, it was like we were sending a message in a bottle out into the world. It was really exciting to see other bands get started that were inspired by us, as we ourselves were inspired by other people."

"Do it yourself means do it for me.
I don't give a shit, just get my video on MTV.
You know exactly what you want.
So don't hide your greed behind me.
Just own it, you little slacker fuck.
Didn't you hear, there's no free money.
It's not magic, it's work.
Yeah, it's cool and it's work.
And it can feel like a choice between pleasure and existence.
—"To the Enemies of Political Rock,"
Team Dresch

To many participants in the early homocore scene, the grassroots ideology that got the movement off the ground was just as important as getting their music out into the world. "We didn't think about doing it on major labels," Bleyle says of Team Dresch's records. "The point of it wasn't making money. It would be great to reach as many people as possible, but that wasn't the initial goal.

"The idea was just to meet anybody, to reach out to anybody," she elaborates. "Underground movements are different from the mainstream in part because this art isn't one-way communication. The idea is to inspire everybody to get involved and make things and participate. We didn't want to start a band just so our band could be big. We wanted to find and build a community so we could have friends and date them and go to parties."

"We live in a culture that basically tells you that you can't do anything, or that you have to do them by these certain rules," Wilson adds. "For one, you can do it yourself, goddamn it. There are so many things you can do that you maybe you didn't think you could, and don't let society tell you you can't, especially as a girl.

"Secondly, major labels are just so freaky," she continues. "The whole fuckin' machinery of it and the insincerity of it all—I don't think it appealed to any of us. We wanted to have something that wasn't tainted—and just have complete control and just be able to say, 'We made this.'"

Like *Personal Best,* Team Dresch's second album, 1996's *Captain My Captain,* was put out as a joint indie release on Dresch's Chainsaw Records and Bleyle's Candy Ass Records. (Bleyle had started Candy Ass with the money she made performing with Hazel as a way to give other bands a chance to get their music out into the world.) To Bleyle, her label and the queercore scene were both tools for providing guidance to young gay kids struggling with their sexuality. "This scene is about reaching out to people," Bleyle says. "To kids who see nothing of themselves in the world when they look in magazines or listen to records. They're invisible, because no one tells you you're allowed to be gay. Or the only visible gay people are trying to sell you vodka or a trip to a golf tournament. We all experienced that. We need to build communities where kids can come out into something positive and say, 'Wow, life isn't so bad. I don't have to hate myself. I can do it. I can be gay and be myself.'"

"The characteristics of this scene are creating your own art, inventing your life, doing it the way you want," she continues. "It's a totally different scene than, like, a jazz scene, which is based on the music itself. Yeah, there's the music, and the music is important, but the music is not the defining characteristic of this scene. You can play any musical style. If you feel like you belong in this scene, you belong. And it's filled with people who are queer, some of whom are singing about it, some of whom are expressing it in other ways, and it all fits."

"Whole lot of things to say.
But I can't seem to hold on.
Moves away and pulls me back to
what I miss.
Like talking, talking to the mad
queen
about emotional evolution."
—"Freewheel," Team Dresch

Team Dresch, in its various incarnations, continued along until 1996, when Wilson decided it was time for her to strike out on her own to concentrate on writing and recording solo material. Drummer Melissa York left shortly thereafter, and guitarist Amanda "Jack" Kelley and drummer Marci Martinez (who had been a member of the band during the recording of *Personal Best*) were brought on board to keep the band going. Over the next two years, the group released four more seven-inch singles on the Outpunk record label and continued playing shows for its rabid fan base. Unfortunately, by 1998, things in the band had reached an turning point. Dresch and Bleyle, who had become girlfriends shortly after starting Team Dresch, had split up in 1996, and though the two women remained very good friends, there were definitely ripples within the band. "There was a lot of pressure," Bleyle concedes of those difficult times. "It's very overwhelming to be so public and so political," Bleyle adds. "It wasn't like going to a normal rock show, where you play a show and sell some T-shirts and leave. You're meeting all these people who have really heavy stories to tell you, and you want to listen, and you are telling your own heavy stories in your music.

"It was really hard to be that open and try to help each other," she admits. "And then to deal with all the silly things that come along with rock music and all the attention that comes along with it."

By 1999, as the press began to leave queercore behind and move on to other trends and movements, Team Dresch had officially disbanded—leaving in its wake a legion of disheartened fans who'd claimed the band's music as their own. For many in the scene who had followed the band so religiously, it was the end of an era.

"It's where the obvious turns dumb and clarity turns off.
I'm standing somewhere near the back of the room.
I'm on her left and I'm in between her.
She's amazing, her words save me.
She holds her head as if it's true."
—"She's Amazing," Team Dresch

"I learned so many things playing with those girls," Wilson says of her experience playing in Team Dresch. "I learned so much,

musically speaking—a ton of musical skill and knowledge, and a lot of things about being in a band. But more importantly, I got a stronger sense of identity and confidence. And I just got to be part of something that was so highly influential within this little niche of freaky queer punk people. It really had an effect on the world, and I was pretty fuckin' lucky. I feel extremely grateful to have been a part of that."

When it is suggested that the members of the band might be role models for queer youths, Bleyle is refreshingly modest. "I'd be honored to have anybody think that something I did or something Team Dresch did was worth looking up to and that they were inspired by it. Nothing would make me happier."

Bleyle speaks of many fans who sent e-mails and came up to the girls at shows and thanked them for giving them a voice—not to mention, she laughs, "the shows with all the crazy girls, including me, taking off their shirts and going crazy." And though it may not be known what kind of an effect the queercore scene had on gay culture in the long run, it's obvious that the lives of many people who identified with the scene were affected in very real and very important ways. Wilson recalls the adoring fans who showed up show after show—and who followed her into her new band, the Butchies, as well.

"Team Dresch really had a profound effect on queer youngsters," she says. "After Team Dresch, I got so many comments from kids coming to Butchies shows saying, 'Thank you so much for your music. Team Dresch changed my life.' It just had a huge impact—a really personal kind of effect on queer kids, especially emotionally."

In fact, it's one of the reasons Bleyle is so quick to identify herself with the movement. "I proudly identify with queercore and homocore, because it's a scene that I care about filled with people making music that I love, and I think a lot of people love the music and love the idea of being yourself, whether they are gay or not," she says. "I definitely felt that we were part of a movement that extended back before us and, I hoped, would continue after us, because, in a broader sense, it's allied with the left in general and punk rock and folk music and the women's movement and gay liberation. I feel so honored to be a part of it."

Though Team Dresch had split up, neither Bleyle's nor Wilson's commitment to the movement ended. While the Butchies had the same spirit as Team Dresch before them, Bleyle remained in the scene with the creation of Infinite Ex's, another queer band that was short-lived. Later, there was Family Outing, a band she started with her gay younger brother, Allen (who is himself a member of the Ga-Ga's, an all-boy, all-gay Go-Go's cover band that also features Pansy Division's Chris Freeman and Best Revenge's Bilito Peligro). Now residing with a girlfriend in Los Angeles, Bleyle still takes the time to show up for gigs, most recently the Team Dresch reunion show for Ed Varga's Homo a Go Go festival in Olympia, Wash., where the band shared a stage with some of today's hottest queercore bands and musicians—including Amy Ray of the Indigo Girls, whose next solo album Bleyle appears on as a guest musician. "That was one of the best shows of my life," Bleyle says. "There was so much great energy in the room. It was just like old times, but even better."

While Bleyle acknowledges that the homocore scene emerged out of a punk, DIY ethic, she says that she feels it is defined more by its focus on the individual stories of the people involved than by the specific kind of music that they play. "It's like reggae music," she says. "I'm not a Rastafarian, but I relate to those songs about freedom and rejecting the social system, and I think this scene is similar. At its core, it's about being yourself no matter what—wanting to be free. And then there are specific songs that are detailed stories about people's lives that are really like folk songs. Punk and folk are related in that way, because they're both stories of people's lives that are like historical documents.

"I listen to all that rock music that the boys and straights make, and I can relate to it," she continues. "What are the songs about? They're about wanting to be free, wanting to be bad, wanting to have sex—all that kind of stuff. I relate to it. And everybody could relate to this queer music, but they won't, because 'it's not about me because it's gay.' And that's bullshit. I can relate to music made by people that are part of cultures that I've never been part of. It's just total and utter bullshit that [some people] can't."

Bleyle gets angry when queer artists are told that using gender-specific pronouns and singing about being gay limits them as artists. "Why aren't straight people limiting themselves [when they sing about being straight]?" she counters. "I tell stories that are true for me, and that should be enough for people to relate to the music. I didn't live Bob Dylan's songs, and I didn't live the Guns N' Roses shit, but I still got their records and listened to them. Why can't I just write lyrics that are true for me? Am I supposed to write about what I guess someone else is experiencing?

"I can't separate it," she continues. "I wouldn't want to—my sexuality, my beliefs, things that are important to me—I couldn't separate that from the music that I write."

"There's a wig-wearing boy named Psychic Al.
What he's looking for, he won't find in school.
He stays up late, flipping through tapes, listening to songs he's heard a hundred times.
But nothing's there.
Hey you! Say what he needs to hear."
—"Musical Fanzine," Team Dresch

"It's still, unfortunately, kinda important to be an out person in this world," says Wilson. "I say it's unfortunate because we all wish we were in a place where people didn't judge you or hate you because you're gay. And I know from being in both Team Dresch and the Butchies that there are kids who are in areas where they don't have access to much of anything undergroundish—let alone gay—and it's really important for them to have access to [openly queer bands]."

"I know that in the United States and in the world, we have a long way to go in terms of equal rights for all people and especially the way we deal with women and being women and with sexuality," says Bleyle. "Back in the early days [of the movement], the music was more explicit because it had to be; otherwise the scene wouldn't exist. Today it's less so. But if some bands—queer people who are telling those stories—do something that resonates with people, all the better."

Both women concede that all bands must choose their own path when it comes to how much of their sexuality they want to include in their music, though both are adamant about the paths that they have chosen. "I just know that it's important to me to be a feminist and be a queer activist, because I'm telling my own stories," Bleyle says. "I'm describing the world I see or the world I want to see, and those are things that are important to me."

Bleyle also asserts that though she understands that some bands may choose to distance themselves from the movement for fear of being pigeonholed or being accused of jumping on a bandwagon, she feels that any band that embraces the scene would be all the better for it. "I can understand people not wanting to be too overly defined while they're in the middle of making something, because everybody wants to feel like what they're doing is not just new but really from themselves—really unique.

"What matters," she continues, "is singing and creating things that are hon-

est—that's what can help us. To react against that, that bums me out—the idea that people would run away from something that is true for them."

For both Wilson and Bleyle, activism was at the core of Team Dresch's mission. "We were all activist-minded people," Wilson notes. "But I know for me, I'm not a very good activist without art and music. Music is where I've been able to feel that I can put something into the world and use my voice. You can have an affect on the world through this kind of thing. Being in a band and being on tour and putting out records is a chance for you to potentially communicate something to the public, and from there it can go so many different ways."

For her part, Bleyle says that her style of musical activism is a "natural blend. I'm a cultural activist. I want things to change. I want things to grow. I want things to be better, especially for kids who have to grow up closeted and afraid and hating themselves. That is so wrong. I just think it's important to reach out intentionally—to try to spread feminist ideas and spread ideas about queer liberation, to try to achieve more equality for all of us. And if that can be done through the music that we make as a community, then that's a pretty fuckin' cool thing."

Punk, Politics, and Pink Triangles

BEFORE HOMOCORE, AND PRIOR TO THE RIOT GRRRL MOVEMENT, THE U.K. PUNK ROCK SCENE WAS MARCHING TO ITS OWN BEAT AND PAVING A PATH FOR QUEERCORE.

Some people in the homocore scene argue that while the movement didn't officially get under way until the late '80s, it actually began quite a while before that, with the anarchist antics and gender-fucked histrionics of the punk scene that sprouted up overseas. "The original punk scene was very gay," says Juan Gomez of Human Hands. "But not really in the way we perceive it today. Punk rock really had this aesthetic of antieverything, antisexuality [classification] included. It was a weird kind of Spartan mentality there for a while. But some of those punk rockers were definitely queer-minded."

Indeed, long before Team Dresch or Pansy Division ever sang about gay rights, other artists who didn't have the good fortune to be part of a supportive scene had already been doing the same thing. In fact, London's Tom Robinson—the first openly gay British rock star—could very well be the original queercore artist. A sorta-folkie whose band Café Society's first record was produced by Ray Davies of the Kinks,

Robinson was so inspired by a Sex Pistols show that he quit the trio to form the much more rock-edged—and radically more political—Tom Robinson Band. (Legend has it that Johnny Rotten stumbled over to Robinson at a club and hissed, "Yeah, Tom Robinson, don't fucking give up, mate. Don't *ever* let 'em make you give up," before vomiting all over Robinson's shoes.) Robinson was notorious for being extremely vocal in the press about his disdain for Margaret Thatcher, accusing her of sanctioning violence against gays and people of color, but the attention he got seemed only to heighten interest in his music. In 1977 the Tom Robinson Band released a live EP called *Glad to be Gay*. The controversial title track was a punk protest song in the truest sense, its antipolice, antihomophobia lyrics delivered in the time-honored tradition of scathing sarcasm:

"The British police are the best in the world.
I don't believe one of these stories I've heard
'bout them raiding our pubs for no reason at all.
Lining the customers up by the wall.
Picking out people and knocking them down.
Resisting arrest as they're kicked on the ground.

Searching their houses and calling
them 'queer.'
I do"t believe that sort of thing happens here.
Sing if you're glad to be gay!"

Though the BBC placed a ban on the song, the band had the last laugh; the EP landed in the Top 20—with Robinson landing on the cover of *Melody Maker* eight times that year. Plus the band's subsequent full-length debut record, *Power in the Darkness,* went gold. Later, the Tom Robinson Band would achieve some success in the States as well, recording a critically lauded record with producer Steve Lillywhite (U2, the Rolling Stones, the Pogues) and opening for the Police at Madison Square Garden. Robinson later left the band and enjoyed a successful solo career (writing songs with the likes of Elton John, Peter Gabriel, and Dan Hartman) and caused quite a stir when he fell in love with the woman who would become his wife and the mother of his children. (Robinson never disowned his past, and he still claims to be bisexual.)

Later, Robinson's outspokenness would inspire another singer to be true to himself in, of all places, Texas. Born from the punk movement of the late '70s, the Dicks—led by the gay Dick Floyd (who often sported a pink mohawk)—rose up from the Austin underground to smash existing ideologies to pieces with confrontational punk rock songs, reconstructing the sexual politics of punk in the process. In the salaciously hard-rockin' tune "Saturday Night at the Book Store," Floyd belted out incendiary lyrics ("You and your fat fucking wife come out of Safeway on a Sunday afternoon and see me standing there and don't even speak to me...'cause I done sucked your cock through a glory hole") with unbridled passion. Floyd later ditched straightforward punk, but he kept the spirit of the music alive in his next endeavor—Sister Double Happiness, an all-gay band that took San Francisco by storm in the mid '80s. That effort inspired many folks in the city—including *Homocore* zine founder Tom Jennings—to lend an ear to the developing homocore scene.

CHAPTER 6

Smells Like Queer Spirit

"Against all odds, we appear.
Grew up brainwashed,
but turned out queer.
Bun-splitters, rug-munchers, too.
We screw just how we want to screw."
—"Smells like Queer Spirit," Pansy Division

Finding mainstream success as a groundbreaking band is no small feat, but it's not a bad gig if you can get it—and if you can withstand the slings and arrows that come with the territory. Winning over an audience with a sonic wallop, however, is undoubtedly much tougher for homocore bands than for mainstream acts. Gay rockers have to win over two markets: straight audiences that may not immediately bend an ear to lyrical subject matter that they're unfamiliar or uncomfortable with, and gay music fans from a scene where monotonous high-energy dance music is the genre of choice.

"Pansy Division was created to address the kind of alienation I felt in not being able to relate to much of gay culture—though it wasn't the primary motivation for forming the group; it was a way, hopefully, to make real connections with like-minded people," says Jon Ginoli, front man and founder of pioneering homocore band Pansy Division, unarguably the best-known all-gay rock group. "And speaking personally, I hoped also to get laid and/or get a boyfriend out of it," he continues with a chuckle while reflecting on the band's 13-year-plus career that includes seven albums with teasing gay anthems like "Fuck Buddy," "Dick of Death," "Beer Can Boy" and "Bill & Ted's Homosexual Adventure."

"We want to push the envelope in being out in rock music, which would help people realize that there are gay rockers and they should get used to it."

"Don't care about heterosexuality.
Rock, rock, rock and roll queer bar.
That's not what I want to be.
Rock, rock, rock and roll queer bar.
I just wanna have some kicks.
I just wanna get some dicks.
Rock, rock, rock, rock, rock and roll queer bar."
—"Rock and Roll Queer Bar," Pansy Division

Whether they were ready or not, mainstream rock audiences did get used to a seeing and hearing Pansy Division when the band was tapped to be the support act on chart-topping pop-punk band Green Day's massive 1994 Dookie tour, which took the camp quartet out of tiny San Francisco clubs and placed it center stage in arenas across the country. The two Bay Area bands were indie-label mates signed to LookOut! Records, and the hetero trio in Green Day had no qualms about teaming with an openly gay band. In fact, Green Day looked at the opportunity as a way to squash homophobia in the testosterone-fueled punk scene.

"Their success came pretty fast," Ginoli recalls of Green Day, which left LookOut! for corporate giant Warner Bros. Records in 1994. "They already had a large grass-roots following based on their two LookOut! albums—and they had an adverse reaction to mainstream jocks and idiots getting into their band. They thought we would be a good weapon to inflict upon the more narrow-minded segment of their audience. And they loved our songs! There was an MTV special on them, filmed at the end of 1994, where they are seen on their tour bus singing our song 'Groovy Underwear.'"

"Tight briefs on your sexy butt.
White fabric surrounding your nuts.
Bike shorts put it on display.
You're wearing it to the left today.
Sweatpants clinging to your crevice.
Boxer shorts for easy access.
I'm digging your groovy underwear..."
—"Groovy Underwear, Pansy
Division"

The lightweight ode to cute boys in tighty whiteys may have made for good camp on MTV, but it was a whole other story out on the road, where songs like "The Cocksucker Club" were sometimes met with indifference—or flying debris.

"We were pelted with a variety of items at most of the shows we opened for Green Day, but we stood our ground!" remembers Pansy Division bassist and founding member Chris Freeman.

"Each night we received a mixed reaction—more hostile than not, but with visible pockets of support out in the crowd," adds Ginoli. "However, we were protected by excellent security. Detroit, at massive Cobo Hall, was really the only show where the audience was overwhelmingly hostile. We went around after the show collecting all the change that had been pelted at us—we figured they were trying to tip us!"

"I made $40 in change that I picked up onstage!" continues Freeman. "I also got a

year's supply of lighters, some clothes."

"The second worst experience was in Allentown, Pa., where the sound man from the venue walked away from the sound desk after two songs once he heard what we were singing about," says Ginoli. "Green Day's sound tech noticed this—the sound was apparently dreadful—and stepped up to mix our set, which was very nice of him."

"Come to think of it, the L.A. crowd was pretty hostile too," adds Freeman. "Our drummer at the time got hit in the head with a coin, and he had a trickle of blood running down his face. We always managed to finish our set, though, and succeeded at making those taunters look foolish. Green Day were awesome to us and so was their crew, so there was nothing wrong there. The worst experiences we've ever had were at our own shows.

"But usually people are friendly," Freeman continues. "And what's really incredible is when someone comes up to tell us how our music has helped them or touched their life in some way. That makes me feel like we've done something important. And that all came as a side effect of just playing the kind of music we wanted to play."

The band's founder, singer and guitarist Jon Ginoli, started playing the music he wanted to play in 1991, performing in San Francisco gay performance spaces and at club nights as a solo act under the moniker Pansy Division, using preprogrammed bass and drum tracks as a virtual backup band.

"In high school he'd spend hundreds of hours
fantasizing about boys in the show-ers.
Billy was hung, Rick was thick,
Daniel had a most upstanding dick.
But Eric was the one with extra yardage to love,
by joining the cocksucker club."
—"The Cocksucker Club," Pansy Division

"At my first solo show, dykes fled the room when I played 'The Cocksucker Club,' Ginoli says with a chuckle. "When I decided to start a band, there really wasn't a pool of gay rock musicians to pick from. I didn't know a single one, even in the big gay mecca of San Francisco. At the time the only other gay rock musicians I knew of were Glen Meadmore, a gay country-punker from L.A., and Tribe 8, a San Francisco dyke band."

Like putting a note in a bottle and tossing it out into the ocean, Ginoli took a chance and placed an ad in several papers in San Francisco looking for "gay musicians into the Buzzcocks, Ramones, and early Beatles."

At the time, bass player Chris Freeman was also a staple of the San Francisco club scene. Like Ginoli, he was another musician frustrated by the experience of being ostracized by other musicians for being gay and by other gays for being into rock and roll. Freeman had all but given up on pursuing a career in music when he came across Ginoli's ad in the *S.F. Weekly.* The meeting of like minds invigorated both musicians. Their first jam session together kick-started rock's loudest and most visible in-your-face homocore band. The group's signature style is a melding of catchy pop-rock melodies with humorous stories about sex, boys, and rock and roll. Of course, there's an occasional punk rock parody thrown in for good balance—like "Rock and Roll Queer Bar," the band's lavender-tinted take on the Ramones' "Rock and Roll High School," and a clever camp spin on Nirvana's "Smells Like Teen Spirit." The title alone—"Smells Like Queer Spirit"— would have made hetero pro-gay rocker Kurt Cobain proud.

"I thought that nobody wanted a gay bass player and that I was too old," recalls Freeman. "I'd get auditions, and they'd want me in the band until they found out I was a fag, then they'd say that they had 'other people to try out.' I quit everything for six months and went stir-crazy. Then I saw that ad and came out of hiding. There isn't much tolerance for being a rock musician—or even liking rock, for that matter—in the gay community. Then when I met Jon through the ad and listened to his demo tape, I knew I had to join the band because it was just going to be too much fun, and having fun with music rather than taking it seriously was my focus at that point."

"We tried to turn our alienation into something positive," says Ginoli. "Instead of being depressed about it, we tried to make music that would make us—and our audience—happy. We could laugh about it, so we put that joy into the music."

"One of our first shows was playing with Tribe 8 and Malibu Barbie—both dyke bands—and we were thrilled!" Freeman continues. "'Yay, we're not alone!' Before that there really wasn't much around in the way of gay bands, except Two Nice Girls from Texas and Fifth Column from Toronto—also dyke bands."

"Initially, I had more hope for success than Chris did," says Ginoli. "He thought I was dreaming when I talked about plans for records and tours. His attitude was 'Sure—go for it,' not expecting it to happen. But little by little it did—actually, it happened pretty damn fast! It took a year and a half to get a record deal and just under two years to have our first album out. I thought we were unique enough and our songs good enough to get the kind of attention we wanted. I thought there must be a place for a cult band doing our kind of stuff; the thing is, I

thought someone else would come along to do it, not me! Before we met, both Chris and I had been keeping our eyes peeled for an out gay rock band. When it didn't happen, it fell to us to do something about it."

"We're here to tell you, ya better make way.
We're queer rockers in your face today.
We can't relate to Judy Garland.
It's a new generation of music calling.
We're the butt-fuckers of rock and roll."
—"Anthem," Pansy Division

After serving as a support act on Green Day's tour, Pansy Division headlined club gigs and recorded virtually nonstop for the next five years. Along the way the band recruited a permanent drummer, Luis (just Luis, like Cher…), and a lead guitarist—Patrick Goodwin—to round out the all-queer quartet's lineup. Pansy Division wrapped its most recent tour at the beginning of 2004, performing tracks from its seventh release, *Total Entertainment!* while further expanding its fan base in grassroots style. The band tours the country by van to bring audiences its hard-rockin' queer anthems, like "I'm Alright"—about falling for the wrong guy—and "When He Comes

Home"—an ode to infidelity and its consequences. *Total Entertainment!* is the band's most experimental album to date and finds the rockers toying with studio production tricks, like using a vocoder to give Freeman's vocals electro-funk distortion on "No Protection," and expanding their punk rock sound with an infusion of dance-pop bliss on this same track. The bubbly delivery on "No Protection" contrasts sharply with the song's subject matter and serves a dual purpose: to inspire a dance floor to get hot and sweaty while providing a cautionary tale about the risks of bareback sex.

"We wanted to deliver that message like good friendly advice rather than a lecture," explains Ginoli.

"We thought it might have a chance at being played in gay dance clubs, so we wanted to send those on the dance floor a message: There are still far too many guys seroconverting, and there should be none at this point," says Freeman.

While Pansy Division's songs are primarily tongue-in-cheek efforts about love and sex, the subject matter isn't always something the band members have experienced firsthand. Such is the case with the sonic sex romp "When He Comes Home," which relays the tawdry tale of one man's tryst with a hot trick whose boyfriend doesn't know about his infidelity.

"The song is more of a composite of a few different situations I knew about," says Freeman, who is lead vocalist on the track. "I tend to twist the angle of perspective until I feel that it makes a good song regardless of how it really is. Like on 'James Bondage,' I've never been a bottom in an S/M situation—always the top—but that perspective of 'doing something to someone' in a song is too much like Mötley Crüe. So I turned it around so that it was being done to me, and then it's entertaining and disarming."

**"Down to his dungeon for a little session.
With his whip in hand, he's gonna teach me a lesson."
—"James Bondage," Pansy Division**

Entertaining, educating, and inspiring a generation of queer rockers and fans are merely sideshows for the members of Pansy Division. Their primary intent is simply to play the music they want to play without being censored by the mainstream. When it comes to punk rock ethics and DIY drive, Pansy Division may just be the closest thing we have to a truly original rock and roll band on par with superstars like Green Day and Blink 182. The only difference is the guys in Pansy Division happen to be out and proud.

"When we started the band, we realized that we didn't want to live in a world where you couldn't have a career in music and be out of the closet at the same time," says Freeman. "Today, after 12 years and seven albums, we get to thumb our noses at the music business. Now I want to live in a world where an out gay artist can have a number 1 hit."

CHAPTER 7

Happiness Is the Best Revenge

Linda Perry's Rock Star Records may have stopped spinning, but gay- and lesbian-oriented record companies aren't as rare as you might think. There is a wide roster of new indie labels launching gay and lesbian bands and helping to carry the sounds of homocore out of the clubs and onto the streets from New York to California. A case in point is Los Angeles-based Spitshine Records, a burgeoning enterprise started by Ryan Revenge, former singer and guitarist with and cofounder of popular queercore band Best Revenge and current front man for the punk rock trio Terrazzo.

"Spitshine Records was inspired by the undying spirit of upstart labels like Mr. Lady, Dischord, K Records, Chainsaw, Kill Rock Stars, Outpunk, Heartcore, and Agitprop! And by the DIY ethic of zines like *Scutterzine, Faggo,* and *Holy Titclamps,*" says Revenge. His label continues to help promote and distribute the music of some of the best queer-oriented bands around, including Vancouver's Skinjobs, Revenge's Best Revenge discs, and Los Angeles's IAmLoved and $3 Puta, a dynamic punktronic duo that includes Raquel Contreras and Rudy Bleu, founder of *Scutterzine*

and the queer-bent Scutterfest rock event.
"Spitshine runs on the same octane and defiant
attitude that carried Pansy Division through
years of touring and playing for redneck Green
Day fans across the country and recording
seven albums—and never backing down.
Never 'prettying' themselves or their sound.
Never using the scene as a stepping stone."

"I'm a strong believer in the punk/DIY
ethic, and that led me to want to have my
own label to put out Best Revenge stuff,"
continues Revenge. "Then, after that got
going, I started thinking, *Hey, maybe I should
put out other bands too.* It's about wanting to
document great music. To have a record of
what's happening at a moment in time.
That's what albums are, really—a snapshot
of an artist at a particular point—and I think
it's a privilege to be involved in such a thing.

"But the label isn't really about promoting
just gay bands. It's about promoting bands
that I believe in, and giving GLBT bands the
fair shake that they deserve but often don't get
from other labels. I want the bands on the
label to be about something revolutionary. If
it's about queer rights, that's great! If it's about
something else progressive, that's cool too.
Just be about something. There's already plenty of music out there that's about nothing."

"Studs and leather and combat boots,
that's what you're gonna get.

So meet me at the Rancid show,
and you can grope me in the pit."
—"Punk Rock Fag," Best Revenge

Whether he's promoting other bands on
Spitshine Records or fronting his own
group, Ryan Revenge is not the type of punk
rock fag to mince words or keep his creative
expression hiding behind a closet door for
the sake of appeasing any particular audience. As front man for popular '90s Los
Angeles homocore band Best Revenge,
Revenge also contributed songs and gave the
band its queer edge with tunes that packed a
musical wallop, like "Punk Rock Fag."

"My idea was for the band to be such a
damn good punk band that people would sort
of get the lyrics as they went along," says
Revenge, who formed Best Revenge in 1997
with two other out musicians, drummer Bilito
and bassist KT, with hopes of spoon-feeding
the local rock scene a taste of homocore.

"They call it compassionate as they
slam our hands in the door.
It's nothing new. We've seen it all
before.
They pass the power down from
father to son.
Just wait 'til they see what we've got
in store.
'Cause we're gonna bash back."
—"Bash Back," Best Revenge

"I had the express intent to do a punk band and I wanted to be openly queer in the lyrics. One of the first songs I wrote was 'Punk Rock Fag,' and everything else just kind of followed from there.

"The band I was in prior to Best Revenge was a 'straight' band called Happy Bomb, and I was playing drums," continues Revenge. "At one point I just kind of realized that one of my biggest problems with the band was that I was just tired of playing along to songs about girls and love.

"Although everyone in the band was cool with my being gay, there was never going to be an opportunity for me to step up as a songwriter and at least have the capacity to be honest. It felt like a dead end to me."

"I crossed my fingers for luck, hopin'
we could be alone.
He took me ridin' in his truck, down
a dirty back road.
And in the broad daylight, nobody
else around,
I think I heard Hank Williams, as we
wrestled to the ground.
He's my rockabilly boy."
—"Rockabilly Boy," Best Revenge

Revenge swapped drums for guitar and started writing songs about backroad boys, homo clones, and compassionate hetero alterna-rock hero Ian McKay. He also switched his priorities over to fronting his own band with Best Revenge, and together with bassist KT, he placed classified ads in local Los Angeles music magazines to attract like-minded musicians for a "queer band."

"The world's a mess.
There's nowhere to go, and people
wanna kill me 'cause I'm homo.
When I got my head against the
door, give me something worth fighting for."
—"Ian McKay," Best Revenge

"A lot of people just didn't get it," Revenge says with a laugh of his novel idea for a new band. "We would get people calling who clearly hadn't even read the ad, which said right away that we are forming a 'queer band.' We had to explain to strangers on the phone what 'queer' meant. It was pretty painful."

Later, Revenge and KT turned to Bilito, who they were renting a rehearsal space from, and invited him to step behind the drums.

"We made our debut at Mr. T's Bowl [a straight club] in [the Los Angeles neighborhood of] Highland Park," recalls Revenge. "I was really nervous, thinking about what it's going to be like to play a song like 'Punk Rock Fag.' I was like, 'OK, here it is. It's time to sell it to the audience. Put up or shut up.'

"Some people thought it was really cool.

And some people just blew it off. At that time, I never got any negative reaction. I don't know if it's just because people really don't listen to the lyrics or if they just don't care."

Years earlier, when he was growing up in a small farm town in Illinois, Revenge was fascinated by a punk rock band out of the Bay Area called Pansy Division. "During the summer just before I left for college, a good friend—a straight friend that I grew up with—played Pansy Division for me," Revenge recalls. "It was really this sort of surreal experience because I don't think he had any idea what he was exposing me to and what a big deal it was for me in that moment, because I wasn't out yet.

"He was really into LookOut! Records [the West Coast-based label Pansy Division was on] and he was listening to a lot of LookOut!'s bands. Thank God for mail order, because that's the only way we were getting any of this stuff at the time," he says with a laugh. "And LookOut! Records is where Green Day came from. Green Day had actually taken Pansy Division out on tour with them that year. So a lot of kids that were into punk started picking up Pansy Division records—and most of those kids were straight. My friend thought Pansy Division was cool. He wasn't put off by the gay stuff. And I always thought that that's the way anyone who really considers himself

to be punk should feel about it, because punk is about challenging old ideas and creating new ones.

"The name 'Best Revenge' actually comes from a Pansy Division song," Revenge continues. "When I was thinking of names for the band, I started thinking, *What was one of the important things that happened that made me feel I could do something like this?* And Pansy Division was certainly a part of that, and one of my favorite songs by them is "The Best Revenge."

Pansy Division released "The Best Revenge" in 1998, and Revenge started his band later that same year. And coincidentally, 1998 was also a year when you could feel the mood of gays worldwide immediately change when gay college student Matthew Shepard was found beaten and tied to a fence in Wyoming on the chilly morning of October 7; he died five days later. His murder was reflected in the music of many gay and lesbian artists. In 1999 former Kansas girl Melissa Etheridge waxed poetic on an original rock and roll eulogy to Shepard called "Scarecrow" from the album *Breakdown*. Revenge—who grew up on a farm outside an Illinois town of about a thousand people—saw Shepard as a sort of kindred spirit. He poured his reaction to the brutal hate crime into a song titled "Sacrifice," which found its way onto Best

Revenge's 2000 EP *Begin* and later on the band's debut full-length disc *Starts with You* in 2002.

"I won't be a martyr for your hate.
Or a victim of your gun.
I won't be your human sacrifice.
I won't be the one you leave tied to the fence.
I won't be a headline on your page of news events.
I won't be the one to make you more human."
"Sacrifice," Best Revenge

"I had a very visceral reaction to Matthew Shepard's murder," says Revenge. "I guess it was because, for me, dying in a rural setting at the hands of rednecks wasn't really that far from what could have been the truth for me if I hadn't left [Illinois] and come to L.A. I had a really gut reaction to it.

"I didn't write the song immediately, because when something hits me that hard, I can rarely write about it immediately. It takes a really long time to process," he says. "I finally came to the realization of what the media was making out of it. The way it was being approached was like, 'Gosh, isn't it bad to hurt gay people?' And someone has to *die* for us to realize that? I was like, 'What bullshit! He didn't have to die for you to know that it's wrong to kill fags. That was the feeling I got from it. I was like, 'Fuck you, I don't have to die in order for you to know that, and no one else has to either. And if you don't get that and someone has to die because of it, then you're just an idiot.'

"After I wrote the song I realized that dying for being gay isn't the only thing that happens. People are put through all kinds of sacrifices for it. But you don't always realize that living here on the West Coast."

CHAPTER 8

Cum on Feel the Boys

WHEN YOU'RE A ROCK BAND WITH A GAY EDGE AND YOU OFTEN FIND YOURSELF PLAYING IN
A PREDOMINANTLY STRAIGHT ROCK AND ROLL CLUB SCENE, A GOOD SENSE OF HUMOR IS ONE
OF THE BEST WAYS TO ENDEAR A NEW AUDIENCE AND INVITE THEM TO JOIN THE PARTY. THE
MEMBERS OF CHICAGO'S SUPER 8 CUM SHOT LET YOU IN ON THE JOKE THE MOMENT YOU
HEAR THE BAND'S NAME.

"Super 8 Cum Shot is not afraid of a little humor, and hell, we like our tongues not only in
our cheeks but also in the cheeks of others," says the band's sharp-witted, sexy shaved-headed
vocalist Jinx Titanic, the sole gay member of the band, which also includes straight shooters
Machine Gun Garofalo on guitar, Dax Malkovich on bass, and drummer Posey "T Mint" Parker.

"We're a rock band, and we love having a good time," adds Malkovich. "We like to stay
up late. We like to drink booze. We like to get a little man-to-fan action after a show. We
enjoy a good laugh. And we can appreciate the immense value of the occasional novelty
song, which certainly may be one of our unique qualities."

But just because they have a keen sense of humor and sharp wit, don't think these randy
rockers don't have a softer, serious side. They do. They occasionally tame their party-animal

spirit to give a cleverly phrased hard-rock lambasting to hypocritical Bible-thumpers, archaic homophobic laws, and conformist closet cases, which is something they do in the searing "Manifesto." And in the tellingly titled "Your Hearse Is Here," they decry the shameless glamorization of the drug-saturated circuit party lifestyle and the risks of bareback sex.

But as purveyors of melodic party-rock, the members of Super 8 Cum Shot tend to keep their more somber tone in check. They're all about giving their audience a feel-good buzz and a ringing in their ears with humorous ball-busters like "Check Your Nuts" and "Oh Daddy." In fact, most of Super 8 Cum Shot's ballsy and eclectic rock and punk songs are laced with sardonic wit that's hard to ignore. Songs like "You Smell Like Dinner" from the band's self-titled 2002 debut *Volume I*—and "Everybody Loves a Muscle Boi" and "There's a Porn Star Shining Down on Me" from the 2003 sophomore release *Volume II*—are party anthems that take gay sexual innuendo out of the bedroom and into the center stage spotlight.

"You are the kinda humpy humpy daddy nobody ever called a queer. You are the one and only U.S. male who can deliver from the rear."
—"You Are," Super 8 Cum Shot

Super 8 Cum Shot's amp-rattling live shows have been rocking club crowds and winning over new fans from coast to coast since July 31, 2003. For their debut club performance, the quartet traveled from their Midwest digs to Los Angeles for an unforgettable night at the Whisky a Go Go, the legendary rock and roll haunt that served as a launching pad for groundbreaking L.A. bands like the Doors and Van Halen.

"We were very excited that our first show would be at such a historic club…until we arrived," recalls Garofalo, "and then we realized that we were on a bill with three metal bands. It was like, one of these things is clearly *not* like the other. We cracked up, got drunk, and threw caution to the wind."

"Much to our surprise and relief, the audience was exceptionally responsive," adds Titanic. "People were screaming and dancing. No one seemed put off by the fact that a big drunken homo was barking out lyrics from a gay perspective. The light show at the club was over-the-top, the sound was excellent, and on top of it, there was this earth-mother type emcee who gave us one of the best intros and outros we've ever had. It was all about come and people coming, and people coming out and coming together. She used the word 'come' at least once in every sentence."

The guys may have effortlessly wowed Los Angeles with their brash brand of original, sexsonic songs, but when it came to gaining support in their hometown of Chicago, it wasn't as easy as turning on their amps and rocking the room. When Super 8 Cum Shot applied to perform at Northalsted Market Days, an annual street festival that draws a large queer audience, in August of 2003, the event's organizers, Chicago Special Events, weren't as receptive as the booking agents at Whisky a Go Go.

"Chicago Special Events did not want to book the band and flatly refused to deal with our booking agent," says Titanic. "Several members of the Halsted Street chamber of commerce met with Chicago Special Events and demanded that we play the event. After a little wrestling match, not only did Chicago Special Events concede to the wishes of the chamber of commerce, but we received top billing! It was our first show in the top spot on a bill."

"And it was the largest crowd we've ever played for," adds Malkovich. "It was thrilling to hear thousands of people screaming out the 'fuck you' part of the chorus of 'Everybody Here Wants to Fuck You.' We were called back for two encores that night. It was definitely a milestone show for us."

"Grab yourself a partner, get yourself undressed.

**Shimmy up and shimmy down, let nature do the rest.
Find a place to put your hands, find a place to lick.
Or you can cover it in latex.
But ya gotta keep it slicked to do the Super 8 Cum Shot."
—"Super 8 Cum Shot," Super 8 Cum Shot**

The initial obstacle Super 8 Cum Shot experienced before its Northalsted Market Days debut prompted the boys in the band to create a new venue that encouraged and welcomed homocore bands to rock and roll with abandon. They turned to the popular Chicago leather bar Cell Block for support. There they began hosting a monthly rock night: Super 8 Cum Shot kicks off the punk rock party with a short set before turning the stage over to three or four handpicked local bands.

"We're trying to encourage a scene where good music and a good show are the defining features," says Malkovich.

"And though we dislike the labels 'homocore' and 'gay band,' we see to it that bands with LGBT members are given the opportunity to showcase their material alongside bands with only heterosexual members," adds Titanic. "The night has been tremendously successful for both the bands and the bar."

When Super 8 Cum Shot isn't busy

transforming a leather daddy cruise bar into a monthly rock and roll spectacle, the members like to mix it up and test the waters at local mainstream clubs, injecting the Windy City's straight scene with some loud and raucous homocore raunch.

"We played shows in straight rock venues for about nine months before a gay venue would even book us," says Titanic. "Many LGBT supporters of Super 8 Cum Shot will travel to see us at those straight venues, and by doing so they change the entire atmosphere of the room. From the onset, our audiences have been a beautiful and sexy mix of gay, lesbian, straight, and transgendered. We're very proud of the fact that a Super 8 Cum Shot show really encourages a vibe where not only is everyone free to be who they are, but they are also free to have fun!"

"A Super 8 Cum Shot show is performed with the same energy and in the same manner regardless of the venue or the bill," adds Garofalo. "However, at the predominantly gay shows, Jinx has the best chance of getting laid, where at the predominantly straight shows, Dax, Posey, and myself have the best chances of getting laid," he says with his tongue firmly planted in cheek.

CHAPTER 9

Down at the Queer Twist and Shout

"I try to shock, because shock is entertainment. When people are truly shocked, they're never bored."
—Glen Meadmore, *The Advocate* (1990)

If you've ever been to a gay rodeo, you know that cowboys are usually well-mannered little wranglers schooled in the ways of charm, politeness, and hospitality. They can be quiet, shy, and remarkably reserved, preferring to woo you with a bashful, aw-shucks demeanor instead of coming on too strong. Well, they broke the mold when they made Glen Meadmore.

"Never trust a hustler.
You know it's not too smart.
Even though he's handsome,
and he's got a nifty bone.

Girlfriend, let me tell you,
Just leave the boys alone."
—"Never Trust a Hustler," Glen
Meadmore

A performance artist who sings tongue-in-cheek country songs about blow jobs, hustlers, and really hot young boys, Meadmore has more than just queered up country music—he's raked it over the coals, turned it inside out, and tarred and feathered it. And he's ruffled quite a few of those feathers with his riotous stage shows, one of which even got him arrested for lewd conduct and public nudity. (Apparently someone took offense when the lanky, naked cowboy stuck a chicken head up his butt. Go figure.)

It all started in Winnipeg, Canada. The son of a professional football player (his dad played for the Winnipeg Blue Bombers and the Saskatchewan Roughriders) and a lawyer heavy into Native American politics, Meadmore often had to adjust to new towns and new schools to accommodate his dad's job in sports. An avid music fan, he began composing songs when he was just 13.

"I used to plunk away at my grandparents' piano, and I remember playing any old thing and saying I had just written a song," he recalls. When he was 14, Meadmore went to see Alice Cooper in concert during the

shock rocker's 1971 Killer tour. After one look at bassist Dennis Dunaway all decked out in sequins, Meadmore's rock star fantasies began. "I went right out and bought an old Black Vox teardrop bass because it was the most unusual bass they had," Meadmore says. He landed a gig playing in a blues cover band, then eventually moved on to the guitar—and anything else that tickled his fancy.

Meadmore kept himself very busy with music during his formative years. He formed an art-rock band with pal Jay Willman, who had been in the blues cover band with him. He played synthesizer, sax, and electric piano. Other bands followed—including the Gooferz and a punk outfit named the Psychiatrists. Then in 1977, Duncan Wilson—a musician who had formed a band called Papa Pluto with Guess Who lead guitarist Kurt Winters—caught Meadmore doing a song on a local cable access show he had started with the Gooferz. "He asked me to do a song during their set, and I did," Meadmore remembers. It was then that Meadmore began to cultivate his bizarre stage act. "During one show I did for Papa Pluto, I fellated a banana and squished a grapefruit," he says.

After leaving Winnipeg for Los Angeles in 1982, Meadmore stormed Silver Lake in high drag and with screaming synthesizers.

77

H O M O C O R E

As with other homocore artists like Extra Fancy and Slojack, the Silver Lake leather bar scene served as the launching pad for the emerging alternative rocker in the mid '80s. At the now defunct but legendary cruise bar One-Way, Meadmore—done up in thrashy-trashy drag—made his debut. His sound was a techno-clash melding of Hank Williams and a dog running around yelping like it just had its tail cut off. The edgy performance artist was a little bit country, a little bit rock and roll, and a lot of strange.

After a brief stint in an "arty" band called the Theoreticals ("I remember one show where it was just me warbling 'I'm just a girl who loves to go-go, I'm just a girl who can't say no' over a tape of me playing a grindy Moog riff repetitiously"), Meadmore recorded his first solo record, *Chicken & Biscuits* in 1987. *Squawbread* followed in 1988, and both were released on the independent Amoeba Records.

For the most part, music critics have been deadlocked when it comes to Meadmore's work. In a 1987 *Option* magazine CD review of *Chicken & Biscuits,* critic Peter Margasak said, "If you're into cross-dressing and inane humor you may like this, but it holds virtually no value otherwise." Jonathan Gold's *L.A. Weekly* review of the disc said of Meadmore's efforts: "His music is better than you might think. So are his costumes."

By the time the early '90s rolled around, however, Meadmore was already bored with the now de rigueur drag edge and decided to change his sound and his costumes. He reconnected with an acoustic guitar, traded in his pumps and tiara for cowboy boots and a 10-gallon hat, and trailblazed a new queer-punk sound through the Los Angeles underground. His music featured an edgier, punk-rocking country-singed style and helped usher in L.A.'s always unpredictable homocore scene.

Meadmore took his queer-cowboy punk rock to any stage that would have him—from Los Angeles to San Francisco and beyond. He promoted indie discs like 1991's *Boned,* which featured tawdry tunes about queer love and lust and looking for "beer-can dicks." Along the way Meadmore's musical exploits were covered in every cool periodical, including *Details* and *The Village Voice.*

"It was around this time [in the early '90s] I realized I wanted to get back to playing guitar," Meadmore says of his decision to form a "cunt-ry" band. He recruited musicians from one of his side bands (a thrash-metal outfit called Pedro, Muriel, and Esther—which also included drag rocker Vaginal Crème Davis in its lineup), and coaxed pal Dave Kendrick to play drums in an offbeat country-western band.

Of his decision to go country, Meadmore

says, "A friend told me to put a fiddle in one of my old songs, and I just liked the way it sounded. It made me think that corny music has real power. And nobody has done anything in country that's really subversive, so I just wanted to tweak the country format because it was so conventional. So to me, it was the perfect thing to try and convert." Meadmore says he has a great fondness for the music, having been raised on it by his grandmother. "She used to play Charley Pride and Ronnie Milsap records and took me to see Jim Reeves when I was 4. All I would talk about after the show was the pink and green hair on his backup singers." He also professes a love for bluegrass music, adding, "I like fiddle square-dance tunes and the innocence of the early mountain folk ditties."

Innocence is not exactly something that comes to mind when Meadmore's name is spoken. "I wanted something that people would remember," he says of the chicken head incident. "I'd heard about some performer who'd thrown a dead cat into the audience. So I thought, 'I'll get some chicken heads!' So I went down to the butcher shop and got a couple of bags of chicken heads and threw them into the audience during my show and put one of them up my ass. But people didn't know what they were until the lights came up at the end of the evening, so they didn't know what I was doing. And

then they started throwing them around. It was mayhem."

Another controversial mishap occurred during a Gay and Lesbian Visibility Week show in the cafeteria of the University of California, Santa Barbara, where Meadmore—who was jumping from table to table and going hog-wild with the crowd—exposed his penis while he was singing. A few weeks later, he found himself smack-dab in the middle of a debate about art versus pornography. For the trial, Meadmore says, "My public defender brought in artist and UCSB teacher Ann Hamilton and she gave a great lecture to the jury about the history and excesses of performance art. This put my show in perspective. It was *very* glamorous." Meadmore walked away a free man in the end due to a—ahem—hung jury. Though he recalls the experience as a "stressful" one, he says it gives him satisfaction to have made it through the ordeal. "It was like a rite of passage. Everyone should go to trial at least once in their career. You gotta prove you cut the mustard."

The experience also put Meadmore in touch with his spiritual side, which he decided to use to his advantage. Thus, Glen Meadmore announced that he had been "reborn"—though, admittedly, he uses the term loosely. "My version of Christianity is not the Bible," he states. "It's in my own mind. I use all sorts of different references to get my definition of what Christian is."

"Let me tell you about a boy I know.
We met looking through the glory hole.
Started milking when I pinched his tit.
Sucked me so dry that I could not spit.
He had a face like a saint and a
mouth like a whore.
They don't make 'em like that no more."
—"Glory Hole," Glen Meadmore

With a shift in music and mind-set, Meadmore set about recording a new album, and in 2002 released *Cowboy Songs for Little Hustlers,* a celebration of all things queer—country-punk style. With titles like "Chickenhawk Stomp" and "Never Trust a Hustler," Meadmore skewers the staples of country music in favor of camp and bad taste—but all in good fun.

"I've always felt it was my calling to make people laugh and cheer them up," he confesses. "My music and lyrics and insane onstage banter is meant to amuse—and abuse." Still, not all audiences are in on the joke. "It's hit or miss," he says of the decidedly "mixed" reaction he gets from crowds.

Even some gay people don't know how to take him. After playing a gay rodeo, Meadmore walked away feeling a bit like a leper. "Those guys didn't know what to make of me. They were expecting Clint Black and stuff. And I was doing really wild, kind of techno-y country."

Obviously, Meadmore is not everyone's cup of tea, but that's part of what he likes about his style. "I like a strong reaction—either boos or applause," he admits. Truthfully, he's turned on by the idea of pissing off people whenever he can. Once, when he opened for a punk band in the early '90s, the audience vehemently booed and pelted him with objects during his act. "I loved it," he professes proudly. "I felt I must have really done something right."

And how does it feel to be the redheaded stepchild of country-punk music? Surprisingly, Meadmore doesn't feel at all ostracized by the typical good-ol'-boy mentality of country. "I think the pop and rock world seems to be more homophobic than country," he says. "I think someone like Dolly Parton or Reba McIntyre would get a kick out of me. You have to have a good sense of humor about yourself to get what I do."

CHAPTER 10
Star Power

Imagine this: One day you're just another struggling Los Angeles musician sling-ing hash for a living, and after one fateful audition, you suddenly find yourself jamming with Kelly Osbourne, supporting Robbie Williams on the road, and wrapping up your third European tour a few months later. That's exactly what happened to hard-rocking drummer Alicia Warrington.

"Right before getting the job with Kelly Osbourne, I was going absolutely insane work-ing as a waitress," says Warrington with a giggle. "I was searching for the right musicians to play with and just having no luck whatsoever. I was at the end of my rope. I could not serve food to people one more day! I was constantly in a bad mood, screaming at people. I had a good friend, Carrie, who worked with me. And one Friday, I went in to work and screamed, 'Carrie, where is my band? This is *not* what I'm supposed to be doing!' Carrie laughed and said, 'It's coming. Don't worry.' The next Friday I was on a set shooting my first video with Kelly.

"A friend of mine informed me one fateful Saturday night that Kelly was looking for a female drummer and was holding a small audition. I learned her single 'Papa Don't Preach,' went in for the audition on Monday, and Tuesday I got the job. Friday, we were doing the video for her single 'Shut Up.' It all happened very quickly."

Having been out since she was a teen living in Saginaw, Mich., Warrington had no qualms about addressing her sexual orientation when the subject of relationships was brought up during a random conversation with her new band mates.

"I don't think it's possible to avoid the subject," she says. "For instance, it was brought up the day after my audition for Kelly. Her other band mates were asking me questions and asked about my boyfriend. I told them that I didn't have a boyfriend, that I in fact have a girlfriend. That opened up a whole series of questions.

"When I was around 17, I found that as soon as I told my family, friends, and band that I was gay, everything seemed much better for me," continues Warrington. "I was a happier person. I didn't feel like I had to hide anything. Before, I felt like I was living a double life. I was depressed and wrote much angrier music," she says with a laugh.

"And with my new band, the gay issue couldn't have been avoided. It's not like I was going to leave my girlfriend at home while I went to the American Music Awards and MTV events and everything else. I wanted her to share in all of these wonderful things that were happening to me. I never want to exclude her, because she is an important part of my life. If people can't handle it, that's not my problem. I don't judge other people on the way they live their lives.

"Kelly didn't treat me any differently at all," says Warrington. "She actually asked me a lot of funny questions about it. There were things that she really wondered about, but they just sounded funny coming from her

because she is a very blunt, up front person.

"The only thing I worried about when I first joined the band was if it was going to be a concern of the Osbourne family. I joined right at the height of *The Osbournes* television show on MTV. It turned out to not be a problem in the least bit," says the multi-instrumentalist, singer, and songwriter.

"I've had so many memorable moments with Kelly," Warrington says when asked about the benefits of being a seemingly "overnight" success. "Performing at the American Music Awards was a great time. It was a privilege to share the stage with legends like Elton John, Willie Nelson, and Ozzy, and people like Britney Spears and Missy Elliott. Another very exciting moment was playing my first arena show at the Nassau Coliseum in New York," she says with a big smile. Later she admits that while she's appreciative of her newfound stadium-size success, "I don't want to be a part of someone's backup band forever, you know?"

Nowadays Warrington is concentrating her efforts on recording and then shopping around to major labels her debut solo album, which she works on during her off-time from the Kelly Osbourne Band. Admittedly, Warrington intentionally lost the angry edge that once colored her music with her early band Fudgegun.

"My writing these days is very pop-rock," says Warrington, who is playing all of the guitars, bass, and drums as well as singing on her solo project. "The first few songs that I recorded make me think of Natalie Merchant meets Avril Lavigne and Macy Gray with some rock thrown in," continues Warrington who shares a Los Angeles pad with fellow queer rocker Chris Freeman of Pansy Division.

"I met Chris in 1998 at a venue in Chicago called the Fireside Bowl. I was on tour with Fudgegun and Chris was on tour with Pansy Division. We played a show together and I just thought they were great. It was awesome to see a group of four flaming gay men performing for a crowd that loved them," she recalls.

"I had told my mother earlier that year that I was gay, and I really didn't have any gay-friendly places to go or know many gay people in Saginaw. It was an inspiration to see Pansy Division—such an openly gay band—touring around the country in their van and opening for Green Day."

Like Warrington and Pansy Division, superstar singer-songwriter-producer Linda Perry is challenging the system and making a difference merely by choosing to be open in her professional career.

"I've never not been outspoken about my sexuality," Perry once told *Girlfriends* magazine. "Everyone knew I was gay—I mean, I was on *David Letterman* with DYKE on my shirt!"

Perry rose to fame in the early '90s as the top hat-wearing, dreadlocked front woman for the San Francisco rock band 4 Non Blondes, whose 1993 hit "What's Up" carried the group out of the clubs and into arenas. The band's success was short and sweet, cementing 4 Non Blondes as a one-hit-wonder after Perry split to pursue a solo career before the group could put together a second album. After recording one solo disc for Interscope Records—1996's awesome but mostly overlooked *In Flight*—Perry jumped ship from the major label and released her second solo disc—1999's equally captivating *After Hours*—on her own indie imprint, Rock Star Records. She started Rock Star in 1995 in order to record her music exactly the way she wanted and as a springboard for other gay-friendly artists and queer rockers. She enjoyed moderate critical success along with label mates like lesbian rockers Stone Fox and 2 Lane Blacktop.

But monumental commercial success didn't come for Perry until years later when she wrote and produced several tracks on pop superstar Pink's best-selling 2001 album, *M!ssundaztood,* and after she penned the 2003 transatlantic self-reflective hit ballad "Beautiful" for Christina Aguilera. These gigs elevated Perry from one-hit-wonder status, and she's since become one of the most in-demand songwriter-producers in the music business. With her meteoric rise to fame taking up much of her time, Rock Star Records has since folded, but Perry's star is sure to burn bright over the mainstream music biz for quite some time.

CHAPTER 11

Fear of a Queer Planet

"Put the fear back in queer.
Tell them all: We're recruiting!"
—"Recruiting," the Skinjobs

UNLESS YOU'RE A DIE-HARD SCI-FI FAN YOU MAY MISS THE MEANING BEHIND THE CLEVER MONIKER OF CANADIAN HOMOCORE BAND THE SKINJOBS. AND IF YOU THINK THE NAME SKINJOBS HINTS AT SOME SEXUAL INNUENDO—LIKE "SPANKING THE MONKEY"—YOUR DIRTY LITTLE MIND IS WAY OFF BASE. BUT ALL THAT IS PERFECTLY UNDERSTANDABLE.

"It does have a sexual twist to it, doesn't it?" muses band front man Mitch Fury when asked about his group's sexy name. "The Skinjobs' name came from *Blade Runner.* In the movie, 'skinjobs' is a derogatory term for replicants. I thought it would be a great name for a queer punk band because it's a parallel with the queer world. In the movie, the replicants are robots that look just like human beings, and you can't tell the difference between them and biological human beings. It's like being queer; you don't know who's queer—anyone can be. There's not a look or anything that's specific for people to note. So it seemed like the perfect name.

"It's funny, though," he continues, "because people hear the name 'Skinjobs' and they usually think it's got some kind of weird sexual connotation to it. Sex sells, so it works for us!"

"Davie, Church Street, and Santa Monica, Christopher, Folsom—I want to cruise them all..."
—"Peep Show Love," the Skinjobs

Sure, sex sells. But when it comes to trying to win over straight rock audiences with queercentric songs—and endearing yourself to the discofied gay audience with brash and edgy punk rock anthems—a healthy dose of good-natured fun doesn't hurt either. After all, if you're delivering a tongue-in-cheek attack on queer stereotypes and rainbow-tinted pride propaganda in a song like "Burn Your Rainbow," humor tends to soften the bombastic blow to the senses.

"I think we're all bound by comedic relief in this world, and I think it's a good way to get people to open up to things," says Fury, whose openly lesbian band mates—bassist Mason Newlove and drummer Lee Hendon—share his quiet pride and keen sense of humor. "Some people think that we're actually over the top and a bit too serious about the queer angle. But to me it wouldn't be funny if it wasn't that way.

"It's important to document your history in your own way, on your own terms, so people don't try to document your history on their terms, in their way."

"When I was 5, I used to play with dolls and switch their heads and all their clothes.
Such a fuss about what to wear.
Screw them all.
I don't really care what they think or what they have to say.
Just give respect and get the pronouns straight—
that's Ms. Fury to you, boy."
—"Gender Bender," the Skinjobs

"In the beginning, the Skinjobs was just a project about writing music together," continues Fury. "Lee and I wanted to start a band, and then when we started writing these queer, fun songs, we were like, 'Hey, let's do a queer punk project!' And so the band became specifically queer and punk in focus. And it's supposed to be fun and shared with our community in Vancouver. Now we want to take it abroad. We want to take it to the next level."

The Skinjobs' glam-slam shows have already captured the attention of Vancouver's gay and straight music fans. Their bold and ballsy melodic punk rock anthems and colorful mix of down-and-dirty drag queen backup swingers have turned the band's shows into a B-52's-like party of club kids and punk rock boys mixing and moshing in perfect synchronicity.

"It was an incredible mix of people that came out to our very first show, which was in a seedy queer bar in Vancouver," recalls Fury. "We specifically organized it to be at a queer bar and have other bands that were queer playing with us. It was a lot of friends—from squeegee punks to leather daddies. It's not often you get to see such an interesting, diverse mix of people together in the same room. It made our first show one of our best—better than we had expected. It was packed. It was a very inspiring show to play. We created this space where queer punk kids could gather together and have fun and dance."

"Later on, when we played our first show that wasn't queer-specific—we played on a bill with some other bands—we sort of went, 'Uh-oh, I wonder if our songs are gonna go over with a straight crowd. Are they gonna be wigged out or offended or uncomfortable?'

"Then, to our benefit, the opening act was this solo performer called Mr. Plow, who was this guy with an acoustic guitar who sings these mellow, beautiful-sounding songs but with the most perverse lyrics. He got on stage and we had no idea what kind of music he played. And then when he started we just thought he was hilarious. We were like, 'If he's going to be singing songs about some girl pissing on him or these crazy-ass perverted songs he has, we figured our stuff is going to meld with this or end up being tame in comparison to some of the stuff he was doing.' And the audience liked his stuff because it's different and it's good. The gig was good in pushing us forward and dealing with our sort of insecurities.

"Honestly, on a personal level, at first it was a bit uncomfortable thinking, *Oh, my God, what's it going to be like playing these [predominantly straight] shows? Our songs are so overtly queer, how is the crowd going take it?* But that's the real challenge, and that's actually where it needs to be taken so that it becomes normal dialogue in the straight community.

"We like to celebrate our queer punk community and have a fun, safe space to do it," continues Fury. "But there's also an element where we like to mix it up and play different shows so that the 'straight' crowds are exposed to it as well. Sometimes the 'gay punk' label works for us, and sometimes it's great when we play shows that are just 'punk rock.' That's where the really interesting things happen. That's where our crossing over into different audiences has a positive effect.

"And actually," he remarks after a moment of reflection, "we've never had anything negative said to us in any environment we've played in—straight or gay."

Onstage, Fury is just as passionate about his music. He has the ability to be both a captivating showman with a sense of humor and a serious musician dedicated to his art and its direction—which compels audiences to take notice of the Skinjobs. His roots as a pioneering queercore musical artist are planted deeply in punk rock, which helped him smash open the door of that proverbial closet when he was 23 and fronting the predominantly straight band Sparkmarker.

"I grew up really getting into heavy metal and then punk rock," Fury says. "I was into bands like Corrosion of Conformity, DRI, and the Accused. I got really involved in punk rock because I liked the fact that it was really good music, it was really heavy, and there were intelligent lyrics. It appealed to the intellectual, political side of me that needed to be nurtured. And through punk rock I developed a certain level of self-confidence because it's all about doing what you want to do and being who you are and not always trying to fit in. It was an incredible concept to realize that music could be so open.

"So by the time I did come out of the closet I was pretty adamant that no one's going to be homophobic to me, because I've been into punk rock since I was 14. I was quite confident about who I was in that scene and being able to express myself. But coming to terms with my sexuality and finding role models—people who were into that kind of music that were queer—was initially hard because there very few like me, or they were very obscure. As far as bands go, there would be rumors that Bob Mould in Hüsker Dü might be gay, but I never actually read it as fact. And then hearing that the keyboardist in Faith No More, Roddy Bottum, might be gay. But I never read an official acknowledgement of it. Later on, when I was out and actually read a quote in print about Rob Halford from Judas Priest being gay, I was very inspired. It was awesome. Judas Priest was the first concert I ever saw, so it really had an impact.

"The whole queer liberation movement has moved so slowly, and I think that Halford was probably trying to be as out as he could be for the time period [of the '80s]. I mean, if you look back in retrospect, he was really fucking with people with his leatherman image, but it just wasn't written down as such. I guess I tend to want to fight the whole concept. Do people's sexual identities or gender identities need to be black and white, and do they need to be labeled so clearly? And if they're not, will people just assume you're straight and narrow?

"But fortunately, when I was finally coming to terms with my sexual identity, I discovered other queer people out there that made it easier to come out. Like Mike Bullshit of *MaximumRocknRoll* in the mid '80s who was a hardcore punk kid who wrote a column in that zine that was all about him being gay. He had a band called GO! And he wrote in his column about his queer life. I identified with his writing. People like Mike Bullshit were inspiring because they were out and they were in the New York-hardcore-tattooed-mean-tough scene that was very aggressive and very homophobic, and for him to be out was very fucking cool! It was very inspiring."

Fury's passion for change through music reverberates in his songs. After one listen to the Skinjobs' *Burn Your Rainbow* it's nearly impossible to resist the band's contagious choruses and equally infectious sense of humor. Their powerful pro-gay personal and political beliefs insinuate their way into your senses like an audio intoxicant. And what else can you say except "rock on!" to a young gay and lesbian punk band that includes on its debut album a song like "Recruiting," an awesome queer anthem about coercing the mainstream masses into homosexuality?

"The time is here.
The time is now.

Tell all your friends, 'cause we're recruiting.
Door to door, school to school, show to show—yeah, we're recruiting.
Every color and every size and every shape—yeah, we're recruiting.
There ain't no war. There ain't no fight, just tons of fun...
It feels so right, it can't be wrong, so scream along: 'We're queer!' "
—"Recruiting," the Skinjobs

"That song was inspired by the [queer activist group] Lesbian Avengers in Vancouver, who used to put up posters around town that said, 'Lesbian Avengers. We're Recruiting.' I loved that poster," says Fury. " 'Recruiting' is a kind of a sarcastic jest for people who are living in fear in this world—the conservative right wing of society—and who are saying that, you know, their sons and daughters are going to get recruited by whatever queer culture they imagine is out there. We figure, if they think that way, let's give it to them—let's put their worst fears into a song and make them cringe." Fury breaks into a bout of laughter.

"It's great if the song can put some fear in the people who actually believe you can be recruited to be queer, and it's a good joke for everyone who is queer and understands and appreciates the humor, because our songs are very tongue-in-cheek and layered, and that's what the queer world is—it is very layered and there is a lot of different kinds of humor. Everything is not so black and white. And that's the kind of fun, silly songs we like to play. I think that 'Recruiting' makes everyone kind of laugh when we play it live, and the drunker they get the more they want to scream, 'Yeah, we're recruiting!' And we couldn't ask for a better audience response than that."

Just as quickly as they endear a gay audience with a song like "Recruiting," the Skinjobs can cause a few brows to furrow with the ballsy anti-gay-stereotypes anarchy anthem "Burn Your Rainbow," which is arguably one of the most memorable and mercilessly melodic tracks on a disc of many. While a blisteringly hot and aggressive guitar hook rips through the undercurrent of the song, Fury sings, "We're more than color by numbers. Celebrate—you're one in a million. Don't imitate—stop trying to fit in. If everyone looked like everyone, then tell me: Just who would you fuck?" To borrow a line from Fury in that song, the track is "punk as fuck." And pretty fucking brilliant—if you can take a joke.

"Our music is meant to be fun and it's all about having a good time. I never really thought about it from a marketing/business level, or that this must be a successful venture," Fury says when asked whether he wor-

ried a song like "Burn Your Rainbow" might alienate gay audiences.

"A lot of the gay community is reflective of people with money—white, male, rich. An advertiser's dream," he continues. "But that doesn't reflect my community or my politics or my experiences growing up. So we decided to create a project—the Skinjobs and Burn Your Rainbow—that critiques that and reflects something different, because there's many different perspectives in the queer community that don't have the money to advertise or put their page in a magazine or document themselves. We're just putting another little piece in that multicolored rainbow that for some reason doesn't show up on coffee mugs."

As a consequence of the reverberations from homocore bands like the Skinjobs—who are single-handedly changing the landscape of their local gay community—a new sort of sub art community has developed in cities across the land. In Vancouver, homocore has spawned a music scene called the QP (Queer Punk) Collective, a supportive, Warholian group of like-minded musicians and artists.

"We're definitely a soundtrack to the QP scene," says Fury. "There's a bunch of other bands that identify as queer or lesbian or are political and have queer members in them, bands like CHE, Chapter 127, and the Stunts.

And the Skinjobs is kind of the result of a supportive community that existed in the QP Collective. All of these artists have always been there, but once we attached the label 'the QP Collective' to this network of supportive like-minded artists, it became more of a noticeable scene. Not just a scene, but it's something that allows people to know that there is a bunch of other queer people they can connect with and find out what's going on and establish a bit of history to watch grow. And I think that's very important that we're documenting that history and have places to celebrate it and share it.

"The Skinjobs began as a part-time project and we just wanted to have fun with it but also do something kind of queer," Fury continues. "In itself, I don't think that's being political. We were just being ourselves, but because of the political climate of the world where queer issues are still cutting-edge in nonurban areas—and even in some urban areas—it becomes political because people think, *You're making a political statement. Why did you have to talk about your sexuality?* Well, we're just talking about our lives, you know? When we talk about our sexuality and gender, that's just us taking about our experiences and our lives, and that becomes political because nonstraight sexuality is still oppressed in many areas of the world.

"We specifically label ourselves 'queer' as a way of kind of broadening the scope of the terms 'gay' and 'lesbian' because we don't necessarily identify with just the sexuality or gender roles being so specific. We like the word 'queer' because it is inclusive and it is open and does leave room for people to have their sexual or gender identity be fluid. And I think that's a really important fact for our band and why we use the word 'queer' on our CD and include a spoken-word piece about being queer and how we feel about that word."

The text of the spoken-word piece—"Hands in the Air"—borrows from and puts a rocking new spin on Jesse Heiwa's 1998 essay, "In Defense of 'Queer.'" The track, buried deep within the solid set of powerhouse punk on *Burn Your Rainbow*, provides a good balance to the energy of the album, following fun and funny songs about same-sex lust, gender bending, tawdry tranny tales, and looking for "Peep Show Love." It kicks off after the fifth track, with Fury layering a smokin' guitar track over bassist Newlove's quick-paced, fluid spoken-word delivery:

"If we really need an umbrella for us all, why not 'queer'?
Let's not be afraid of ourselves...
Let us name ourselves and speak

with our own voices: 'I am a proud queer in solidarity with my brothers and my sisters all around the fucking world!
And I will be accepted as one of you, not who someone else wants me to be!"
—Skinjobs, "Hands in the Air"

Using punk rock music as a soapbox to express personal and political issues is nothing new to Mitch Fury. He was doing it even before joining the QP Collective, while he was a member of the predominantly straight band Sparkmarker, a popular Vancouver club staple in the early '90s. But it wasn't until he hooked up with Newlove and Hendon and put his energies into making a name for himself in the homocore scene that he tapped into his full creative expression as a musical artist. The Skinjobs, however, didn't start to take shape until one fateful afternoon when Fury came to collect on a favor from Hendon, whom he had known from the Vancouver music scene.

"She had borrowed my equipment," Fury recalls, "and I said, 'Hey, well you owe me a favor. Let me use your jam space for a while and we can jam together.' Then we decided to write some queer songs that were overtly gay or homo or queer or whatever, and to just have fun with it. Then we thought, *We should start a band; we should play shows*

with this material. We recruited a bass player—Mason—by putting the word out to our friends that we were looking for someone to play bass who is queer and who would want to be involved in this project. Then everything just clicked. And it immediately felt comfortable.

"For me, being in bands previous, I was always the token queer person in the band," continues Fury. "In Sparkmarker, which had a kind of political mandate that crossed the board of being omnipolitical in some ways, I did one song that was gay specific, and one that was kind of about HIV and AIDS issues. But I never really got to do the queer rock thing in a way that was really celebrated, like I wanted to.

"The other band members were totally supportive. They were my musical peers, and as far as my being queer they were totally supportive, but they couldn't necessarily relate to the full extent of me coming out while I was in the band. They were great about it. But you really can't compare the two—playing in a queer band and being the sole queer member in a 'straight' band. One's not better than the other; it's just two different kinds of objectives.

"But with Sparkmarker, and being out and open in that band, there wasn't really much room for dialogue to talk with the audience after the show about queer issues.

Even if I was up onstage and playing queer songs [in a straight environment], it wouldn't be a response of people going, 'Hmm, cool,' and then coming up after the show to talk. That's why I wanted to create a gay punk scene.

"I've always known lots of lesbians in the indie rock music scene, but not many fags, at least not as many, especially in Vancouver. It seemed like the ratio was like 9 to 1. So that inspired me to want to do more queer things, to create a dialogue or a safe venue, especially for guys, to talk about their sexuality and build a community. And I wanted there to be more fags in music, playing different kinds of music and not just disco. I mean, going to gay bars was neat, but they weren't playing the kinds of music that I listen to. I accepted the music there, but I love rock and roll, and I knew there were other gay guys out there—musicians and rock fans—that felt the same.

"There was one time when Sparkmarker was playing in Italy, and I had a sticker on the back of my guitar that said DAMN HOMO," recalls Fury. "A couple of kids came up and started questioning me because they thought I was being homophobic. I was like, 'Oh, no, no, no. I'm gay. It's just sarcastic humor.' And they were like, 'Oh, OK.' But no conversation came out of it. It was like, OK, homophobia is not cool. But there was no dialogue like, 'Oh, that's cool, you're queer,' and then taking the dialogue on to the next level.

"But now there's just a different culture surrounding the Skinjobs. And I couldn't be happier about it."

CHAPTER 12

Breaking the Mould

"Listen, there's music in the air.
I heard your voice, coming from somewhere.
But look how much we've grown.
I guess I should have known."
—"See a Little Light," Bob Mould

WHEN IT'S MENTIONED TO BOB MOULD THAT IN AN INTERVIEW FOR THIS BOOK, SKINJOBS FRONT MAN MITCH FURY EXPRESSED HIS DISMAY THAT THE ONCE MYSTERIOUS AND AMBIGUOUS MOULD DID NOT COME OUT EARLIER IN HIS CAREER, MOULD JUST SHAKES HIS HEAD AND REFLECTS ON HIS EARLY DAYS IN THE GENRE-DEFYING, GROUNDBREAKING BAND HÜSKER DÜ.

"You know, some of the regrets in my life are when I hear comments like that and realize that, yeah, had I felt like I was more comfortable with who I was and what my sexual identity was, I would've been out sooner." The ex-Hüsker Dü and former Sugar front man came out publicly in a 1994 interview with *Spin*. "But some of us are incredibly self-hating, and it takes time to get to that point. It's especially tough if you're going to be called upon in a way to sort of lend your thoughts about the movement, like now [with this interview] or in Seattle [at the queer-rock Bent Festival]. If I'm not feeling good about myself, if I'm not feeling comfortable with where I am in my life, I don't wanna talk about it because it would be fairly destructive.

"Now I feel pretty full, integrated, whole, not self-hating. Now it's a whole lot easier to talk about.

"I think it's just getting over the self-hating as much as anything," Mould says with a nervous laugh. "I make no excuses for the things I do and the life that I've had, but, you know, I never really was in the [gay] life, for whatever reasons. Maybe not identifying with the gay community that I saw around me in the late '70s. Certainly empathizing and doing what I could through the '80s, again without self-defining. You know, in '94 I had reached a point, I think, of critical mass exposure as far as success in my career and there was no way to delay the inevitable.

"I always thought people knew that I was a homo, and I didn't think that it should matter. I thought that what I was doing with my work was what was important."

"Poison years in my mind.
Got to free myself from this bind.
I know I'm a reasoning guy."
—"Poison Years," Bob Mould

Before Mould came out, there really weren't many other notable rock musicians calling for a more tolerant environment in rock music for openly gay musicians. Legends like Lou Reed and Michael Stipe were still coming to terms with their ambiguity, and the most visible "questionably gay" musician in alternative-rock music seemed to be Fred Schneider, the flamboyant front man of the B-52's. You have to wonder if it would have been different and more comfortable for Mould to come out in his career if there were other rock and roll role models who were out.

"Uh, no. Probably not," says Mould. "Not at that time. You know, the [gay] culture has come a long way since I was 16 years old. I think now it's important. I think back then I don't know if I could have absorbed it any better or worse. But I think society is completely different now. Me at 16 and somebody at 16 right now, it's not even comparable.

"To the best of my knowledge, I never denied my sexuality, but never acknowledged it either," says Mould. "I was evasive until I realized that there was no point in being evasive, and that was in '94 in the *Spin* interview with Dennis Cooper, which infuriated me to no end because that was my 'out' piece, and it was an awful out.

"Dennis is a gay novelist and, I thought, kindred spirit; and maybe he is. I took him into my home for a couple days, and he spent a couple days with me and my partner and pretty much walked away with my life story. And unfortunately, what became the article in *Spin* was about 10 minutes' worth of that. There was a quote where I said something like, 'I'm not a freak, and I don't want people looking at me like a freak, because this is just who I am.' And in the context of everything else that I'd been talking about would appear sensible; out of context it looked pretty horrible, and it made me look like I had screwed up and really insulted a lot of people. And I've been spending the better part of a decade to figure out what I can do to undo that. But, you know, there's no good way to come out.

"However, I don't know if coming out sooner would have changed my work," Mould continues. "But now that I am integrated and out, it does affect my work. But at the time, I don't know if it would've. I know it would have affected my career possibilities.

"And when I came out, I knew it was gonna put a dent in things. And it did. There are components of the [music] business that are not gay-tolerant whatsoever," he says. "And some of those components are really strong pieces of the puzzle as far as commercial success goes. And they started to fall away one by one."

"As the years go by, they take their toll on you.

Think of all the things we wanted to do.
And all the words we said yesterday.
That's a long time ago."
—"See a Little Light," Bob Mould

In 1988, the year Hüsker Dü called it quits, Mould recorded his critically lauded debut solo album *Workbook,* a reflective, moody experimental rock soundtrack to what was happening in his life just after he severed his ties with the band.

Later, in an interview with *Sound Spike* to promote *Workbook,* Mould talked about one of the benefits of being a solo artist: "I find myself not afraid of offending a band mate by writing on a particular topic they might not be comfortable with." And what might that "particular topic" be?

"Life in general, but definitely gay issues too," he replies. "Sometimes when you got a band, even though I may be the leader, you know, I'm sensitive to the content vis-à-vis the people I'm asking to help me get it across. So life issues mostly, but gaycentric issues too."

One of Mould's life issues was kicking booze in 1986, a venture into sober reality that opened up his creative expression and softened the edge of his somewhat somber personality.

"Yeah, well, people like to hear me talk

about pain," he says with a laugh that play-fully mocks some of his early moody moments in interviews. "Being sober and out, you just feel more of everything, then you start to live life and you get the full-ness and you get all the tones and the shades of life."

THREE DOLLAR BILL

"getting to know you"

IAMLOVED
NEVER FORGET

www.spitshinerecords

VOICE YOUR DISSENT.

SPITSHINE RECORDS
EST. 2002

punk & queer zine
faggo

SPIT & GLORY
3

SÖUR

SUPER 8 CUM SHOT

PARENTAL ADVISORY EXPLICIT CONTENT

DD1118L COMP

COMP

DOU 10X

G1 471

#011154

C290CT3

MAKE IT A BUD LIGHT
THREE DOLLAR BILL
DR KILLBOT/APARTM
DOUBLE DOOR/21 &
1572 N.MILWAUKEE/
TUE NOV 18 2003

G1 471 C 0.00 EDD1118L

CN 09159

COMP

ticketmaster.com

Hanukkah Benefit

for the Terezin Chamber Music Foundation

THREE DOLLAR BILL

LORAXX

PUTA-PONS

(AND MAYBE) **EVIL BEAVER**

Saturday, December 4, music starts at 10
LOUNGE AX, 2648 N. Lincoln

gina young

The conference team, my staff, and I think so highly
of Gina that we are looking for an opportunity to
bring her back to OSU next year. I think she is the
best emerging singer-songwriter today.
– Midwest BLGTA College Conference 2003

CHAPTER 13

Rock and Roll Over

It's an unusually chilly summer night in Los Angeles, and an eclectic crowd of rock fans is making its way in to the El Rey Theatre for a sonic showcase of some of Hollywood's best new buzz bands. The final performance tonight proves to be the biggest draw. When SöuR breaks into its set with "Money Shots and Write Offs," the atmosphere in the room becomes electrified. People standing around the theatre-club stop their conversations to focus on lead singer Sativa Novak, whose power-house Pat Benatar-like vocals pique as much interest as her sexy rocker-chick look—teasingly short dress, glittering tiara, and faux fur coat. She's clearly got the chops and the sex appeal to command the attention of the tattooed hard rock hetero boys and rocker chicks in the crowd. But those of us who compose "the other 10%" are focused on Clint Yeager, the band's gay bass player. Dressed in his standard alt-rock-guy gear—Dickies shorts, high-top sneakers, and a tight white tank top that shows off his powerful build and two armfuls of tattoos—Yeager is hard to miss.

Under the hot stage lights of the El Rey, between swigs of Budweiser, Yeager is running his fingers up and down his bass at Cliff Burton-like speed, creating a supersonic wall of sound that has provided a signature style and an indie hit for SöuR. "High Strung," from the band's self-released debut *Exactly What You Think It Is,* has been added to the DJ playlists at college and indie radio stations across the county. Tonight's performance of the song gets an added dose of rock adrenaline courtesy of Yeager, who rocks and rolls to the beat while strangling his bass as if he's trying to get the loudest bang out of it. Every now and then he steps atop his amp to spit his Bud fountain-style into the audience in a move that would make Gene Simmons proud.

Those who came to see Yeager play tonight, however, half expected the gushing beer. His rockin' stage antics and rollicking showmanship have always made for a great live show, whether he was jumping off the amps as part of early-'90s industrial band Drance or spitting fire as member of mid-'90s hard rockers Superfiends.

Prior to joining SöuR, Yeager carved an indelible name for himself in Los Angeles's homocore rock scene when Superfiends crept out of the shadows of support gigs at small Hollywood clubs and made their debut as headliners at the popular biweekly queercore rock event HARD at the Faultline. It was an unusual gig because the gay leather cruise bar that hosted the event wasn't equipped with a stage. Instead bands would set up and play just to the right of a Saint Andrew's cross that was located near the main bar area. Back then, the undeniably sexy Yeager sported a shaved head with one unicorn-style dreadlock and black eyeliner that made his face look like he told someone about a fight club but shouldn't have. The band's half-hour HARD set was a sonic and visual assault of loud guitars and steely drum loops that combined perfectly with the freaky low mood lighting and the band's garish goth getup.

A competent bass player and occasional guitarist who has played in or formed a number of notable local bands, Yeager has long been a prominent figure in the Silver Lake homocore scene. Silver Lake has been home to Beck, Henry Rollins, Concrete Blonde's Johnette Napolitano, and gay alt-rock softie Rufus Wainwright, though Yeager mentions none of these relatively tame rockers when he's asked about his rock and roll inspirations.

"It's all about the KISS, baby," declares Yeager. He's talking, of course, about his early rock and roll influences—the rock gods and trailblazers who shaped his desire to be a rock musician. "I was around 4 years old, and I worshipped KISS. I wanted to be a rock star from that moment on."

One might wonder how Gene, Paul, Ace, and Peter would react to learn they inspired a young gay boy to grow up to be a hard-rockin' bassist in several bands in Silver

Lake's underground rock scene. But one thing is clear: Clint Yeager is here to rock and roll all night—*and* party every day.

As the only gay member of the up-and-coming "disco metal" band SöuR, Yeager is the bassist with attitude—the guy who spits beer, the satanically angelic rocker who snarls at the audience. With his four-gauge earrings and colorful tattoos, he looks every inch the rock and roll superstar, but it's his assured, aggressive playing of his chosen instrument that cinches his inclusion in the queer rock and roll hall of fame—though he is not so sure he belongs there.

"I guess I would have to say that I don't identify myself with queercore probably more because I am not playing in an all-gay band and I'm not tackling gay issues with my music," Yeager says, though he is happy to be known as "the gay one in the band." "I think it's important to be who you are and stay true to your art and your convictions. If I was into shaggin' watermelons, I'd be open about that too. It seems to simplify my life to have everything out on the table."

It's that casual, no-frills attitude about his sexuality—and life in general—that keeps Yeager grounded in the here and now and focused more on his music than on pandering to any one group of people. "I don't restrict myself to only participating in gay culture," Yeager continues, "and in doing

so, not only do I find that I experience a larger variety of ideas, but I also find that my sexuality has little impact on my ability to relate to people and with their ability to relate to me."

Born in Dallas, Yeager found himself living "all over" Texas as well as various parts of New Mexico. "I think my parents had a bit of a nomadic streak in them," he says, adding that he was raised mostly by his grandmother until he was 13, as his mother and father embarked on a journey of spiritual enlightenment under the tutelage of a self-discovery guru who went by the name Rhondell. "I think my parents were kind of done with raising kids when I came along, and it just seemed to make sense for my grandmother to take care of me," he recalls. "My upbringing is in every way abnormal." There was one upside, though. "My grandmother was pretty old and couldn't really chase me around, so I got away with a lot of stuff," Yeager laughs. He idolized Judas Priest front man Rob Halford (who came out years later) and recalls "ogling [him] from the front row of half a dozen shows when I was a kid and not knowing why I was so enamored."

Inspired by the music ("I'm into the spontaneity and lack of structure along with the idea of creating something powerful," he says of his attraction to rock and roll),

Yeager bought a guitar and taught himself how to play. Ironically, the first song he learned to play was Judas Priest's "Livin' After Midnight," which was written and performed by then-closeted Halford. It wasn't long before Clint realized that he would need to get out of Texas if he wanted to take his love of music any further.

At 15, the independent-minded Yeager broke out on his own, bound for Los Angeles. "I felt like there were like-minded people here," says Clint, who resides in Silver Lake. After arriving, Yeager lived "the traditional struggling musician life of several guys in an apartment, all supporting their music habits with retail or food service jobs."

He kicked around with a gloomy death-rock band called Catastrophe Ballet and then a hardcore group named Seminal FK before finally joining the the queer industrial dance-rock band Drance, whose early '90s debut was an underground phenomenon in Southern California. Yeager then formed his own band, a theatrical rock outfit named Daisyface. It was during this time that Clint met his longtime band mate Sativa Novak, who joined Daisyface as a singer. Though the buzzworthy band didn't last (it eventually ended in a storm of personality clashes), the friendship between Yeager and Novak did. At Novak's request,

Clint quit another of his own bands—the theatrical rock group Superfiends, which he describes as "super animated, hi-fi porno"—to back Novak and band mates DD Ehrlich and Tom Curry in SöuR.

"I saw a lot of potential [in SöuR]," Yeager says of his decision to jump ship to jam with Novak and company, though Novak's involvement was the deal clincher. "I would be a liar if I said I didn't like playing with her," he adds. It's primarily the reason why he doesn't feel out of place as the only openly gay musician in a band full of hard-rockin' heteros. "It's like all the other bands I've been in," he says. "It's just normal. I think I relate to the people I play with first and foremost on a creative level. If we click in any other areas, that is a bonus that can only be helpful."

It's a thought that is shared by Novak, who, when asked about Yeager, becomes positively gushy. "If you are lucky, maybe once or twice you meet someone that truly knows what you are trying to do and wants to collaborate," she says. "Clint knows rock. He knows about the haute couture value of dirty rubber and yet will drag his own electronics around in the lonely, rainy hours after a show that no one cared about. He does this because he has to. He doesn't have your morals. He's not listening to someone else's story. He is an artist on all planes, and his most untouchable talent is to one-up you."

Yeager's fondness for his band mates is obvious to anyone who attends one of the band's performances, but it's notable to report that Yeager almost didn't end up in SöuR because of a certain shock-rock personality whose outrageous stage antics and controversial lyrics often overshadowed his music. Following Daisyface's breakup, a somewhat disillusioned Yeager came across an ad in *L.A. Weekly* announcing auditions for Marilyn Manson's band. Thinking he was ready for a new scene, Yeager put together an audition kit that included photos of himself in outrageous costumes and one in particular that featured him in a mock self-sodomy position. A month later, he and a musician buddy, Don Cilurso, received calls from the Manson camp. They were told to learn the music from Manson's debut EP, *Portrait of an American Family,* and show up at Trent Reznor's recording studio within a week.

"It was exciting and horrible," Yeager recalls of the experience. "Auditions are always horrible. You are put on the spot and scrutinized by a group of strangers who already have a bond with each other." But, having learned five of the songs from Manson's CD in just a week (and dedicating himself to mastering Manson's goth-tainted

rendition of Patti Smith's "Rock and Roll Nigger"), Clint showed up and did his best with a surreal experience that included Trent Reznor walking around aimlessly with toilet paper and Manson sideman Twiggy Ramirez perched on the couch beside the Antichrist Superstar himself. Later, after collapsing onto his motel room bed from exhaustion and stress, Yeager was awakened by a call from Manson, who said, as Yeager recalls, "He liked my playing and watching me play and that it would be fun to be in a band with me." Sadly, that didn't come to pass, as Yeager never heard from the Manson bunch again.

"Of course I wish it had turned out differently," Clint says now, though he takes some comfort in the fact that the guy who got the spot lasted only for one tour. "It would have been an honor to play with Twiggy. Manson is a huge creative force to be reckoned with, but musically it's all about Twiggy. I wish I'd prepared myself a little bit better and been a little more calm when I was there."

"Fuck your worthy cause;
I don't give a shit what you believe.
Yes, it's all about my crotch.
And I think it's time for you to leave.
With money shots and write-offs,
I'm becoming Jesus Christ
Supercrotch.

With money shots and write-offs,
I'm moving on."
—"Money Shots and Write-offs," SöuR

Watching Yeager perform onstage can be quite an erotic experience. A confident musician with rugged good looks and a decidedly mischievous stage presence, he's a gay Gene Simmons for the new millennium. Tearing through SöuR's set list, he alternates between aggressive menacing and playful taunting of the crowd, making sure to keep them entertained at all times. The consummate bassist, he plays off Novak's sultry sex kitten moves, making sure not to steal the focus from her seductive gyrating but remaining a prominent presence throughout.

"Sexuality is always present in what I do," he says. "Almost every aspect of me is channeled into music. It's hard to define what elements are present sometimes, because so many emotions overlap with each other. Sometimes self-destructiveness manifests itself as sexuality; sometimes love manifests itself as sexuality. Sometimes sexuality is just an expression of love. The lines become very blurry to me. I suppose the difficulty is in figuring out what is motivating the sexuality. But there's a huge amount of emotion present in the music, so sexuality is always front and center."

It's not surprising, then, that Yeager wound up composing film scores for the adult movie industry. Friends who worked for Catalina Video approached him to do one, so he "did it, and just continued occasionally doing things from then on." He eventually composed the scores for Catalina's *Night of the Living Bi Dolls, The Hills Have Bis, Sexual Suspect, Voyager,* and *The Rascal* and reports that the experience wasn't all that different from writing for a rock album. "It wasn't much of a leap at all," he says. "Most people think they write from the heart or the mind, but I'm extremely visceral and generally write from the crotch. That's where all the best music comes from."

Though Yeager only cowrote two of the songs on SöuR's debut CD *Exactly What You Think It Is,* he composed all the tunes during his tenure with Superfiends, and he's becoming more involved with SöuR's music. "Ideas come from literally everywhere," Yeager notes. "Something may start off as a drumbeat in my head or it could be a guitar part or vocal snippet. I usually try to record a rough version of the idea just to catalog it. Sometimes they inspire other parts and grow and evolve into a song, and sometimes they never make it past that initial phase. Some don't even make it out of my head. I'll be out with [someone] and get lost in my head, putting an idea together. It can really hit you anywhere. Kinda like epilepsy."

"I know how to get it done.
It's not gonna be pretty.
You know I'm up-front about that.
I'm a little high strung. Strung out.
Pissed—when I get cut down to size,
yeah."
—"High Strung," SöuR

Yeager is one of the lucky ones. He hasn't had to contend with much homophobia in the music business, partly because he's not fronting a queer band, but also (and more likely) because of his rule to never suffer fools gladly. (It doesn't hurt either that he looks like one of those edgy straight rockers you'd love to meet up with backstage after a sweaty gig.) He does recall two instances, however, in which there were negative reactions to his sexuality. The first time occurred during a sound check for a Daisyface show at a rock club in North Hollywood, where an agitated sound guy rubbed Yeager the wrong way and a confrontation ensued. "I don't think he liked my vibe and was a little disturbed by my appearance," Yeager posits. "All I know is that it led to a very agitated phone message from him on our band line threatening that the next time I played in his club I would be in a wheelchair. I distinctly remember the phrase 'faggot motherfucker' being used." True to form, the ever-mischievous Yeager decided to turn the experience

into catharsis—not to mention art. "For the next six months, we opened all our shows, including one at that same club, with that message," he says with a wicked grin. For Yeager, using the message was not only an empowering act of rebellion but one that helped him to shape his onstage antics. "That was when I started feeling comfortable enough onstage to really start playing with performance ideas," he says.

And the other time homophobia reared its ugly head? "I was kicked out of one band because one of the founding members was threatened by my sexuality," he reports with a laugh. "The irony—being kicked out of a femmy, girly goth band for being a fag. It kinda makes me chuckle."

Interestingly, Yeager doesn't have much use for the queercore movement, though he is quick to give credit where credit is due. "There are bands out there like IAmLoved that I think are amazing. I think there is a real genuineness to their expression." But Yeager remains skeptical of the queercore scene, specifically of bands (he cites Pansy Division and Nick Name as examples) that define their music primarily in terms of their sexuality. "Don't get me wrong; I respect what they are doing if it pleases them. I just can't relate to them. I think that if all you address with your music is gay-related, it makes me question whether you are being genuine or whether you live in a gay bubble."

What does he think gay bands should spend more time on? "Art is subjective and everyone is different," he says. "I guess this is going to sound selfish, but I do what I do for me, so as long as I'm happy with what I'm doing, that is the most important thing. I think when you start trying to calculate what people want you to say or what they want to hear, then you are already creating for a different demographic. I approach music and creativity in general as expression. I find it much easier to express myself than to express someone else."

If his rock and roll agenda is any indication, Yeager spends a lot of time trying to express himself. In addition to SöuR, he is also the front man for a side project he calls Speed Queen, an attempt "at stripping away the layers of what is 'current' for me. I just want to achieve that nonmodernized basic rock 'thing' that is honest and can speak candidly about where I am at this point in my life with this band." And, as if in contrast to his desire only to express himself, he has also taken up producing duties, helping gay Canadian-born rocker-lounge singer Micah

Barnes on an upcoming solo project. Yeager says producing Barnes's music gives him a deeper appreciation of his own craft. "I like being part of something so personal and intimate," he says of Barnes's plush, lyrical melodies. "[Barnes's music] is so far from anything I have done before and so lyrically accomplished that I feel kinda like what I am doing is just guiding things. It is a real honor to have someone let you in and seek your opinions."

As for his own career, "I'm still trying to write that perfect song," he continues. "The one that is sincere and speaks accurately for you and expresses your most powerful emotions. The one that haunts me when I listen to it. I don't know if that's even possible."

One thing he does know for sure is that music is and always will be his first true love. "Rock has always been a driving force," he says. "Rock, to me, is all about instinct and emotion. It's about being spontaneous and about making your own rules. It's the place where I feel at home. I love the notion that a bunch of flaky people can combine their individual sonic chaos into one united wall of sound."

CHAPTER 14

Join the Club

AROUND THE TIME OF THE BIRTH OF AMERICAN HOMOCORE ERA, BIG-CITY GAY AND STRAIGHT CLUBS BEGAN HOSTING QUEER ROCK NIGHTS, WHICH MORE OFTEN THAN NOT PACKED THE JOINTS SHOULDER TO SHOULDER WITH LEATHER GUYS, SHAVED-HEADED PUNK BOYS, AND GOATEED ALTERNA-ROCK HIPSTERS LOOKING FOR A WELCOME CHANGE FROM THE DISCOFIED GAY CLUB SCENE.

While Seattle drew the world's attention to its loud and raucous grunge scene, there was a time, from the early to the mid '90s, when homocore bands seemed to be coming out of the woodwork in Los Angeles's Silver Lake neighborhood. It wasn't uncommon to pick up the *L.A. Weekly* and see in the club listings popular homocore-identified acts like Slojack, Extra Fancy, Glue, Black Fag, and Glen Meadmore, who were rocking the stages of popular mainstream venues like the Viper Room, Spaceland, and the famous Whisky a Go Go.

The winds of change swept through Chicago's club scene in the early '90s, when Joanna Brown and Mark Freitas debuted their club, Homocore Chicago, in 1992, creating a creative space for queer punks to rock out with abandon. The event ended in 1997, and in the five years it existed it helped bridge a community of musicians and queer activists and established a network of like-minded bands and fans who even today continue to share a common culture through indie music, queer-rock zines, and political actions.

On the East Coast, club promoters Pat Briggs and Michael Schmidt had New York's hard-rock drag queens stompin' their leather stiletto heels to the beat of Squeezebox, a gender-bending drag-rock party hosted by club empress Mistress Formika that took place Friday nights at the SoHo club Don Hill's from 1994 to 2001. Between DJ sets of glam, metal, and glitter rock, Squeezebox kept bouffants bopping and heads banging to shows by local bands and occasional surprise sets by notable artists like Debbie Harry, Courtney Love, Green Day, and Marc Almond. The real stars of Squeezebox, however, were drag-rocker chicks like Mistress Formika, Jackie Beat, and Miss Guy (of the Toilet Boys) who chose to toss aside the expected lip-synching and take the center-stage mike to front their own live rock performances. Squeezebox also served as a launching pad for openly gay rocker Pat Brigs, who teamed with Don Hill's bartender Tommy Salmorin and formed the gender-bending glam-core band Psychotica. That band's moment of mainstream rock success included stints on the 1995 Lollapalooza tour and a profile interview in *The Advocate* the same year.

One hard-rocking gender bender from the Squeezebox scene even managed to rock her way right out of the club and into the mainstream spotlight as the star of her own hit musical, *Hedwig and the Angry Inch,* which enjoyed a usually celebrity-packed SRO run at an off-Broadway theater before becoming a Sundance award-winning film. Hedwig is the tortured gender-bent rocker chick; John Cameron Mitchell is the soft-spoken rock and roller who created her. He also wrote the rock musical, along with guitarist and music composer Stephen Trask, whose band Cheater served as the Angry Inch backup band to Mitchell's Hedwig when an early incarnation of the show debuted at Squeezebox in 1994.

Around the time Hedwig was introducing her rock prowess to fellow Squeezeboxers, another outrageous and unusual rocker chick, Vaginal Crème Davis, was keeping Los Angeles's motley crew of queer rocker boys amused at Sucker, the weekly punk-rock queer beer bust held at the Garage on Santa Monica Boulevard in Silver Lake. Along with drag vixen Davis, DJs Frank Rodriguez and Dale Johnson hosted the event. While Davis served as queen empress of Silver Lake's homocore scene in the '90s, Club Sucker pulled in some of the West Coast's most popular homocore and mainstream acts, including out rocker and ex-Faith No More keyboardist Roddy Bottum's Imperial Teen, Silver Lake queercore powerhouse Slojack, and popular lesbian alt-rock duo the

Murmurs. Club Sucker ended with a bang—quite literally—in 1995, calling it quits after five years of beer-busting, gender-bending, ear-splitting Sundays. Los Angeles's Extra Fancy reunited to close out the final night with out front man Brian Grillo pounding on his metal oil-can drum and ripping through a sweat-soaked powerhouse set of the band's classic queer-themed signature songs, including the S/M mosher "Yes, Sir!"

Another successful and groundbreaking queercore event to shake up the Silver Lake scene was the wild and unpredictable club HARD, which was held Saturday nights from 1995 to 1997 at the popular gay leather cruise bar Faultline. You always knew it was HARD because the sounds of Joan Jett and Nirvana drew in a younger crowd of flannel-wearing, tattooed, and pierced muscle cubs to graze with the regulars—generally burly older bears and leathermen. The best part about HARD, however, wasn't just the mix of men it attracted but rather the rockin' midnight concerts by local and visiting bands from across the country, including every underground phenom from New York City's Toilet Boys and Portland's Foreskin 500 to L.A.'s Babyland, Superfiends, and the gender-bending bands Cholita and PME (Pedro Muriel and Esther), the latter two featuring drag dynamo Vaginal Davis. Even MTV-friendly pop-punkers the Dandy

Warhols took a tour detour to the leather bar to turn in a set at HARD in 1997.

After HARD went soft later that same year (creators Enrique Marie Presley and Jeffrey Hilbert decided to pull the plug and end the party on a high note), the only real rock party left in Silver Lake was the long-running drag-rock spectacle Dragstrip 66, a loud and lively monthly event now held at the club Echo. With club promoter and former Extra Fancy band manager Paul V. (usually in his alter ego drag persona, Tureena Soup) at the turntables, it's common to see alterna-rock boys shaking it up with drag rocker chicks on the dance floor as AC/DC melds into Madonna. The eclectic mix of music and merriment has kept the place packed since January 1993. The highlight of the monthly sonic soiree is the midnight live show that features dragsters parodying rock songs by everyone from Bowie to Benatar plus sporadic visits by queercore bands.

Despite some glowing success, the homocore club scene has traveled a rocky road since its infancy. Clubs like Squeezebox at Don Hill's and Homocorps at CBGB's in New York, Rock and Roll Fag Bar at L.A.'s Troubadour, the Freak Show at Gauntlet II leather bar, and HARD at the Faultline (the latter two in Silver Lake) have come and gone. They'll never be forgotten, however, as these early pioneering, hard-rocking queer events set a rock solid foundation in the homocore scene that has inspired a DIY drive in bands and fans to continue to bring the raucous sounds of queer rock to their hometown.

Silver Lake scenester Rudy Bleu, front man of the homocore band Hot N' Heavy and founder of the hip queer-punk periodical *Scutterzine,* launched the Scutterfest music festival in 2001 at Los Angeles's Fais Do-Do. The annual Scutterfest serves as a community-bonding event that raises money for two $1,000 scholarships that are awarded annually to gay and lesbian high school students who are planning to study the arts in college.

"The first two years, the event was held on the same weekend as L.A. gay pride," recalls Ryan Revenge, whose band Best Revenge performed at the debut of Scutterfest. "I think it was Rudy's intent to give people an alternative to the pride event. It's for people who feel the pride event isn't really for them.

"The bands involved with Scutterfest kind of took a different turn from what other gay bands in L.A. were doing previous to it," continues Revenge. "They'd play 21 and over clubs and try to fit into the mainstream like all the other rock bands that descended upon L.A. Scutterfest is different

in that the bands involved, we put on our own shows and we take care of our own causes. It's very punk."

The edgy punk sensibilities and do-it-yourself enthusiasm of bands like Best Revenge may not jibe well with the cookie-cutter dynamics of the rainbow-tinted mainstream gay scene, but they're certainly not alone. Like Bleu, Revenge, and the organizers of Scutterfest, small groups of gay artists and homocore fans in cities across the country are creating queer collectives by bringing homocore out from the shadows of the underground and to the stages of popular mainstream venues.

In Berkeley, Calif., a place known for its laid-back attitude and indie rock scene, the local landmark punk club 924 Gilman Street has one key rule in effect at all times: It doesn't book racist, sexist, homophobic, or major-label acts. That, of course, is an open invitation to queercore indie bands to drop by, plug in their amps, and rock out at the alcohol-free venue, which hosts all-ages shows. All the cool bands, including Tribe 8, Bikini Kill, Pansy Division, and Sleater-Kinney, have visited 924 Gilman Street to bring their music to the Northern California masses.

Que Sera, the Long Beach, Calif., lesbian bar that provided Melissa Etheridge a place to showcase her talent early on, continues to give lesbian bands a chance to increase their fan base at a monthly Friday night showcase hosted by queer-focused Abstak Entertainment.

New Yorkers who long for the days of Squeezebox and Homocorps can visit Brooklyn's Dumba performance space, which routinely hosts all-ages queer-oriented rock concerts that have featured bands such as Le Tigre, Tribe 8, Patsy, and Los Crudos.

Boston's hard-rock drag queens looking to stomp their pumps to punk do it at Raw Bar at Jacque's Cabaret. On the second Friday of every month, Raw Bar, a club showcasing female impersonators, hosts a punk rock cabaret featuring live sets by off-beat queer bands, solo musicians, performance artists and the expected assortment of camp crusaders, including gender-bending blond rock and roll chanteuse Leah Callahan.

These cities aren't the only places where punk rock-loving gays and lesbians dwell. In other large and medium-size cities as well as small towns from coast to coast, club bookers are reaching out to touring queer bands with hopes of bringing their homocore sound to their town if only for a memorable one-nighter.

In Denton, a small city in north Texas, the lesbian bar Mabel Peabody's Beauty Shoppe and Chainsaw Repair continues to corral top touring queer female talent for its stage. The past few years have seen hard-rocking girl bands like Evil Beaver, Bonfire Madigan, and Radio Berlin rock, rattle, and roll into town. The club's booking agent, Pearl Fish, is an avid fan of homocore and female-fronted bands and actively enlists them to introduce their sound and style to Denton.

"My goal as a booking agent and promoter is to raise the musical consciousness of north Texas," says Fish, "to create a scene that is all inclusive, and to make Mabel's the stop for all the rad queer/girl bands that are on tour."

Twin Cities indie scene-makers Brett Johnson and Dave Peil felt like outcasts in their local queer community because of their hard rock leanings. So in winter 2003 they started OUT Cast Inklusion, a monthly homocore event at Minneapolis's Triple Rock Social Club, with DJs Johnson and Peil spinning rock, metal, and punk between live shows by bands like Johnson's own RADA, other local, and traveling queer bands and performers.

Since debuting in St. Louis in winter 2003, Elegant Discourse Night at the Hi-Pointe nightclub has attracted touring female-fronted and queer and pro-queer bands to perform at the monthly event, the only night of its kind in the St. Louis area.

In Eugene, Ore., students at U of O banded together in May 2003 to launch the debut of Boifest, a music festival showcasing gay male rock musicians and offering support and exposure for Northwest bands. On the bill at the kickoff were gender-bending goth-rockers Madame Morte of Olympia, Wash., punk outfit Rad Community, and Portland singer-songwriter Rory Merritt-Skitt. The show's producers (the University of Oregon Cultural Forum and the University of Oregon Lesbian, Gay, Bisexual, Transgender, Queer Alliance) are planning to make the male counterpart to New York's annual Lesbopalooza fest a yearly event.

Borrowing its format from other popular Olympia music events like the original Ladyfest and Yoyo a Go Go, Homo a Go Go is a four-day festival held at various venues throughout the city and showcasing the indie music, film, art, and radical activism based in the Northwest. The biennial event benefits the Olympia-based Gender Variant Health Project, supports a grant fund for queer artists, and features a revolving roster of homocore bands, like past performers Tribe 8, Fagatron, Lip Kandy, and Boy Pussy USA.

In 2002, Seattle welcomed the debut of its own spectacular queercore music event, the annual Bent Festival, which like L.A.'s Scutterfest coincides with the city's discofied gay pride weekend. In 2003 the event grew from one gig into a four-day music festival held at various Seattle clubs and attracting some of the biggest and most respected names in homocore, including Imperial Teen, Bob Mould, and Sugar.

"The allure above all for me is that the Bent Festival coincides with pride weekend in Seattle," says Mould. "And as a homosexual, a lot of times gay pride events do not speak to my sensibility. For someone to be putting together a festival which basically lines up completely with my sensibility and to time it in a way that it's positioned concurrent with the older, traditional pride weekends, I saw an opportunity to try to help to bring a little more diversity, at least in terms of music, to Seattle pride weekend.

"I couldn't think of a better situation than to be playing alongside people like Imperial Teen and Thalia Zedek [formerly of Come and Live Skull]. It was a win-win situation. There was nothing to lose. It's an indie rock festival of queer bands next to a pride festival. I didn't see that happening when I lived in New York. I wasn't aware of that happening in other cities in America. I imagine in places like Berlin and Amsterdam it's a common thing. But not in many American cities. I saw that Bent could be an impactful thing and that was a big draw for me. It drew me to it pretty strongly."

Cofounded by Seattle club bookers and promoters Frank Nieto and Dave Meinert, the Bent Festival has already made a deep impact on Seattle's queer scene and beyond in the short time it's been around. In a 2003 interview with RollingStone.com, Nieto reflected on the 2002 inauguration of Bent: "There was this one parent who brought her daughter down from Vancouver for an all-ages show. She came up to me and said, 'Thank you for putting on the festival. You've given my daughter someplace to go.' It made me cry."

CHAPTER 15

Homo-palooza

"It's raining, it's pouring, gender roles are boring.
So fuck that shit; we're sick of it.
All the girls are snoring."
—"Can She Bake a Cherry Pie?" Gina Young + the Bent

"IT'S A DAMN SHAME THAT THERE ARE DOZENS OF QUEER PUNK, ROCK, AND ALTERNATIVE BANDS IN CITIES AND TOWNS ALL OVER THE UNITED STATES, PLAYING MUSIC THAT'S HONEST, LOUD, AND GREAT BY ANY MEASURE—AND TODAY, NOT ENOUGH PEOPLE ARE GETTING TO SEE THEM PERFORM," SAYS NEW YORK CITY-BASED MUSIC PROMOTER AND BAND MANAGER ANNA JACOBSON-LEONG. "AND NOT ENOUGH RADIO STATIONS ARE WILLING TO PLAY THEIR SONGS—THANKS TO THE REIGN OF CLEAR CHANNEL. AND THE GREAT LABELS THAT DO SUPPORT THESE BANDS—MR. LADY, CANDY ASS, CHAINSAW, KILL ROCK STARS, AGITPROP! AND HEARTCORE, AMONG OTHERS—OFTEN HAVE PASSION TO BURN, BUT BARELY ENOUGH MONEY TO SURVIVE FROM ONE DAY TO THE NEXT."

Frustrated but determined to make a change, Jacobson-Leong decided to do something about the stagnant homocore scene and to champion queer bands her way in a valiant DIY effort.

Inspired by New York City's legendary but now-defunct Homocorps (a queercore night at CBGB's), Los Angeles's Scutterfest, San Francisco's 1996 Dirtybird Queercore festival, and Queeruptions in London, New York, San Francisco, and Berlin, Jacobson-Leong created the Queercore Blitz Tour. According to Jacobson-Leong, the tour, which debuted in Boston in spring 2004, has one mission statement: "To showcase outstanding queercore musicians who crank out hard-hitting music that's powerful enough to knock the boots off of music aficionados of any sexual persuasion.

"Queercore music is important, influential, diverse, and poorly supported," continues Jacobson-Leong. "This ongoing inequity and the desire to promote great bands such as the musicians featured on this tour fueled the inception of Queercore Blitz."

The Queercore Blitz Tour founder tapped three of New York's most popular homocore bands—grindcore grungemeisters the Dead Betties, riot grrrls Gina Young + the Bent, and metal monsters Triple Creme—to share a concert bill with brave new bands from across the country. The tour included Portland's pop-punkers Davies vs. Dresch (featuring Team Dresch's Donna Dresch); San Francisco's dark, melodic new wavers Boyskout; and post-punkers the Kitty Kill and classic retro-rock-ers Secret Cock, both from Boston.

Joshua Starr, front man and bassist for the Dead Betties, understands the frustration of Queercore's music-loving promoters and jumped at the chance to participate in their grassroots effort.

"New York is a sad scene right now," laments Starr. "It's very Disneyland: Over here you've got your fags, and over here you've got your blacks, and over here are the DJs, and over here are your trust fund kids, and here are the indie kids—everything is very segregated, and we work hard against that because we want to see all the kids doing something real."

Starr's frustration reflects the sentiment of a musician intent on expressing himself and building community through music without sacrificing personal integrity or, on the other hand, embracing any PC labels that the media tend to attach to gay musicians. Though he is out in his music career, he refuses to wave a rainbow flag at the risk of pigeonholing himself and his band into any specific category. Instead he and his Dead Betties band mates—out guitarist Eric Shepherd and drummer Derek Pippin (who, for the record, is straight)—bring their music to the masses by carefully balancing their tour schedule between gay and straight rock venues. In addition to playing New York City rock landmark CBGB's, the Dead

Betties have toured mainstream East Coast clubs like Boston's Milky Way Lounge and Philly's Pontiac Grille, while still saving time in their schedule to participate in homocore fests like Homo a Go Go and, of course, the first-ever Queercore Blitz Tour.

"You jack off at your desk
and watch the poor fucking janitor
clean up the mess
'cause you're a soldier for the
American army,
the land of the free never got rid of
slavery.
So hold your hand to your heart
and watch the world on the news
fallin' apart.
Safe and sound right by your TV.
Death is coming and watching it is easy.
Freedom is dead."
—"Social Office Science," the Dead
Betties

"The band as a whole really enjoyed being a part of the first leg of the tour," says Starr of Queercore Blitz. "We played five out of the six dates on the tour. There was a definite difference from city to city. New York was the best show for us, partly because it's home and partly because the crowd was very enthusiastic. The crowd in D.C. was great as well, and I must say that every band had a great set that night. Boston was a night of strong performances and a good audience, but there were a few technical difficulties and time constraints. And the show in Philly was very successful. It was a very rewarding experience all around, and it's always a plus to perform with bands that complement your sound and vice versa. I really enjoyed Gina Young + the Bent's performances."

The camaraderie and community of homocore music fests like the Queercore Blitz Tour apparently leave a lasting impression on fans and musicians alike. It did for Gina Young, another New York-based queer musician who was featured in the Queercore Blitz lineup and who is making a name for herself as both a solo artist (singer-song-writer-guitarist) and musical playwright as well as with the Bent, an all-girl band for which she handles lead vocals.

"I'll never forget the first time I went to a show where the musicians were openly queer," says Young. "It was a benefit in Washington, D.C., and I stood in the front for a hippie-esque grungy punk band called EstroJet. The lead singer was a beautiful woman with dreadlocks who didn't shave her legs and spoke openly about being queer, and I just remember my jaw being on the floor the entire time. I think it was the first time I had even been face-to-face with an openly queer person, and she was so fucking cool that I didn't know what to do with myself.

"Later it was the emotional and explicit lyrics of out punkers like Team Dresch and Tribe 8 that empowered me immensely—even though I didn't understand half of the terms they were using until years later," she continues with a laugh. "And then there was Ani DiFranco. I heard the album *Imperfectly* when I was in high school. When she sang about having sex with women, it gave me chills. I had never heard anything like it and I didn't know where to put all the feelings it raised in me."

Wunderkind DiFranco from Buffalo, N.Y., also left a lasting impression on another of Queercore Blitz's participants: Christina (just Christina, like Cher), front woman and vocalist for the all-girl band Triple Creme. "I saw an article in a magazine about Ani DiFranco when I was probably 20 or 21 and I literally ran to my neighborhood record store and had them order her CD immediately," says Christina, who formed Triple Creme with guitarist Robin, drummer Tif, and bassist Terry in 1998. "When I found out Ani was queer I was elated."

"When I realized that Rob Halford from Judas Priest was gay, my mind was blown," Terry adds about the inspiration behind her molten metal bass riffs. "I was so fucking excited because I had been only exposed to gay musicians through 'womyn's music fests'

and I'm not really a fan of folk. He rocks *and* he's gay? I was psyched."

"Me and my baby, we are celebrities, stars in the movies, stars of your fantasies.
We're only everything that is worth being."
—"Charlize," the Dead Betties

"Imperial Teen is an out band that affected me in a really positive way," says Joshua Starr of the power of music and celebrity. "They taught me that their sexuality had nothing to do with it—they are just a damn good band. I think it's probably very positive for unexposed straight guys to listen to 'out' musicians who are just as hard hitting as their 'straight' contemporaries. It forms a common ground."

"That's one of the things that was really cool about the Queercore Blitz Tour. There was a common ground because all of the musicians were not only queer but also into punk and hardcore too," adds Young, whose band played Boston; Northampton, Mass.; New York City; Philadelphia; and Washington, D.C. on the tour. "I think the LGBT music scene has stratified in really particular ways. Lesbians have gravitated heavily towards folk-rock, whereas the gay boys are all about that pumping house music that makes my girlfriends and me giggle, roll our eyes, and say, 'Babylon,'" continues Young, giving a nod to the disco-saturated gay Showtime series *Queer as Folk*. "I know tons of out musicians, but very few who gravitate toward the harder, punk edges of sound."

Triple Creme is one band that shrugged off folk and gravitated toward guitar-heavy rock, creating a cache of postpunk anthems that combine esoteric poetry à la Radiohead with a sonic fury and passion reminiscent of the Yeah, Yeah, Yeahs and PJ Harvey.

"It felt really good to finally be a part of a group event with the Queercore Blitz," says Christina. "Touring is fun as it is, but when you're touring with a large group of amazing, talented people, it's just something really special. Not only do you have, fun but you learn. We are enthusiastic to see what comes of the Queercore Blitz Tour over the next few years. We feel really grateful to get to be a part of it. There has been a lot of support and interest from outside sources and hopefully it will grow into something like an on-the-road Ladyfest or Homo a Go Go."

"We love that we are a part of the queer music scene, especially after touring with the Queercore Blitz Tour and Homo a Go Go," adds band mate Tif. "It's great to be around other bands that are talented and to be a part of a movement. At the same time, we don't want to pigeonhole ourselves as

only that. Our music is accessible for everybody. The human experience is something that we all share no matter what your sexual preference."

"I'm tired of this fight—who's on the left? Who's on the right?
What's on first? Where's coming home?
We're different but the same—just one big game.
Get out of your pigeonhole.
Use your mind and don't lose your soul."
—"Different Like Everybody," Triple Creme

"Who wants to be pigeonholed?" adds Triple Creme's Terry. "No one. We are doing what we want, for the most part, and hoping that there are people out there who like it, can rock to it, identify with it, and are inspired by it. If we are rejected because we are queer or not in the mainstream aesthetic, then that's just fine because I don't want to be catering to some 'world of rock' image. That would suck."

"I don't think Triple Creme necessarily started out as a queer-on-purpose venture," adds Robin. "Tif knew us all and knew we wanted to play, so she introduced us to each other via e-mail and we talked about what it was that we were looking for in terms of music, our influences, and our experience playing. We were all coming from slightly different places in terms of musical experience. Tif and I had played together in my living room—I had a junky old Ibanez that I was learning to play and she would beat on the kitchen mopping bucket and we wrote crazy songs about the pizza delivery girl and the subways and not watering an ex's plants. We mostly just laughed. So there were no auditions, just four girls getting to know each other and figuring out how to arrange hooks and ideas and lyrics into full songs.

"I don't remember there being any kind of discussion in a serious way about the band's queer identity until we started to book gigs for our tour in May 2003," continues Robin. "Before that we were very out queer, played [lesbian club night] Meow Mix a million times, played New York gay pride and at queer events or rock nights in New York and Philly. We started to feel though like we wanted to branch out a little and not just be seen as a queer band but as a good band that happened to be queer. So we started to mix it up a little and booked some 'straight' gigs. We really started thinking about how to get our music out to a wider audience without compromising ourselves."

"We decided we wanted to play to the most all-inclusive audiences and not pigeonhole ourselves as a 'gay band,' adds

Christina. "We were out already, and we weren't concerned with hiding that."

"I'm moving down without a sound.
It's so hot; sun in my eyes; desert dry.
I'm not dreaming.
Desert dry, all in my eyes.
Is it real or in my mind?
I wanna be your cowboy girl.
Would you be my cowgirl boy?"
—"Double Dutch," Triple Creme

"And now that we have a little experience under our belts, we prefer to be known first as a band, secondly as homocore; but I think homocore is a pretty good term in itself," says Robin. "Sometimes we have a hard time defining our sound, but 'homocore' tends to give people a pretty good idea of what we're about."

"'Homocore?' Well, I like the term, but yeah we are a band first," agrees Terry. "How about looking at it as I'm a musician who happens to be queer? Or I'm a brunette who happens to play bass? Or I'm a bass player who happens to have a day job…"

"I embrace the term, but I don't want to be known only for that," adds Tif. "Triple Creme is about playing music together and having a good time. We are all queer, so by default we end up in this amazing niche; but we'd like to be able to cross into other genres as well."

"It used to bother me that I had to 'label'

myself, when straight performers don't need to identify themselves as straight," says Young. "But eventually I realized that if I don't take the power of definition into my own hands, other people will do it for me. They then have the power to assume I'm a lesbian and comment on it in a derogatory way, or to assume I'm straight because hetero-normativity prevails, and then silence who I really am repeatedly and violently. I won't give away the power to define myself. As for the band, we are all very out in our lives, so it's only natural that we be out in our music."

"Supergirl lives a double life; pretends she wants a husband instead of a wife.
Ducks into phone booths to change her clothes so her momma won't see the ring in her nose.
Changes her persona and changes her name so her daddy will believe she's one and the same, as the daughter he raised to be simple and plain.
Good Catholic values like mine following in shame."
—"Supergirl," Gina Young + the Bent

"I came into my queerness and my art simultaneously—they feed off of and inspire each other," says Young, who formed the

Bent in 2002 with guitarist Kathi Ko, bassist Tracy Dicktracy, and drummer Kelly Addison, three out musicians she met through riot grrrl gatherings in New York City. "In fact, most of my early songs and poems were oblique attempts to deal with my emerging sexuality. Like in high school, I was writing queer songs before I even knew I was queer! One of my first, 'G.I. Joe,' has a first verse that goes:

'G.I. Joe was my hero.
I never played with Barbie much.
I don't know why she didn't like me.
I always found her kind of butch.'

"At the time I just thought this was hilarious. Next thing you know, I'm playing this song at the talent show and coming out to my all-girls Catholic school, wondering why all of the other students and teachers aren't as excited about it as I am."

Young's high school coming out concert may not have gone the way she had hoped, but her conviction and unflinching drive for creative expression led her to audiences that enthusiastically appreciate her strength and courage as an artist.

"I made my official 'debut' as a singer-songwriter at a queer girls open mike called 'Grrrls Night Out' in New York City," continues Young. "Having a bunch of queer girls smile and laugh and clap at my two songs definitely gave me the inspiration to keep going. They *really* got it, they completely understood where I was coming from, and that felt really validating. Since then I have played at hundreds of events—some all-gay, some all-straight, most falling into a mixed/queer-friendly middle—and I feel pretty fluent in the different approaches needed to reach different audiences."

Seducing any audience with original music is, of course, one of the rewards of being an artist with something powerful and transcendent to offer. On the flip side of the situation, however, out queer musicians who are working to make a name for themselves in the predominantly straight mainstream rock and club scenes run the risk of encountering homophobia and possibly alienating straight audiences who may be uncomfortable with gay subject matter. Thus queer artists arguably have a more difficult time than their hard-rocking hetero counterparts in building a bigger fan base.

"I don't care about that at all," says Young. "I have never understood the concept of trying to reach the largest possible audience by appealing to the lowest common denominator. I would gladly have 10 really smart dykes coming to my shows and have it mean something, rather than sell 10 million records."

"So-called str8 grrrl, you look unhappy.
I've heard the rumors.
You've got my sympathy.
Is this a lie you're living?
Is this a sin that we're committing?
...'cause if you think you're straight, how come I know how you taste?"
—"So-called Str8 Grrrl," Gina Young + the Bent

"I'm still not sure why you can't gain acceptance in the world of rock if you're not straight," says Triple Creme's Terry. "I just want to go for it. Do what we do. Be who we are and rock."

"If acceptance into the mainstream meant we would have to return to the closets from whence we came, we wouldn't do it," adds Terry's band mate Christina. "We were really lucky to have continuous and almost automatic support from the queer community, without whom we might be another under-recognized all-girl band struggling for gigs. Places like Meow Mix and the now-defunct Rising Café gave us the opportunities to play and create a fan base. Eventually we started booking shows at other venues, and although our fan base is predominantly queer, it's always nice to meet and talk to audience members who are there just for the music. We are not a political band by design, only by nature. Our first and foremost concern is making interesting, solid music."

"In one way, having the instant queer audience has been great, and in another way it's difficult because a lot of people are afraid to go to a gay bar to see music," says Tif. "For instance, our straight guy friends have felt awkward at Meow Mix. As far as being accepted in the mainstream music world, we're still working on that. It's really hard to get heard when you aren't on a major label. I think that the world is in a more accepting place now than in the past, but I'm not sure if a major label would know how to market us."

"Ideally, we would like for anyone who likes our type of music to enjoy it without reservation, without a concern over labels," adds Christina. "We can't force people to change; we can only do our best at what we do and accept ourselves. We just hope the rest will follow."

"In regard to potentially alienating straight audiences, I've always felt the opposite," says Joshua Starr. "Controversy opens up any performer up to a wider fan base, and the more dialogue we can add to this topic, the better."

"I don't know if I would use the world 'alienate,' because we're not trying to hide the fact that we're queer, and we would want our straight fans to know that, though it wouldn't have to be our primary identification," says Triple Cremer Robin. "It's more about getting better exposure outside of the queer circuit and being available to a wider fan base, which I think entails promotion with less of a 'queer' appeal, if there is such a thing. We do care about this in the sense that our music deserves to be heard by all kinds of people, and we have a lot of songs and a sound that would appeal to people outside of the queer community."

"As far as confronting any obstacles or homophobic backlash as a band, we haven't," adds Starr. "If we did, we'd just turn it around and use it to our advantage."

"I think I encounter far more homophobic violence in my day-to-day life than I do as a musician," says Young. "I get harassed on the streets and on the subway all the time, but it almost never happens to me onstage. Music seems to open people up more and makes them more generous and willing to listen to a different point of view. Music is transcendent and beautiful. Several times I've played for audiences that I thought would be hostile and had people come up afterward saying, 'Wow, I never really thought about that stuff 'cause I don't really know any gay people, but now that I hear what you're saying, it makes a lot of sense.'"

"She talks commercials.
She fucks cheap porn.

She's been cable-ready pretty much since the day she was born."
—"My Girlfriend the TV," Tracy Young + the Bent

For the Dead Betties, the issue of sexuality is a mere sidebar to the band's identity. Though the trio is two-thirds gay, the band members' intent was not to start a homocore band. It just kind of turned out that way.

"Rumors have strung you from a fence.
For a love they wouldn't let you live.
On TV screens you choke to death over laugh tracks.
Take your last breath.
Your blood they hosed away in the streets.
Made mockeries of your defeat."
—"Dead Lover," the Dead Betties

Starr formed the Dead Betties in 2000 during his senior year in high school. Starr tapped his drummer buddy Derek Pippin to help him create the rhythm section for a band Starr envisioned as combining the punk rock crunch of Sonic Youth, the ballsy lyrical assault of Rage Against the Machine, and the raucous energy and sonic drive of Babes in Toyland. In early 2002 the Dead duo hooked up with guitarist Eric Shepherd. A tight-knit trio with a power-

house of energy and contagious hooks, the band seamlessly melds together a molten-metal mishmash of heavy, spiraling guitars, hard-thumping bass grooves, and skin pounding that'd make Dave Grohl envious. It's all delivered with an underground, punk-propelled ferocity that led Homocorps founder and Velvet Mafia lead singer Dean Johnson to laud the charismatic Starr as "the gay Kurt Cobain" in a 2003 article in *HX* magazine.

"We never thought about it," Starr says when asked about the gay identity attached to the Dead Betties. "It only comes up when other people bring it up. But sometimes I do think we really scare the pants off of all the straight college-rock guys by being louder, meaner, and tougher than they could ever be. I love out-cocking homophobic rockers—it's so demeaning to them.

"But regarding the gay issue, I believe that people should not let their activities define who they are," Starr continues. "Sure I am a male, and I also engage in homosexual activities, but as an individual I feel it much too limiting to wear any sort of label. Life isn't one-dimensional. Our drummer Derek is an example of what the world needs more of—he definitely prefers heterosexual activities, but has never limited himself to that in response to any sort of social stigma. As a band we just simply love to play live, so give us a show and we'll play it. Derek plays 'gay' rock clubs and festivals just as Eric and I play 'straight' venues and bars. The three of us don't live in a black-and-white world where everyone is safely segregated. It seems a little silly to even have to dwell on such a minute issue. If only people could look past who one takes to bed.

"As an individual living in a society that thrives on making one choose which cookie you are going to be cut into, I find much, much more freedom as an artist by simply not subscribing," Starr goes on. "I don't want my art to be quarantined, filtered, and safe. I am quite open with my sexual preferences, which do give me some sort of edge. If my behaviors are offensive, I take the apprehension of others and use it to my advantage. I use this tension artistically; satirizing anyone who is willing to view an 'out' artist as being either fringe or cottage industry material. Being 'out' in my music career affects my creative expression in a positive way because I am able to expose an artistic angle that is outside of society."

"We get so angry when they call it 'girl band night'
and they let the boys play.
That's so fucked up.
We get so pissed off.
Boys rush us off the stage.

Token girl up in front.
That's not a girl band;
We think it's a crock—
use a girl to front your cock rock."
—"4 Boys," Triple Creme

"It's really hard in general to make it as an 'alternative' or DIY band," says Triple Creme's Robin, "and I think the queer factor may make it harder. However, with so much lesbian exposure on the scene right now, with things like *The L Word* and the *Queer Eye* shows, who knows, maybe someone would see us as an opportunity to give our community a wider creative outlet. Maybe we're riding on what appears to be a growing acceptance of queerness in popular culture."

"Getting signed to an indie label would be great," adds Christina, "because I don't think we're major-label material. But I don't think we are interested in that world except of course to host *TRL* on MTV," she says with a laugh. "The thing about us is, we are always content with where we are and what we are doing, so we rarely feel disappointed. This is why we stay together and are happy with what we're doing. But we really do want to tour Europe, because we *love* Italian girls."

"We just want to make good music, ultimately, and get our music out there," interjects Robin. "It always comes back to the creativity, the music itself—that's where the love is. And in the fans, the community that revolves around the music scene."

"The camaraderie of being in a queer band feels unmatched," adds Christina. "There is this deeper bond that is more than the music we create. When we play the music well, it's like this energy builds up around us that spells victory, and it is so dynamic and invigorating. It's like you always know you are queer, and it's always there in the back of your mind and, when we are all together creating as one, the difference is a beautiful powerhouse. It just erases all the moments of crap you had to live through because of that difference."

CHAPTER 16

Superkool!

"Kids, let's get political. We're generation critical.
Don't let them piss on your leg and tell you that it's raining.
D.I.Y. T.C.B. 3DB will set you free!"
—"Never Stop," Three Dollar Bill (3DB)

"I'VE ALWAYS PREFERRED HARD ROCK AND PUNK ROCK MUSIC OVER ANY OTHER TYPE OF MUSIC BECAUSE IT'S SUCH A HEALTHY, AGGRESSIVE RELEASE OF ENERGY AND EMOTION," SAYS BISEXUAL ROCKER JANE DANGER, WHOSE PUNK ROCK PASSION AND COURTNEY LOVE-LIKE GROWLS FUEL THE ENERGY BEHIND THE HARD-ROCKING QUEERCORE BAND THREE DOLLAR BILL. "OF COURSE THERE ARE A LOT OF DIFFERENT TYPES OF GAY PEOPLE, BUT IT DOES SURPRISE ME THAT THE MAJORITY OF QUEERS HAVE ALWAYS PREFERRED LISTENING TO DANCE AND DISCO RATHER THAN ROCK. YOU'D THINK THE ANGER AND AGGRESSION IN PUNK AND ROCK MUSIC WOULD BE MORE UNIVERSALLY FELT EMOTIONS WITHIN THE GAY COMMUNITY AND A WAY TO CONNECT WITH OTHER HOMOS GIVEN OUR STRUGGLE WITH EQUAL RIGHTS, POLITICS AND GOVERNMENT."

Started as a creative outlet and sociopolitical soapbox for the all-queer band members, Three Dollar Bill was launched in 1997 by Danger and pal Chris Piss, who along with Danger shares both vocals and guitar duties in the group. After an initial lineup change, bassist G. Rex and drummer Chip Lash currently round out the band. The mix of three sexy, tattooed out girls and their cute and quirky gay male sidekick makes for one hell of a fun, eclectic party-rock showcase. In fact, the Chicago band, which fans often refer to as simply 3DB, has created a good buzz throughout the Midwest. Three Dollar Bill has been a popular act on the Windy City scene ever since it put out its 1998 self-released debut EP, *Getting to Know You,* a slick six-song selection of cool and contagious pop-punk tunes. Song on the album address everything from same-sex infatuation ("Girl-O-Matic") and crusty closet cases ("Self-Loathing Queer") to Hollywood homophobia ("Must See T.V.") and even a "Retarded Drag Queen."

**"Don't laugh at Ed if he don't look so good in his sequin dress.
At least he took the time to curl his wig and wax his chest."
—"Retarded Drag Queen," Three Dollar Bill**

"At the time that we formed Three Dollar Bill, we thought that the hard rock-punk style we loved would also appeal to other queers who might be tired of folk or disco or who just like a variety of music," says Piss. "I admired the attitudes and do-it-yourself ideals of punk rock but wanted to avoid being preachy or self-righteous. Three Dollar Bill allowed me to speak out against

stuff I didn't think was right while still maintaining a sense of humor. We also thought queer audiences would like to hear rock music that said something to them about their lives."

"The main reason I even started a band was because I wasn't hearing the type of music I wanted to hear anywhere else," adds Danger. "I liked rock music, but I craved better lyrics to sing along to—or at least ones I could identify with in some way."

"When I was growing up I couldn't really identify with popular bands of the time because I was unaware that *any* famous musician was queer," says Piss. "I liked the Smiths, the Who, Styx, and even Melissa Etheridge, but no one was out back then. If I had known any of these people were queer, it might have helped me accept who I was sooner than I did."

**"Where are all the queers—you won't come out and play.
Haven't you heard yet, that 10% of us are gay?!"
—"Must See T.V.," Three Dollar Bill**

"I get a kick out of it if I learn a celebrity or musician is queer, or even pro-gay," continues Piss. "And it's not like I want everyone to be gay. I just want everyone to be open and honest and confident about who they are. I also get a kick out of knowing who's a socialist, who's a vegetarian, and who's against the war [in Iraq]. It doesn't mean I'll like their music any more or less, but I have to love somebody like Melissa Etheridge who has the guts to say 'Yes, I am' when so many others would rather say 'I'm a private person' or 'That's nobody's business.'"

"I don't feel that I suddenly like the person more just because they've come out," says Danger, "but I do respect people who are out and proud and are trying to be a positive role model for others in any way possible."

When Danger and Piss were first introduced to each other through mutual friends, both were new to songwriting and each had written a few original songs that they wanted to perform with like-minded musicians looking to form a hard rock band with a queer edge. The duo joined forces and began scouting for prospective band mates at clubs and rock shows and via their circle of musician friends. But it was in the most unexpected arena that Danger met the musicians that would come to make up Three Dollar Bill's rhythm section.

"Tells me how she hates her skool;
'Fuck shit up' is her golden rule.
Dreams of a place, could this be true?
Where all the girls rule Superkool!
—"Superkool!" Three Dollar Bill

"We've mostly had luck just finding friends who are musicians and friends of friends," says Danger, "but I met our current bass sensation, G. Rex, while playing tackle football on Chicago's first ever pro tackle women's team, the Chicago Force. Drummer Chip had some friends on the team too and was really motivated and a hard hitter, so we couldn't resist."

"There's no shortage of great people in Chicago," adds Piss. "Also, some of our former members have been straight. We are very accepting of straight people as long as they are fun to hang out with and are hard-hitting on the drums."

"Ironically, most of the members of 3DB have been female and have been queer, although we never specified either as a requirement," says Danger. "As long as each person is dedicated, responsible, and into making music it doesn't matter what their sexual preference is as long as we're all having fun and the music is sounding good.

"But as far as our band being composed of bisexual, gay, and lesbian members, it kind of just worked out that way and I really love it," continues Danger. "I'm all about integrating crowds and getting people together who normally wouldn't meet, so having both a gay male and lesbian female vocalist speaking for the band is awesome! It attracts a lot of different people."

"You could guess, but I'll confess,
archaic rules are a mess.
All the world is different now,
yet some still own and some still bow.
Apathy and atrophy—
we can't stand complacency."
—"Never Stop," Three Dollar Bill

"Even before Jane and I had met each other, we each were strongly in favor of queer women and men hanging out together," adds Piss. "The historical separation of these two groups was not something we could support and I felt like our dual leadership of this band was intended to foster an inclusive scene.

"In the beginning I didn't worry at all about finding an audience," Piss continues. "I thought gays and lesbians would like this, and we didn't expect to get any radio airplay anyway. But we ended up getting a very mixed audience, with at least as many loyal fans who are straight as who are gay. We also unexpectedly found out that straight male DJs were happy to play our music on independent radio and on local music shows on the corporate stations. They weren't threatened by who we are."

"I never worried about our audience because we formed the band mainly as a personal and creative release for ourselves," says Danger. "We thought that the gay community would like us. We never had expec-

tations of becoming 'rock stars,' we just wanted to write and play songs and hoped to be able to play some shows around Chicago every once in a while."

"I'm perfectly happy with this sexuality.
Oh, why can't you fuck off—stop trying to convert me.
I already know I do not fit the part,
but I'd rather die than give in and
have to start."
—"Phallic Symbol," Three Dollar Bill

"We just wanted to write some gay-themed songs and perform them at the Fireside Bowl, which is a wonderful filthy little all-ages venue in Chicago," adds Piss. "Our first show as Three Dollar Bill was at the Fireside Bowl and we didn't have a bassist, so I borrowed a bass guitar and Jane and I switched off on bass as much as we switched off on vocals. We could barely play guitar yet and we were even worse on bass. Our straight-but-not-narrow friend Elliot Dicks of the Chicago band the Nerves was filling in on drums and proved to be the only competent musician out of the three of us. Jane and I probably sucked, but we didn't care. We had something to say and we wanted to rock, so we did. And it was exciting enough that it made us keep going and find new members and record more CDs and get better as musicians. People who remember that first show are very polite when they say we've come a long way since then! But we have, actually. We recorded our first EP and started getting bigger and bigger shows and a little airplay."

"With a subtle lisp and pouty lips, your face could launch a thousand ships."
—"Nathaniel," Three Dollar Bill

"I still get tremendous satisfaction from just having a creative outlet," continues Piss. "Being in a queer band like Three Dollar Bill only helps me be more free and open in my writing. My first few songs were all about gay characters: 'Self-Loathing Queer,' 'Dud Boy,' 'Retarded Drag Queen.' A straight band might have responded to my writing by asking, 'Does everything have to be *gay*?' I would have said, 'Yes. My first few songs *have* to be gay.' But with a queer band, my 'gay songs' are a nonissue, and so are my songs that are not gay-themed. We have no limitations on our writing."

"Your brother says he's gonna kick your faggot ass when he gets out of jail.
Your daddy knows all about the subscriptions to *International Male*."
—"Self-Loathing Queer," Three Dollar Bill

"There are no rules in Three Dollar Bill," reiterates Danger. "In the beginning, I wrote more songs with queer themes because that was a major issue in my life at the time. While still coming from a similar perspective, my more recent songs are less likely to be 'obviously gay' just because I've gotten a lot of that out of my system. I am a personal writer, however, so there are always common themes recurring in my songs depending on my mood and state of mind. While '4/99' and 'American Dream' may have a queer voice, they still deal with issues and events that I think a lot of people can relate to regardless of their sexual identity.

"Three Dollar Bill has never been about making money, because face it, no band really ever does," continues Danger. "You've got to love the music. When I first taught myself how to play guitar and write songs I never dreamed we'd play all the places we have and would meet so many cool folks along the way, but I'm a motivated and inspired person and I've always wanted to record and publish my own albums, so things just kept happening naturally. I believe that anything is possible, and positive feedback from fans really helps."

Letting things happen naturally has been working out quite nicely for the band. Three Dollar Bill is a staple of Chicago's eclectic music scene, performing at both straight and gay venues—often bringing its pro-gay rock anthems up from the underground and to the mainstream masses at clubs like the all-ages Fireside Bowl and Chicago's legendary Double Door.

"My most memorable show was at the Double Door," says Piss, "because it's such a great club and because we got to perform on a stage that amazing people like the Rolling Stones and Nina Hagen have performed on. But I also really love playing at benefits and parties. At Chris Kellner's Hook Torture Gallery in Chicago, we played on a stage shaped like a mouth. We were surrounded by all of this sadomasochistic artwork and a polymorphously perverse crowd of leathered-up men and women—straight and gay. When we can contribute to a true alternative like that or play at a benefit to raise money for queer youth or to finish an independent film, I feel like what we're doing makes a difference to someone."

Like several other popular queer-oriented bands—Super 8 Cum Shot, Evil Beaver, Stewed Tomatoes, the Prescriptions— Three Dollar Bill is adding a lively splash of hard-to-ignore, lavender-tinted tunes to Chicago's mainstream music scene. Along the way, the band is netting headlining gigs at clubs, expanding the boundaries of rock and roll, and helping to keep alive the spirit of Chicago's lively homocore community that began in the '90s.

"Chicago's queer music scene pretty much exists within the straight indie music scene," says Danger. "It really isn't as specific as it used to be when various local promoters like Homocore Chicago would host a night of all-queer punk bands in homocore's heyday of the early 1990s. Coffeehouses and open-mike nights still thrive, and although the music isn't 'loud, brash, queer punk rock,' it's still nice to see these things happening and for there to be an outlet for queer-positive voices. Like in any big city, things change and bars open and close and people get older and find new interests. Chicago is a huge city, and I think most of the music groups are associated more by musical style than by a specific sexuality or gender. The community of Chicago indie rockers is pretty tight knit and supportive— both gay and straight. It's always a pleasure to see new queer-focused bands starting up. More! More! More!"

"Crush all destructive machinery
which is our ugly society.
Beware to bashers and senators.
This is the new culture."
—"Homo Insurrection," Three Dollar Bill

In addition to making its way onto local radio stations in Chicago and on various homocore CD compilations, Three Dollar

Bill's music has been surfacing in various creative venues. The queer punk rock quartet composed and performed homocore tunes for the 2002 revival of Chicago's Nomenil Theatre Company's original musical *Pushin' Up Roses*.

"*Pushin' Up Roses* was Nomenil's first play in the early 1990s," says Piss. "Nomenil Theatre Company is my partner Allen Conkle's company, and it's a gay troupe. There is a band in the play named Sugar Puppy Cum, but back then Allen didn't know a band, so they used actors and prerecorded music. In 2002, Allen asked Three Dollar Bill to be in the play and perform live music. It was great fun."

More recently the band was tapped to add some sonic juice to various indie films like G.B. Jones's 2003 project *The Lollipop Generation*. The gory 2004 gay camp horror flick *Hellbent* features a number of Three Dollar Bill's rousing numbers—including "Homo Insurrection," a haunting and moody song with spiraling guitars that finds Danger and Piss grinding their axes together while they spar on lead vocals.

In between collaborating with filmmakers and stage directors on side projects and cranking out several club performances every month, Three Dollar Bill found time to record its second full-length CD, 2004's *Parody of Pleasure*. Its blossoming success makes Three Dollar Bill the coolest thing to come out of Chicago since the Smashing Pumpkins.

CHAPTER 17

New York State of Mind

"She wanted the love I needed to give.
I needed the life that she wanted to live."
—"Missing the Earth," Alla Ivanchikova

BUFFALO, N.Y., MAY BE NOTORIOUS FOR ITS HARSH WINTERS, BUT ITS LOCAL MUSIC SCENE IS A HOTBED OF HIGH-CALIBER TALENT THAT HAS PRODUCED A NUMBER OF POWERHOUSE BANDS AND ARTISTS. LATE FUNKMEISTER AND SUPER FREAK RICK JAMES, THE CHART-TOP-PING GOO GOO DOLLS, LEGENDARY BASSIST BILLY SHEEHAN (OF THE DAVID LEE ROTH BAND AND MR. BIG), AND BISEXUAL INDIE-ROCK SUPERSTAR ANI DIFRANCO ALL HONED THEIR SKILLS IN TINY CLUBS IN BUFFALO. THE SWATH OF MUSIC JOINTS STRETCHES FROM DOWN-TOWN'S BUSTLING CLUB ROW TO ALLENTOWN, A HOMOCENTRIC SECTION OF TOWN A MILE AWAY THAT IS THE HEART OF THE CITY'S CREATIVE LIFE.

From the same sonic circle of Buffalo-based talent comes Alla Ivanchikova, an out singer/songwriter and Russian transplant who has taken her classically trained music know-how and added a hard and heavy punch of rock and roll. Before she even embarked on her first tour outside of Buffalo, the buzz surrounding Alla Ivanchikova prompted the editors of *Art Voice,* western New York's premier arts magazine, to put her on the cover, with an accompanying feature interview. In his interview with Ivanchikova, *Art Voice* writer Matthew Holota summed up Alla's debut release, *Missing the Earth,* in two words: "damn good."

"Buffalo's music scene is quite diverse— there are a lot of women musicians, songwriters, performers—lesbian and straight," says Ivanchikova, who's pursuing a master's degree at the State University of New York-University at Buffalo while making a name for herself in the local music culture. "There are also venues where you can experiment, try yourself out for the first time. A friend of mine, Tim Baldwin, used to organize all-women shows at Nietzsche's, a straight venue in Allentown, almost every Sunday. He would invite one artist from elsewhere—New York or Toronto—as a main act, and five or six local artists. People would get to know each other and eventually jam on each other's songs and sing along. It was a really good space to meet other female musicians. It was very democratic too. There isn't a noticeably 'big, supportive community,' really, but there are perhaps isles where you can

go and meet other artists and, most importantly, listen to them play."

Because Ivanchikova is an outspoken (and out) female musician performing politically conscious songs, comparisons to fellow Buffalonian DiFranco were inevitable. GirlPunk.net said Ivanchikova's "great voice" has "shades of Hynde, DiFranco, Harvey…" And one critic for the University at Buffalo's *Spectrum* newspaper went so far as to say that Alla's "musical sophistication far outstrips those of DiFranco's early efforts."

Getting this kind of attention as an unsigned artist is impressive—even more so when you consider that Ivanchikova doesn't compromise her music for the sake of mainstream acceptance and brazenly addresses gay and lesbian issues in her songs. In fact, remaining mum on her lesbian identity was something she never even considered.

"I had this self-important 'I am going to tell you something really special and you better listen' attitude about the whole thing, and it worked," says Ivanchikova. "In the beginning, I wasn't concerned with [her lesbian identity] at all. I was just writing what I wanted to be writing about, whether people were going to like it or not.

"It is extremely important for me as an artist to be personal in my lyrics, and being personal means being honest about the experiences I have had," continues

Ivanchikova. "My songs are loaded with female pronouns, like:

'She wanted a love I needed to give.
I needed a life she wanted to live.
I satisfied her interest
In foreign countries and frontiers,
she satisfied my urge for someone
who was near.'
—["Missing the Earth"]

"I have to talk about the situations in which I find myself in the world," says Ivanchikova. "I don't hide anything, but I don't insist on my perspective either. If I fell in love with a man, I would write about that too. I found that if you are really honest, people are accepting, because they can identify with what you are saying.

"Labels are limiting, and you can't afford to limit yourself according to whatever labels are out there in the world at the moment. Writing a song, for me, means forgetting who I am, but in a very personal way. As a gay artist, I want people to become less rigid, but I also have to learn how to be less rigid myself. And there is a lot of rigidity and intolerance amongst us [in the GLBT community] as well. For me, playing for *everyone* means also learning something from them: learning tolerance, learning about other people's experiences, being attuned to the world.

"I have a song on my first album called 'Woman I Love,' and it's about falling in love with an older woman who turns out to be heterosexual but goes along with it for a while," continues Ivanchikova. "Every time I say, 'Woman I love is 38; woman I love, she is probably straight,' everybody loves it, and most of the people who request the song are men. Because it's funny, and also because ultimately it is a song about rejection, and everybody can relate."

"Actually, my debut show with a full band was at a straight venue, and I remember that people were really listening, and some of them started laughing when we played 'Woman I Love,'" says Ivanchikova. "This song is like a 'coming-out' song for me every time I play it; so I only play it when I am comfortable in a venue.

"Playing for gay audiences is always exciting, but it can sometimes turn into a huge fiasco," she says. "In 2002 we played at this large queer event. Ninety percent of the people left long before the show started, because they were just not interested. The rest left while my band and I were setting up onstage, because they wanted to join the others in the bar. That was perhaps the only time in my life when nobody came over to me after the show to say anything, except for the organizers, who were extremely nice.

"It was a beautiful summer evening,"

continues Ivanchikova, "and just such a great night of live music and beer. We gave a great show and went home. None of us wanted to join 'the rest' in the bar in a drunken celebration. It was frustrating to realize that lesbians who were supposed to be my community just don't get it. Unfortunately, I think a lot of musicians can relate to this kind of experience.

"I like playing for mixed audiences the best. It's good to have a fair share of both crowds. I like playing with other all-girl bands—gay and straight—in a regular rock club. When you create music, or any kind of art, really, acceptance by your community is desirable, but not necessary."

CHAPTER 18

Karma Chameleon

"He's a sinewy silhouette overshadowed by his complexities,
rambling around like a tattered paper doll dressed in his androgyny.
Is he a she or is she a he?
Why won't you let her keep his mystery?"
—"Satellite Baby," Kelly Mantle

WHETHER HE'S TEASING HIS AUDIENCE WITH THE LYRICS TO HIS GENDER-BENDING SIGNA-
TURE SOLO SONG, "SATELLITE BABY," OR DONNING A DRESS AND TUCKING IN HIS PACKAGE TO
OBSCURE HIS "MASCULINE PARTS" TO SING BACKUP VOCALS WITH LOS ANGELES ROCK BAND
SEX WITH LURCH, KELLY MANTLE IS AN EXPERT AT PROVING THAT THINGS AREN'T ALWAYS
WHAT THEY SEEM. INDEED, MANTLE REVELS IN TOYING WITH SOCIETY'S CONCEPTIONS OF
MALE AND FEMALE——SOMETHING THAT HE'S BEEN DOING SINCE HE WAS A YOUNG, IMPRES-
SIONABLE YOUTH DRESSING UP IN HIS MOM'S CLOTHES AND PUTTING ON SHOWS FOR HIS
CONFUSED FAMILY.

"I was extremely musical as a child," Mantle recalls. "I used to put on my mom's old 45s
and sing into my Mr. Microphone." The priceless musical toy was a Christmas gift that
Mantle received when he was 5—one that he says convinced him that he wanted to pursue

music when he grew up—even though others tried to tell him he wasn't cut out for it. "When I was in high school, my choir teacher urged me to enter these dreadful, cheesy solo choir competitions, and the judges would always rank my scores extremely low and give me terrible critiques on my singing. And, of course, I thought these people were like singing experts or something, so I finally concluded that I couldn't sing."

Fortunately, Mantle decided to give his first love another chance. "When I got out of high school and started singing in bands, I began to discover my real voice," he says happily, "not the formal, overly operatic musical theater/show choir voice that those judges wanted to force on me."

Though Mantle took piano lessons and sang in a choir, he didn't learn to play the guitar until much later. "When I was in college, a friend of mine gave me her classical guitar because I enrolled in a guitar class. I was determined to learn how to play. But I found myself focusing more on the Kurt Cobain-esque dirty boys in the class than on my guitar technique, so I came out of that class with very little guitar skill under my belt." Still, all was not lost. "I did come out with a few hot boyfriends, though," he adds with a chuckle.

It wasn't until he caught Stevie Nicks performing on an episode of VH1's *Storytellers* that he finally decided to become serious about his craft. "She talked about the day she wrote 'Landslide.' She described particular events that occurred that day, and how she went home that evening, sat down at her piano, and wrote the song. That's when I decided that I wanted to know what that felt like. At the end of the day, I wanted to know how to put my experiences to music," he recounts. So he dusted off the guitar, sat down and opened up a guitar chord book and taught himself three chords. Later that night, he found the chord tablature for "Landslide" on the Internet and taught himself to play that as well. "The next night," he says, "I wrote my first song."

"Art is why I get up in the morning. But by nightfall I'm still marketing the scraps you see of me.
Have you heard my CD?
Or bought my DVDs to see behind my scenes?
Can you guarantee me all your money?"
—"Spotlight," Kelly Mantle

Years later, after graduating from the University of Oklahoma, Mantle decided to leave the heartland behind and go west, where he had the opportunity to combine his fascination with dressing up in women's clothes with his love of music when he was invited to join popular Los Angeles indie "glam surf rock" band Sex With Lurch as a background singer and dancer—in drag. "I jumped at the opportunity," he says. "We had so much fun."

All the while Mantle was writing songs, and he eventually decided to lay them down on a record. He asked some friends to back him up and recruited Pansy Division's Chris Freeman (whom he'd met through their mutual friend Vicky Hamilton, the woman responsible for discovering Guns N' Roses in the 1980s) to produce and play on the album as well. The subsequent self-release— 2001's jangly art-rock record *Ever Changing*—was a bewitching, effortless blend of rock, pop, and folk, a predominant-ly acoustic record recorded with a band. Featuring 15 songs (several of which were written with Freeman) dealing with the complexities of love, heartache, and the ambiguity of gender roles ("Satellite Baby" is one of the record's high points), the album displayed Mantle's obvious knack for emo-tionally incisive lyrics. He also proved to have a natural instinct for hook and melody.

But while Mantle was proud of the effort, he still thought something was a bit off. "Even though the record was recorded with a full band, it was more or less a collection of songs I had written to perform solo on my acoustic guitar, so it never really added up to me to hear these songs 'rocked out' because they weren't rock songs," he says. "I love the CD for the moment in time that it represents, and it made for a great learning experience."

What he learned was that he wanted to take his music in a different direction, one that combined the intimacy of his acoustic songs with the fullness of a band sound. Soliciting the assistance of a brand new crew of musicians, Mantle decided to redub the band simply Mantle and start over. Fleshing out the music with a more expansive sound and more challenging arrangements, the band wrote a fresh batch of songs and, after they felt comfortable enough with them, they went back into the recording studio to churn out 2003's six-song EP *Rock-N-Glow*. The indie album isn't so much a departure from *Ever Changing* as it is a fully realized expansion of it. Thankfully, the music retains its jangly freshness (imagine the Partridge Family fronted by art-pop crooner Lloyd Cole recording modern rock songs while on acid) while building on the prom-ise of the first album. That said, the songs on the second album do allow a slightly more sinister and moody darkness to creep in around the edges. Which is exactly how Mantle wanted it. "I wrote songs with a spe-cific sound in mind," he says of the second record's genesis. "I wanted to capture that darker shade of the '80s 'British pop' sound that influenced me growing up. But I also wanted to mix it up with hints of '70s androgynous glam rock like that of Bowie, Jagger, and the Velvet Underground."

Maybe I want too much.
Maybe I ask too much of life to give.
But I just can't settle for 'it is what it is' 'cuz it is what it is.
It's gotta be bigger than this."
—"Bigger Than This," Kelly Mantle

"Kelly doesn't necessarily need to write about politics in his songs to convey that he's an activist," says out singer-songwriter Micah Barnes, who performs with Mantle at the monthly Los Angeles lounge-rock cabaret Silver Lake City Limits. "He doesn't necessarily need to picket at rallies to portray his activism. His very being embraces an obvious and outward statement on gender revolution. That is her political statement."

Mantle agrees. "I'm an activist for individuality," he states. "I hope to overshadow and delete normalcy through my music."

Though he says he embraces the queer-core movement, Mantle prefers not to limit himself to it. "I've never really belonged to any one movement or community," he says. "I always find myself feeling just a little on the outskirts of any defined movement. I

find it very difficult to define myself as just one thing, one idea. I find myself being completely individualistic and yet comfortable in a wide variety of many different communities."

Like the title track to *Ever Changing*, Mantle contends that his sexuality is in a constant state of metamorphosis. He acknowledges that he's been in relationships with "gay men, heterosexual men, bisexual men, gay women, heterosexual women, and bisexual women," and says that while he defines himself as queer, he chooses not to restrict himself to the archaic notions that the term can often inspire—or to let it interfere with his craft. "Being queer definitely has an influence on what and whom I write songs about," he says. "But you have to understand that my sexual orientation is a vast and complex thing. It's very difficult to define or label—like my music."

Regarding the responsibility he feels to gay people, Mantle is consistent in his pledge to promote such uniqueness. "It's my responsibility to encourage everyone to embrace the complexity of their individuality," he says. "We are all complex individuals. Transparency and beauty have become one and the same. Complexity is [regarded as] ugly because it's harder to explain. Therefore, it's my responsibility to celebrate the freaks and queens and queers everywhere—as well as the gypsies, tramps, and thieves that came before us."

"Why do you have to talk about
what's wrong from right?
To make you feel so mighty real and
clever?
Will your pessimism keep you from
your flight?
To reveal yourself for real into forever…
The path of least resistance is the
nature of our existence.
But Iamwhoiam when I'm not who
I'm supposed to be."
—"Iamwhoiam," Kelly Mantle

Mantle stands on the stage with a guitar strapped around his sinewy torso, his silken voice haunting in its simplicity yet mystifying in its range. One moment his vocals are deeply masculine, a rich tenor of unwavering beauty; the next, his voice hits a high note that sends chills through the spines of the audience members. As he sings the lyrics to "Satellite Baby," calling for the acceptance and understanding of androgyny and gender individuality, he draws the audience onto the stage with him—not physically, but certainly in spirit. Looking around, you can see the moment it happens—a collective submission to the power of such an extraordinary performer whose sincerity and unmistakable talent defy definitions of gender and sexuality.

"I have found myself in situations where I'm performing for a club full of heterosexual male rock and roll types who are always a little weary of me at first because they think I'm gonna get up on the stage and pussy out," Mantle says of his experience playing to a crowd. "But when the show begins, I find that they end up being some of my biggest fans, because when you believe in yourself and your vision and your music, it's contagious. It crosses any lines or closed minds that may exist. That's the power of music."

CHAPTER 19

Sisters Are Doin' It for Themselves

"Don't you tell me how to live.
I don't want to be like you.
You should fucking get away.
Don't tell me what to do.
I don't wanna look like you.
You just shot me out of me.
Why don't you set me free
from your monstrosity?
—"M.I.A.," Sugarpuss

"LESBIANS HAVE ALWAYS BEEN INTEGRAL TO THE QUEERCORE MOVEMENT," PROCLAIMS FORMER TEAM DRESCH GUITARIST-BASSIST JODY BLEYLE. "QUEERCORE IS GIRL-ROOTED. THE BANDS THAT STARTED THE SCENE—THEY WERE ALL LESBIANS. THERE WERE ALMOST NO GUYS."

Indeed, from the aggressively punk histrionics of San Francisco's Tribe 8 and Toronto's Fifth Column to the garage-band rock of Team Dresch and the Third Sex, "dyke rock" literally put the core in queercore. These grrrls propelled the small gathering from its grassroots beginnings to the gay media-fueled "movement" that it would eventually become.

"We *were* the fucking movement," Bleyle exclaims. "I think it's really funny that people associate the queercore movement as being guycentric."

There's no denying that the humble beginnings of what was to become the American queercore scene were rooted in the riot grrrl movement that began in the early '90s with bands like Bikini Kill, Bratmobile, and L7. A response to the prevalent macho posturing of punk, the riot grrrl scene boasted full-blooded, aggressive femininity at its center, confronted issues such as rape, domestic violence, sexuality, and female empowerment, and applied a grassroots, independent sensibility to its manifesto. "In the early '90s the queercore and riot grrrl scenes were so intertwined," Bleyle says. "That was a very strong part of where queercore came from."

While several of the female performers who participated in the riot grrrl scene were, in fact, gay (Bikini Kill's front woman,

Kathleen Hanna, for instance), and the riot grrrl zines often dealt with the topic of homosexuality, the focus of the movement was not lesbianism, and participants were understandably angry when their music was dismissed as "dyke rock." Perhaps because of this, several of the homocore scene's key players branched off to form bands that were made up chiefly of lesbians, and, with the help of Tom Jennings's seminal zine *Homocore,* the queercore rock movement was born.

As the movement began to surge forward, with Pansy Division and Extra Fancy bringing mainstream attention to the scene with their high-profile gigs (Pansy Division opening for Green Day; Extra Fancy landing a major-label record deal), the lesbian bands began to come and go. Team Dresch folded in 1998 when Kaia Wilson and Melissa York went on to form the Butchies. And Tribe 8 went under shortly before 2000. Fifth Column and Third Sex weren't far behind. Into the picture came new bands to take the places of the old ones—though, this time around, the all-gay lineups were dropped in favor of a more inclusive mix of members. Kathleen Hanna began Le Tigre, another pansexual effort, while—also in Oregon—Sleater-Kinney featured gay Carrie Brownstein, bisexual Corin Tucker, and straight Janet Weiss. Britain's Skunk Anansie had the lesbian Skin as its lead singer, and San Francisco's Veronica Lipgloss and the Evil Eye is made up of two lesbians and two straight men.

But all-lesbian bands are, of course, still around. The Butchies have been the most recognizable underground lesbian rock outfit, boasting a hardcore following carried over from Team Dresch, while New York's Triple Creme has been carrying the torch that dyke rock queercore bands ignited during homocore's heyday. And after one listen to the music of two up-and-comers on the current queercore scene—the hardcore rock effort Sugarpuss and the art-pop outfit Boyskout—it's apparent that homocore need not worry about losing its grrrls. They're still out there rockin', and they still know how to stir up one hell of a damn good riot.

"Can't you see I am free?
You and I will never be.
You raped my soul; you raped my mind.
Can't you see it's my first time deep inside.
You're leaving me with no pride.
I'm not yours to taste.
I'm not your fucking human waste."
—"Victim," Sugarpuss

"We don't fit into the queercore genre," proclaims Lisa Kinnear (a.k.a. "Lisafer") of the hardcore Los Angeles-based punk band Sugarpuss. "We don't write music about being gay. We do not label ourselves as a queer band. It's hard enough to get respect for being female in this industry. We are just three chicks that rock our asses off who happen to be gay."

Sugarpuss's 2003 debut CD, the hard-hitting *Victim*, was a studiously low-fi venture, a throwback to the riot grrrl records of the early '90s, complete with death-metal lyrics and fully empowered delivery.

In fact, according to the girls in the band, their first gig was playing at the Riot Grrrl Festival at Koo's Café in Orange County, Calif. And like predecessors Bikini Kill and L7, Sugarpuss is about taking rock music back from the patriarchy and spreading the wealth around to the women who also want a taste of the rock and roll life.

The three women musicians in Sugarpuss—drummer Pat Calvelo and bassist Dora Sandoval round out the band—don't go out of their way to reveal their sexuality, nor do they trumpet queerness as part of their band's makeup. They say they're happiest when they're accepted just on the merits of their music rather than their gender or sexuality. "Being in a girl band, people automatically tend to think negative, like, *Oh, they probably don't know how to play their instruments* or *Oh, no, not*

143

another girl band," Sandoval says. "So that in itself is a struggle. And being gay on top of that just adds to the fire. There's been a couple of times that I can remember at our shows when I heard someone say, 'Not another lesbian band,' but it doesn't bother me much because the same person that has something bad to say is always the person that ends up really getting into our show."

"You fail to see what's inside of me.
You take the pretty pain and shove it
deep through me.
I'll swallow the air you breathe
as I watch you pray.
You choke your life away
while I sit and breathe.
Your words pierce through me
as my mind slips.
You can never heal what's inside
of me."
—"Pretty Pain," Sugarpuss

All three Sugarpuss band mates say that while they think the queercore scene is a positive thing, they do not necessarily keep tabs on it—nor do they want to. "I don't really pay attention to which bands are gay and which aren't," Sandoval admits. "I think that it's a good thing that we as musicians can be part of a movement because of our sexuality, but on the other hand, sexuality has never been an issue to me. This really hasn't been a focus

in my life. It's like, who cares if we're gay? We just want to fuck shit up!"

"I don't need your sexist regime.
I don't need to be something I'm
not.
Rough edges fade.
Scars never heal.
This is who I am.
So take me as I come."
—"School of Etiquette," Boyskout

"I always wanted to create a girl band that made songs about relationships with other girls," says Leslie Satterfield, the lead singer and mastermind behind Boyskout, an ironically named outfit that consists of four female musicians playing moody pop music in much the same vein as the Cure and Siouxsie and the Banshees, but with some riffs from Sleater-Kinney and Pretty Girls Make Graves as well. The music is dreamy—pure art-pop that sounds as fresh and as invigorating as anything else to come along in the last several years.

The band formed in San Francisco in 2001 and released its debut CD, *School of Etiquette,* in January 2004 on indie label Alive Records. After parting with the band's original members over creative differences shortly after the disc was released, Satterfield kept the beat going by recruiting Piper Lewine to play bass, former Tenth of Always drummer Alana King to pound out the percussion, and Zola Goodrich to do guitar and keyboard duties. Satterfield taught the new lineup the songs from *School of Etiquette* and wrote some new ones, and Boyskout was re-formed. "The members of Boyskout before were pretty much my friends that joined the band, and they didn't know too much about being musicians," Satterfield says. "But the new members are really solid and they know their stuff."

Indeed, Boyskout is primed to break out big with its mix of old- and new-school goth pop—if it can just dodge that darn "dyke rock" label. "I don't think that our music fits well into what comes to mind when you say the phrase 'lesbian band,'" Satterfield offers. "We'd prefer not to be labeled as one particular thing in general. Our influences are so mixed, and labels are often so limiting."

Lewine, who is straight, says that she has a problem with the band's music being defined by sexual orientation, declaring, "I don't want to be labeled as anything except a fucking great rock band." She says that she feels very comfortable being the only straight girl in the mix "because I feel like the other girls are my friends. [And they are also] individuals. When I look or think about them—or us—I don't think to myself, *Gay*. I think, *Great band, awesome girls,*

rockin' music." Lewine does add, however, that she feels Boyskout has much to offer gays and lesbians: "Boyskout is out there playing music. We are playing our hearts out, and Leslie is mostly singing about sex with girls."

For her part, Satterfield says that regardless of the band's reluctance to embrace the homocore label, it's important that Boyskout be known for being queercentric. "I do feel that it is Boyskout's responsibility to embrace the fact that [most of us] are openly gay," she says. "It is important to spread the message to kids questioning their sexuality that other people feel the same way they do and that they are not alone and that a community does exist outside of small-minded towns or unaccepting groups of people."

"A lot of bands have had gay members who have not been too vocal about their sexuality, like the Smiths, Queen, and Judas Priest," Goodrich adds. "I just think that with Boyskout, no one feels they have anything to hide."

"Oh sweet sweet sweet sweet little girl,
I still want you.
For a little while.
Another case of identity
caught by your style and my fantasy."
—"Identity," Boyskout

"There are always going to be exceptions to every rule, and I think the hetero definition of rock music is becoming less of a rule," Alana King says of Boyskout's role in rock music. "The more visible queer bands are out there, the less of a big deal it is. Homosexuals are becoming trendy."

For Satterfield, rock music is the perfect place for a band like Boyskout. "In some ways, rock music is hetero-defined because it has traditionally been dominated by straight men," she says. "But rock music has also been defined by people who go against society's norms, and that is something that any queer person can relate to."

While the girls might not like being lumped together with other bands simply because of sexuality, it's clear that their ideals are indeed rooted in movement's mission. "I feel that if you are making music, you have a responsibility to create the best music you can and to remain true to yourself as an artist," Satterfield says. "The main message of Boyskout's music is about living your life in a way that you are being as true as possible to yourself."

CHAPTER 20
Revenge of the Canadian Loudmouth

"Loud noise like apocalypse in your head
Laying with the night.
Loud boy never had nobody to love.
I went to my knees.
Will not let it breed.
I'd get every kiss I ever missed and always wanted.
If loud boy DJ ruled the world."
—"If I Was the DJ," Barnes

MICAH BARNES IS WHAT SOME MIGHT REFER TO AS AN AMALGAMATION: EQUAL PARTS AGGRESSIVE PUNK ROCKER AND QUIET, CONTEMPLATIVE PIANO BAR CROONER, BARNES DEFIES CATEGORIZATION WITHIN THE MUSIC WORLD AND DANCES TO HIS OWN BEAT. IT'S ONLY FITTING; AFTER ALL, HE DOES COUNT BILLIE HOLIDAY, FATS WALLER, AND LAURA NYRO

AS HIS MUSICAL HEROES. IN THE SAME
BREATH HE NAMES PATTI SMITH, TRENT
REZNOR, AND EXTRA FANCY AS EQUALLY
IMPORTANT INFLUENCES.

Of course, when you're the child of a
European intellectual bohemian who won
awards for journalism, fiction, and television
writing and a Jewish-Canadian jazz musician–cum–classical composer, you're bound
to have diverse tastes when it comes to culture. Add to that some of your own experiences in the entertainment trade, and you
have a very complex musical character
indeed. "I was in dance and acting class as a
kid and working onstage and TV before I
was even a teenager!" recalls Barnes, who
was born in Vienna and moved to Toronto
with his parents at age 3. He says music was
a big part of that creativity as well: "Growing
up, I met and was around musicians who
had played with Charlie Parker and Billie
Holiday, and folks like Willie Dixon and
Charles Mingus were actually coming to my
house. Music has always been the thing we
did in our family."

In time, the music bug would bite a pre-
teen Barnes as well. "The music was bursting
out of me and it drove me internally like a
force of nature," he says. "It was a larger
world of imagination and creativity that
included dance and theater and visual arts
and film. I was lucky enough to be encouraged by my parents, so I ran with the ball.
They were encouraging of my moving
around the furniture to create sets and drap-
ing a sheet over me for costumes and making up operas and ballets in the living room.
I wasn't really into girls through my teens,
but I wasn't into boys either. I had my love
affair with music instead. Looking back, it
gave me a safe haven from the world of
teenage discovery. I was pouring all that
energy into my first songs."

By the time he was 12 he'd realized that
his passion was playing the piano; by 13 he
was performing jazz and blues tunes in coffeehouses around town. Playing the songs of
his musical heroes (Holiday, Waller, and
Nyro songs were staples in his sets), Barnes
mixed it up by tossing in some of his own
compositions. He was a hit. In junior high a
friend recruited him for a glitter-rock band
called Mantis and acquainted Barnes with
the music of Lou Reed, David Bowie, Iggy
Pop, and Patti Smith. On the side, Barnes
smeared on some mascara and sported a
Robert Smith hair style and performed as
part of a family act (the Micah Barnes Trio)
with his drummer brother, Daniel. "We
formed a cabaret group doing campy queer
and new wavey material when we were still
in high school," he says.

Punk music played a big part in Barnes's musical evolution as well. He started working the door at local performance art venues, where he got an eyeful—and earful—from then-unknown experimental acts like the Talking Heads and Laurie Anderson. "I opened my head to the world of rock and roll and the ideas that punk performance rock inspired in me," he says. Upon graduation from high school, Barnes fell in with the blossoming alternative theater scene, working with punk-queer company Buddies in Bad Times, which spawned notoriously "out"-spoken acts like Fifth Column and iconic underground photographer and director Bruce LaBruce (*Super 8, Hustler White*). "We screamed our spoken word pieces seminaked to middle-class patrons out to be shocked," he says with a chuckle. "It was great."

During this time, Barnes and his brother struck it out with the Micah Barnes Trio, which soon expanded with new members and was eventually renamed the Micah Barnes Band. Having generated a healthy buzz in and around Toronto, the band went on to open for international touring acts like Nik Kershaw ("Wouldn't It Be Good?") and Natalie Cole and Canadian sensations Parachute Club, Carol Pope, and Jane Siberry, who shared a manager with Barnes. Unfortunately, Barnes could not manage to

"break through" himself. "There were few out gay men in the Canadian rock scene, and I stuck out like a sore thumb," he says. Though he tried, he couldn't secure the support of a reputable label—though he says he did turn down some "lousy" record deals along the way.

In 1990 two things happened that changed the course of Barnes's life. His lover, choreographer Rene Holliday, had been battling AIDS and finally succumbed to the disease not long before Barnes was asked to join a cappella singing group the Nylons, who had been performing on college campuses and in concert halls around the world. A still-grieving Barnes accepted the invitation, and says he found a haven for his pain in touring and performing with the group ("I had this very safe bubble to travel around in and sort of heal in through singing for the people," he says). But the new gig didn't come without drawbacks: Though it was common knowledge that the members of the group were gay, the Nylons were not out in a public way, and Barnes, being the "ACT UP faggot who lost my lover to AIDS," had a hard time keeping his sexuality under wraps. "Simply put, I was the Patti Smith fag and they were the Judy Garland fags…who were used to a generationally different sort of expression of their sexuality. It was very difficult for me to be comfortable in that kind of closeted energy, though I was learning from the guys."

Barnes held his tongue in his dealings with the press and tried to fit in among his group mates, but it wasn't long before his long-simmering anger reached the boiling point.

"God ripped my lover from my bed.
Left an angry faggot fierce and damned.
A savage heart in a ravaged land.
An open bleeding wound.
I reach for pleasure, sick for flesh.
My soul is numb, my brain is sex.
I suck on life in the face of death.
And crash into your arms.
Your beating heart.
The touch of skin on skin tonight.
All I want is the heart of your body, the heat of your blood.
Do I get what I want?
Do I get what I want?
Do I get what I want?
—"Do I Get What I Want?" Barnes

Barnes recorded two albums (*Four on the Floor* and *Live to Love*) with the Nylons and did his best to practice a bit of stealth when talking with journalists. But following the AIDS-related death of the group's lead singer, Marc Conners, just six months after Holliday's passing, Barnes had had enough of the silence surrounding the AIDS epidemic and decided he needed to speak up. "I knew I had gone too far in a few interviews because of grief and anger of the death of my lover and our singer," he says. "I was a mess trying to make sense of what was going on in my heart, and I said some overly political things." A right-wing Canadian paper took his words out of context and twisted his statements to make Barnes sound like a queer radical—much to the chagrin of his Nylon mates. "It was not good for their squeaky-clean image," he laughs. "I was horrified to be the bad boy but kind of getting used to it. But the Nylons not being officially out was starting to look more and more ridiculous, especially in context of k.d. lang and Melissa Etheridge [coming out]."

Though he managed to smooth things over with the other members of the group and stick it out for several more years, Barnes knew that he'd only put a Band-Aid on the sore that would only continue to fester if he continued to stick around. After six years with the Nylons, Barnes had had enough and decided that his time with the group needed to come to an end. He left in 1996 and formed a writing collaboration with the group's producer Brad Daymond, who had come on board during the recording of *Live to Love*. As Barnes tells it, "[It was then] that I was able to express my anger and queer identity by coming up with the hard-hitting, in-your-face material that became my first solo record, *Loud Boy Radio*."

"They tried to silence me.
Do violence unto me.
I am the song they said would never get played.
Inappropriate dinner conversations.
The thing that's never mentioned.
Exploding in your face like
Armageddon day.
This is the sound of the free zone.
This is the sound of the century turning. (Turn it up!)
Loud rock radio. (Rock radio)
Punk rock radio.
Loud boy radio."
—"Loud Boy Radio," Barnes

Freed from the claustrophobic constraints of the Nylons, Barnes concentrated on his solo career, channeling all his suppressed rage and grief into songs that openly confronted what it was like to grow up gay and to deal his lover's death (and to speak out about these experiences). He dropped his first name and started going by simply Barnes. Songs like "Loud Boy Radio," "If I Was the DJ," and "Do I Get What I Want?" came quickly. After hooking up with executive producer Andy Goldmark, Barnes and Daymond couched the songs in loud, raucous arrangements that recalled the raw

urgency of early Nine Inch Nails. They also dabbled in R&B and electronic pop, calling on such influences as Seal and Erasure. But for the most part, the record was unmistakably punk: a raw, urgent, self-produced effort that allowed its creator to leap forth from a place of anger and unleash it on the world.

"*Loud Boy Radio* was born after much silence and frustration," he reports. "Losing a lover and having to keep touring and recording other people's songs meant I had a lot of feelings bottled up inside of me. Expressing my sexuality at that point was an aggressive and intense kind of liberation. [Recording that album] was like a bloodletting."

The songs also forced Barnes to take control of his life in other ways—though doing so eventually backfired on him. "It was in performance that things got really intense," he explains. "I found I had to toughen up in order to give the songs their life. And so I shaved my head and worked out and got into a whole powerful fag persona that really challenged my audiences in Canada.

"They had seen me on their TVs as a nice cuddly Nylon for the better part of five years," he continues, "so they weren't buying it." Neither was major-label rock music. Goldmark approached "all the major labels" with the six songs that made up *Loud Boy Radio*, trying without success to score

Barnes a record deal. Though the songs generated a good deal of buzz, Goldmark was, sadly, faced with rejection after rejection. "Too many people were nervous about it," Barnes says. "'Boy With a Secret,' specifically, was getting a lot of people in the industry excited about supporting me as this little gay-boy/Alanis Morissette thing, and I was laughing because I knew damn well that the gatekeepers wouldn't allow it.

"I had people in the business tell me, 'This belongs on the radio, but it will not get on the radio,'" he continues. "At one point a major manager told me it would be 10 years before anyone broke an openly gay male act." That's when Barnes decided it was time for a change of scenery. Even though the music industry had turned him away, Barnes felt that Los Angeles would open him up to new opportunities. So he packed up his stuff and wound up in Venice Beach. Barnes immediately looked up Paul V., who had managed the queer-fronted, buzzed-about Extra Fancy. Barnes had heard the band's music back in Toronto and recalled its "intensity" as something that had ignited a fire within him. "It made me feel like a queer rock act could break through," he says. "I felt empowered."

As it turned out, Paul V. dug Barnes's stuff and took him on as a client, urging Barnes to put *Loud Boy Radio* out as an independent release in 1998. The CD, released under Loud Boy Records, met with instant critical acclaim, and went on to receive three 1999 GLAAD Awards nominations (with nods for Best Male Artist, Debut Artist, and Out Recording for "Boy With a Secret") and a win for Best Club Song for the title track). Barnes went on tour to promote the CD, playing in "every underground club and venue in Manhattan, Chicago, San Francisco, and anywhere else I could get booked."

A few years later, after temporarily toying in dance music, Barnes hooked up with fellow Los Angeles scenester Kelly Mantle, another out singer-songwriter with an unusual approach to performing (usually in drag), and began unveiling new cabaret-rock tunes in a monthly club they dubbed Silver Lake City Limits. The raves began pouring in. "Bowie meets Brecht in a dark alley," gushed *L.A. Weekly,* while the *Bay Area Reporter* proclaimed, "Barnes' vocals combine the dramatics of Freddie Mercury, the passion of Eddie Vedder, and the mournfulness of Morrissey with the sweetness of Michael Stipe."

Soon, Barnes decided he was ready to record the songs and connected with Clint Yeager, the gay bassist for power-rock band SöuR, who agreed to try his hand at producing some music for Barnes. The album that emerged from their collaboration—the self-titled *Micah Barnes*—is both a return and a rebirth for Barnes. The songs on his sophomore efforts are a moving and celebratory combination of personal storytelling, a deep love of dramatic performance, and an uncanny wit that, though it's been through its share of heartache and adversity, has miraculously managed to remain intact.

"I say that I like girls; feel like a girl
inside.
Kids in school know something is
queer.
Cornered at the Y; he wouldn't let
me go.
Sucked me off where nobody
could see.
I tried to be like other boys.
Sprung a hard-on in the shower.
Something strange is growing inside.
Boy with a secret.
A nasty habit, a filthy heart.
And a dirty little mind."
—"Boy With a Secret," Barnes

Barnes recalls that from a very early age, he had a sense that something was "not quite right" about him. "I knew there was something quote-unquote 'wrong' with me from the time I was a toddler," he says. "It's just that in my family I was extremely creative and very special. I wasn't ostracized for

being that way. It's just that being gay wasn't something that was acknowledged at all."

Fortunately, over the course of his sexual development, Barnes had his music. And to a little gay boy growing up in Canada, rock music represented something akin to a great big queer road show. "Queerness is so a part of rock and roll—from Little Richard's pompadour and mascara to Elvis's girly eyes and lips and hips," Barnes says. "From Blondie's tongue-in-cheek smarts to PJ Harvey's art-school-girl-gone-bad. I have never felt rock and roll to be closed to me.

"My pal Howie played me Lou Reed, David Bowie, Patti Smith, and Iggy Pop when I was 13, and I understood that it was all somehow radically queer music in the largest sense of the word," he elaborates. It's only in how others in the music business—namely the major-label executives who had turned him away for being "too gay"—perceive him that his sexuality becomes a problem, since, as he says, "they hold the purse strings." But he hasn't let it stop him from being who he is: "I am a big, tall, strong, out gay man, and I always have been, since I was a teenager, no matter what I do about it. The fact that I don't smell 'rock' to someone is their problem, not mine. It's just a pity that I once believed that [those music execs] were in a position of power."

To that end, Barnes says he is only too

happy to be identified as a queercore artist, though he is quick to add that he doesn't make his music only for a queer audience. "It's only if I start preaching to the choir that I feel I've failed at giving something to the audience," he says. "I'm not just queer because I sleep with men; I'm queer because my life experience is marked by that identity, and so my art reflects that whether I want it to or not. Artists are freaks, and to be true to what makes us tick, we have to be true to our hearts and our blood."

"It's always wonderful to feel community," Barnes says of the queercore movement. "It's so rare that kinship can develop in this highly competitive field. I always look to bridge the gaps between us, and of course, out queer artists have a special batch of difficulties in getting their music out of the ghetto. I applaud the work of many, the success of all, and am thankful for the growth and mutual support and respect that the movement engenders."

CHAPTER 21

Ray of Light

"I hear the rock show winding down at the high school.
Kids out on the sidewalk are waiting for a ride.
All the punks and the queers and the freaks and the smokers.
Feel like they'll be waiting for the rest of their lives.
Alright, I hear what you're saying to me.
Alright, I hear what I just can't do.
But I got this spark; I got to feed it something,
or put it out for good."
—"Put It Out for Good," Amy Ray

WITH A LOT OF GAY- AND LESBIAN-ORIENTED BANDS HAVING A HARD TIME GETTING ANY
ATTENTION FROM MAJOR LABELS, IT'S OFTEN THE JOB OF SMALLER, INDEPENDENT LABELS TO
PICK UP THE SLACK AND GIVE QUEER ARTISTS A CHANCE TO MAKE AN IMPRESSION ON AUDI-
ENCES. FOR AMY RAY—ONE HALF OF PIONEERING FOLK-ROCK DUO THE INDIGO GIRLS—
STARTING HER OWN RECORD LABEL WAS A WAY OF GIVING BACK TO THE INDIE CULTURE THAT
GAVE HER BAND ITS START. "THE INDIGO GIRLS HAD BEEN PUTTING OUT OUR OWN RECORDS,
AND THEN WE GOT SIGNED [TO EPIC RECORDS], AND I JUST LOOKED AT THE WHOLE THING
AND I WAS LIKE, 'I DON'T REALLY WANT TO LEAVE BEHIND WHAT I'M DOING IN THE INDE-
PENDENT COMMUNITY,'" RAY RECALLS. "I REALLY ENJOYED PUTTING OUT OUR OWN RECORDS
AND BEING PART OF THAT."

So when Ray—who had been struggling to make ends meet while independently releasing Indigo Girls records—received a sizable chunk of money after Epic signed the duo, she decided not to spend it on frivolous things like a bigger house and a great car. Instead, in 1990, she used the money to stay true to her indie roots by starting Daemon Records, a grassroots record label based in her hometown of Decatur, Ga. "To me, it was like putting money in the arts," Ray says of her decision to start the label. "I had all these friends at the time who were in bands [without recording contracts], and there wasn't as much access to recording your own stuff and putting out a record. And I had this big influx of money from being signed, and I just wanted to have my own label and I wanted it to be an activist label and be part of the community."

Relying partially on the support of friends and volunteers who were eager to see her dream succeed, Ray got Daemon off to a promising start. She immediately signed two acts: Atlanta-based musicians Gerard McHugh and the Ellen James Society. Soon after, she got a distributor and started hitting the proverbial pavement, shopping the records to college radio and independent record stores. "At first I did everything by myself with my manager and some friends helping me out," she recalls. "I would be on tour with the Indigo Girls and just wake up every morning and start working—raiding college radio and retail promotion and just making lots of phone calls. We never spent a lot of money on ads. It was really the antithesis of corporate stuff." Eventually she was able to hire her friends on as employees, though running a record label still requires the use of interns to get a lot of the work done. "The label tries to not run at a loss, but it's pretty hard," Ray admits.

Before long, other acts were signed to the label, including local Georgia favorites Dede Vogt, Kristen Hall, Michelle Malone, and James Hall. Ray, having benefited from the experience of putting out her own records with the Indigos, decided to use Daemon as a way of educating artists on how to handle their careers.

In the beginning, Ray wasn't concerned at all about profits. "I wasn't worried about the risks when I first started off, because I had so much money," she laughs. "I didn't want it to be profit-based or motivated by anything beyond the art. And that's the mistake I made."

She clarifies: "I didn't start the label and go, 'OK, every product has to break even.' I said, 'These are all worthwhile projects. If they don't break even, it doesn't matter.' I sort of started with the antithesis of a good businessperson. And then after the first couple years, I started realizing that even though I could afford to lose money, it didn't feel good for the bands or for anybody to be associated with that kind of business sense.

"It's not like we need to sell a bunch of records to meet some kind of money-hungry goal," she continues. "But just on a pragmatic level you want to feel like you're being smart. And the bands want to feel in control of their lives, and if they feel like they're in the hole and they're never able to break even or get any kind of royalties, it's just kind of a bad thing. So I started to be more aware of that and got smarter about recording costs."

Ray says that her biggest hurdle in running the label has been the distribution end of things. "It's like, how do you get records in the stores and how do you get a distributor that you think is really paying attention to you?" she says of her struggles over the years.

"Testing 1-2-3 in the marketplace.
It's a demographic-based disgrace.
And a stupid whiteboy handshake
that we'll never be a part of.
So when it's DJ Blow and the morning show,
I'll give you 100 reasons to just say no.
Come on, girls, let's go right now,
'cause Lucystoners don't need boners.
Ain't no man could ever own her.

With the boys she had the nerve
to give the girls what they deserve."
—"Lucystoners," Amy Ray

Though both the Indigo Girls and Daemon Records have been fairly successful, Ray is aware of a slightly homophobic bent in the press that both ventures have received over the years. "It's always been this struggle of, like, when the gay press talks to us, we're going to talk about the movement and politics probably as much as our music, and that makes sense in that context," she begins. "But when we get reviews in the mainstream press, there's often more information about who's in our audience than about our music—and that bugs us. At that point, you don't have control over what they're saying—and the reason they're saying it is subtly homophobic."

Like other queer-minded artists, Ray says it bothers her when writers choose to focus on her sexuality rather than her music. "It's when your sexuality is taking away from their ability to talk about your music that it becomes an issue," she says. "That is the thing that makes you not want to be defined by your sexuality. That's the thing that makes artists not want to come out."

Both Ray and Emily Saliers (the other Indigo Girl) officially came out in 1993. Though it came as no surprise to their fans or even to the press, it was a decision that was a long time in the making, and one that made perfect sense for Ray. "For me, it was never worth it to be in the closet," she declares. "You've got to stand for something. If you don't, you won't have an audience." The Indigos lost none of their core audience by coming out (their outdoor arena concerts frequently sell out), though being out did have other consequences. In 1998 a high school principal in Columbia, S.C., buckled under pressure from concerned parents and canceled a concert the Girls were scheduled to perform on campus. A week later another principal canceled a show, citing one utterance of the word "fuckin'" in their song "Shame on You" as the reason for his decision. Five students walked out of their classes to protest the move, and they were suspended for their rebellion. The American Civil Liberties Union offered the students legal advice, while both Rock Out Censorship and Artists for a Hate-Free America stepped in to offer solidarity and support. Undaunted, the Girls found other venues in the area for their performances, and they thanked supporters for their help. The experience only strengthened their resolve to speak out on the causes most important to them—as well to be forthright about their response to homophobia.

"I think sexism is at the root of homophobia," Ray says, adding that the media have not been kind to nonglamorous women in particular. "Women who aren't glamorous or marketable aren't really received well in the press, whether they're gay or straight, and the reason is that it kind of goes against our sexual paradigm. And men that are queer are looked down on if they're more feminine, because they're more like a woman—as if there's something wrong with being a woman.

"I think it's this combination of the way the market is perceived as being a market that can't handle certain kinds of women and certain kinds of men," she adds. "If you're queer and you're out, it's hard. And I think that the market is perceived as feeling that way, so the people in charge of record companies don't want to take that risk and present artists to that market because they don't think it's going to be well received and they won't make any money." It's an ideology that irks Ray. In 1998 she included the song "Lucystoners" on her first solo CD— the harder-edged, punked-up *Stag,* which she released on Daemon. The song specifically cited *Rolling Stone* editor Jann Wenner as a culprit in shafting women and gays. Not surprisingly, *Stag* was never reviewed in *Rolling Stone.* "When Emily first heard it, she was just like, 'Well, we're never gonna get written up in *Rolling Stone* again.'" Ray says with a laugh. "And I was like, 'We *never* were anyway.'" (Interestingly, the Indigo Girls' most recent record, 2004's *All That We Let In*, did get reviewed in *Rolling Stone*.)

Ray has been very vocal about her disillusionment with the major-label music business. Her ongoing frustration has led her to develop theories about why gay artists are often left out in the cold. Addressing how record execs and magazine editors have dealt with openly gay artists, Ray says, "As the industry has consolidated, they've come up with this idea of these really specific demographics. Everything boils down to this one demographic for this format of radio or this type of magazine that carries these types of ads that are for this certain type of man.

"You're not allowed to be multidimensional," she adds. "Radio is afraid to be that way, and magazines are afraid to be that way. I think a lot of consolidation means that the more corporate something is, the narrower it becomes. And gay people get really disenfranchised by that."

Which is perhaps one reason that Ray believes that having a "movement" is essential for queer artists. "There was an article in *The New York Times* a few years ago in which the Indigo Girls were interviewed about how folk music was the voice of the lesbian community. The writer named Ani DiFranco [who's bisexual] and Dar Williams

[who is straight] as examples," Ray recalls. "That's why we can't get anywhere as musicians. When they say [something reductive like that], they're not saying it in a celebratory way. They're talking about its mediocrity and how it's this lowest common denominator and how anybody who is gay can get an audience just because they're gay. And I'm like, if that was true, we'd all be rich and we'd all be on the radio and interviewed in *Rolling Stone,* and that's not happening. And because that's not happening, we do need a queer movement. We need our own record labels and supporters."

Which is why Daemon Records has become a haven for queer artists looking for a home. Ray says she is only too happy to accommodate them if she can, though she adds, "I don't know if we're doing enough yet, but I definitely want to enhance the queercore movement, and I want to be there as an infrastructure for it.

"It's an important thing, and I'll always support it even beyond Daemon, just as a musician," she continues. "I think it's an important thing. It keeps you motivated to look at a bigger purpose." Ray says that Daemon has been approached by several queer-oriented musicians who have been turned away by other labels—even labels previously known for taking on queer acts. "You'll go through these waves where there are a lot of indie labels that are available to queer bands, and a lot of the times there's not. Right now we're seeing a lot of queer bands [on Daemon's roster] in a short period of time because all of these queer bands started approaching us. And I was just like, 'Well, I want to do as many projects as we can do, because it feels like there's a need for it right now." Ray cites Georgia-spawned Athens Boy Choir and the New York-based group Girlyman as just two of the openly gay acts signed to or distributed by the label, adding that, "I don't put out bands just because they're queer. But if the band is good and they're queer and they're being turned away everywhere else, I'm a haven for them. And right now there's just a lot of good stuff out there."

For her part, Ray says she understands why some musicians might have a problem being associated with a particular movement—especially when it's being derided by the media—though she's not so sensitive to the issue herself. "I hate when people compartmentalize the movement in a way that's derogatory," she says. "When queer artists talk about the queer punk scene, it's celebratory, like, 'Look at what we have.' It's different than saying, 'Oh, look at those Indigo Girls or that Amy Ray. Everybody in that audience is gay.'" This accounts for Ray's willingness to be included as part of the

queercore scene—even if it's not totally definable. "I haven't been able to figure all of it out yet; I just feel that there is a movement, and I'm always glad to be part of it. If it defines me in a way that's positive and I have control over it, then I'm willing to be defined by it."

"We are talking.
We are driving.
And in this moment we are denying what it costs,
what it takes
for one perfect world
when we look the other way."
—"Perfect World," Indigo Girls

"I was really impressed by Amy's devotion to activism and how involved she is," says former Beastie Boys drummer Kate Shellenbach, who first met Ray while he was touring with her band Luscious Jackson on the Lilith Fair tour. She later performed on Ray's disc *Stag* after joining her on the grassroots Suffragette Sessions tour, a slightly more aggressive and political version of Lilith. "It was cool to see how *Stag* came out and how important the gay themes were and how open she is in her commitment to activism. And not just gay issues, but in the way she lives and in the way she approaches music and her record company. It's all very inspiring."

Ray says she feels it's imperative that musicians look to each other for support and encouragement—even when the higher-ups fail to recognize it. "I feel like there's a sense of community out there, but I don't feel that it's there in a way that's appreciated by the general mass public, because it's not rewarded by the music business or by clubs," adds Ray. "Everything has gotten so competitive, so the idea of a community of musicians has sort of gone underground in a way.

"It's always been underground in some ways, but it's kind of gone back down, but it's there. I mean, I know it's there, because [Emily and I] survive in it, and we're part of it. And I feel like the more things become big mergers and big corporations and big promoters and big *everything,* it's more important that that level of community in the underground get stronger, and it does, actually. And so that's what I feel is going on right now. Just a very strong network of people who are sort of below the radar."

CHAPTER 22

Rockin' in the Free World

To look at Scott Free, you wouldn't expect to hear the words of a sensitive, heartfelt, and openly gay singer-songwriter to come out of his mouth. Built, for lack of a better term, "like a brick shithouse," with a "don't fuck with me" sneer to match, Free looks like he could kick the stuffing out of anyone who dares to mess with him—especially anyone who has problems with his sexuality. Take, for instance, the no-nonsense lyrics to his song "Fight About It," in which he bellows:

"Yeah, I'm a faggot.
You wanna fight about it?
This faggot could beat your fuckin' ass."

Of course, it's exactly that kind of menacing, I'll-wipe-the-floor-with-your-homophobic-face put-on that Free enjoys working with, especially because he knows he'll always come out the winner. "I love to play to straight audiences, because I love to fuck with that," Free admits with a satisfied chuckle. "Usually when I perform at a straight venue, I just go up there and they don't expect 'gay music' to come out of a guy like me. So it's really fun to get up there and scream, 'You can fuck me' or 'Yeah, I'm a faggot; you wanna fight about it?' They get *really* confused." And how do straight audiences take a shit-kicking queercore musician? "After a while, they really love it," he says happily. "Then the fun *really* begins!"

Though his often loud and aggressive music could be compared to that of another hulking rock icon, the hetero Henry Rollins, Free is also adept at exploring his "softer side" when the situation calls for it. Listen to "Not Good Enough," the somber, pensive opening track from his 1999 CD *The Living Dead,* for proof that the seemingly hardcore Free doesn't just want to scream and shout:

"How could we just believe what they said?
Couldn't we see our beauty instead?
How could we get it into our heads that we were not good enough."

"Some folks aren't quite sure how to take me," Free readily admits. "I write in styles that range from hardcore punk to political folk to cabaret jazz. I can sing punk holding an acoustic guitar, or I will play a jazz song on piano about an S/M experience I had, so I do get some blank stares."

Of course, for an artist who has continually shifted musical direction throughout his career, some blank stares are bound to follow. Free has been jumping genres for as far back as he can recall, and he boasts not only a hit house single but excursions into rap, pop, punk, and metal as well.

Free says he has his mother to thank for his musical prowess. As a stay-at-home mom, she doted on her children and encouraged Scott to take piano lessons at an early age while he was growing up in the suburbs of Chicago. Though his father was a scientist, Free excelled at music.

Still, it wasn't until the early '80s, with the onset of punk and new wave, that Free, then a high school student, really caught the musical bug. "Punk changed the entire way I viewed music—and viewed the world," he says. "For me, growing up gay was a very isolating experience, and I definitely had a sense of 'There's no one around here like me.' And there was just something about punk that I immediately related to. It wasn't just, 'Wow, they're wearing safety pins and mohawks.' It really had more to do with relating to their sense of alienation."

Free immersed himself in the world of Devo and the B-52's, cultivated a fashion style that employed leather and chains, and experienced epiphanies at Cramps shows. Ironically, however, "finding himself" proved to be costly to Free, who suddenly realized he was even more isolated than ever. "When [punk music] came out, you lost friends because of your affiliation with it," he says. "There was this huge divide. Either you liked Boston and REO Speedwagon, or you liked the whole punk-new wave realm and you rejected big stadium rock and probably reflected [that culture] in your clothing.

"But certainly musically, Devo was out of left field, and the B-52s were just the weirdest thing you had ever seen," he adds. "And you either rejected it or you got completely into it. You were kind of forced to make that decision. And I got completely into it."

With music as his rock, Free soon found new friends in college who appreciated his eclectic tastes. "My friends and I were obsessed with punk," he says. "We appeared on campus often as Devo. I think we believed we *were* Devo!" He wound up in a punk-new wave cover band called the Tragic Heroes, performing covers of Thomas Dolby, Oingo Boingo, and of course, Devo. "Our first off-campus gig was at my sister's Christian college," he recounts. "They didn't have a lot of exposure to punk on their campus, so we were a huge success."

Upon graduation, Free decided to give the Big Apple a try, and relocated to New York City with the intent of getting a rock band together. Though "nothing of signifi-

cance" ever materialized in the way of a rock band, Free says, he did perform with the Lavender Light Gospel Choir of New York and managed to find an outlet in another musical genre altogether. "Rap was in its infancy, and I loved the genre," he says. "So as a bizarre little twist, I wrote a rap song called 'Beat the Rap' and made a video out of it." The video ended up in rotation on Black Entertainment Television. This was back in the day before the Beastie Boys had come along. "I would brag about being the first white rapper," he jokes, though he adds, "When I look back, I just think it's a really bad song, so I kind of hide it away."

Before long, he got caught up in the burgeoning house music scene and noticed that a good bit of it seemed to be coming out of his hometown. Meanwhile, having been exposed to a much more prevalent gay subculture in New York's Greenwich Village, Free realized that he needed to come out to his family and decided to move back to Chicago in order to do so. "It was an important step for me, and it wasn't something I could just do on a weekend," he says.

And there was house music. "It was an amazing time," he remembers, "when someone could put together a track in their basement, ship it off to England, and then have a hit song." Having come out to his family, Free busied himself as a dance musician, producing singles under a variety of monikers, most notably with his sister (whom he renamed Kajsa) and as an outfit named Transient. Transient's single "Higher" would eventually go on to briefly make the European dance charts, and the experience inspired Free even further. "It was very empowering," he says. "A realization that you could make an impact outside of the major-label record industry."

Still, Free had not yet found his niche, and after sowing his oats in rap and dance, he decided to return to the music that had started it all for him—punk. It was around this time that Free, who had tested HIV-positive not long before, became sick with AIDS. "I thought I was on my way out," he recalls. The experience further motivated him to say what he had to say before his end came. Of course, Free survived, as did his impulse to speak out. And his involvement with the house music scene had actually strengthened his love for punk. "The breaking down of dance music into core hypnotic beats had so many similarities to punk in the way that it rejected the commercialism of pop music," he notes.

Having picked up the guitar in college, he began to write songs for himself to perform: angry, confessional, intense pieces detailing the pain and isolation he had felt growing up gay. That work allowed him to vent his frustrations musically. Suddenly, things seemed to click for him. "I felt like I had more of an identity," he states of being out and proud. In 1997 hc released *Getting Off*, a raging collection of songs about death, sex, homophobia, and the AIDS epidemic built around screeching guitars and electronic sounds that heralded the emergence of an artist clearly on a mission. Two years later, Free followed that CD up with *The Living Dead*, a somewhat gentler (though equally rocking) treatise on, among other topics, body snobbery ("Rejection"), internalized homophobia ("We Serve You"), celebrity worship ("Pride") and long-since-dead friends ("Leather Ghosts").

Glowing reviews followed (the *New York Blade*'s Jeffrey Newman called *Getting Off* "truly one of the most disturbing yet powerful recordings of the AIDS era"), and Free had finally come into his own as a songwriter.

"I'm goin' to the bathhouse with an extra-strength Viagra.
I'm puttin' on my finest towel and givin' my best smile.
And anybody who wants some can have some
'cause I'm so goddamn sick of rejection."
—"Rejection," Scott Free

"My songs are almost always emotion-based," Free says of his writing. "It could be a particular headline I read or possibly something that happened to me, but I have to be charged up about a particular subject to write."

This is abundantly evident in his lyrics, though his words haven't always been received in the way they're intended. Free admits that reactions from gays and lesbians have been mixed, though he notes that it's mostly the adults who don't seem to "get" where he is coming from. "I performed a benefit for a gay youth organization, and I sang a song that I thought would be appropriate, about a guy who had gotten beaten up every day in school because he 'acted like a girl,'" he says. "And when I sang that, the adults interpreted it to somehow mean that I thought the kid deserved to be beaten up. One of the counselors said to me, 'How can you sing a song like that to the kids?' And to me, that was the point."

Free is happy to report that most of the feedback he's received from gay and lesbian youths has been very positive, and it pleases him to know that his music might have an effect on someone in need of a positive role model. "To me, it's just trying to find the stories out there that music lovers can relate to—for people who really use music as a way of therapy or empowerment," he says. "I looked to music. I searched out singer-songwriters that I related to or got something from. Music was a really important part of my growing up experience."

By the same token, Free says he definitely considers himself to be an activist, especially when it comes to the music of gay people. "I believe in the possibilities of music as a force of social change," he states. "Which is why, along with songs about gay rights, I have songs on everything from religious intolerance to the death penalty." But Free's main goal these days is "increasing the awareness of queer music as a viable form of artistic expression," though he says he sometimes gets frustrated that it's harder to get the gay audience interested in the music of its own people than it is the mainstream world. "My focus is aimed at the gay community mostly because our own community is not aware that gay musicians exist. In the meantime, the music world at large is coming to recognize us for the musical contributions we are making," he says.

"Queer musicians are creating great music, but the community has been slow to recognize it," he continues. "I always make a comparison to gay filmmaking, where an independent producer and director, with no-name actors, can create enormous interest in the LGBT community when they release a film, just because the subject matter is gay. The same is not true for gay musicians who release CDs or go on tour. The interest is not there at this point. And because of the enormous talent out there, it should be."

For this reason, Free says he "loves" the queercore movement and its "focus on gender queer and trans issues, the environment, and animal rights. The energy and DIY attitude is so inspirational; they have their shit together, don't they?" It's his fondness for the movement that has led him to host a weekly queer performance series that he calls Homolatte and to create his own annual queer music festival, the aptly named Queer Is Folk Festival, which is housed in the Old Town School of Folk Music in Chicago and benefits a local

AIDS charity. The festival has been running strong for four years, and Free is ecstatic about its progress. "I've been able to build an audience," he marvels. "They just kind of trust the talent that I bring in. It's really cool that I can pack a house and help build up a queer music community at the same time."

It was Free's desire to bring attention to queer musicians, in fact, that led him to stage a recent protest of Chicago's gay pride festival because fewer than half of the musicians performing on the mainstage were gay or lesbian. "The organizers were not pleased," he chuckles. "I mean, who protests a street fair? But it was necessary to raise awareness that we are not being represented as we should be."

CHAPTER 23

Straight Outta Silver Lake

"He's been making plans, saying things I don't believe.
He's trying to be so sweet, and this is what I need."
—"Anyway You Can," IAmLoved

"WE'RE NOT AN AGENDA BAND," PROCLAIMS IAMLOVED FRONT MAN JIMMY JASMINE BETWEEN TAKES DURING THE RECORDING OF THE BAND'S SOPHOMORE ALBUM. "WE'RE LIKE RIP TAYLOR ON CRACK—IT JUST KINDA TRANSLATES THAT WE'RE GAYS, YOU KNOW? BEING GAY REALLY DOESN'T ENTER THE EQUATION, THOUGH, UNTIL LIKE 8:30 OR 9, WHEN WE START THE AFTER-PRACTICE ORGY."

Of course, all it takes is one listen to IAmLoved's music and it's obvious that the group is queer as a $3 bill. On its powerhouse 2003 debut CD, *Never Forget*, the Los Angeles indie band rocks the house with supercharged songs about growing up gay, vengeful concubines with firearms, and homo hustlers just trying to make a buck. All of these experiences are conveyed with the band's distinctive brand of scathing wit and raucously loud sonics. Surrounded by scads of queer cachet (the disc was produced by Pansy Division front man Chris Freeman and released via queer record labels Agitprop and Spitshine), the boys in this band have been building a name—and a reputation—as a group of homo hipsters with attitude who are poised to break out of the gay ghetto and into the mainstream.

And though the majority of their songs aren't necessarily in-your-face queer, the members of this band aren't afraid to mix in some hard-rocking homocore tunes with their more mainstream rock songs. After all there's no mistaking the tongue-in-cheek queer sentiments in songs like "He Has a Hole" and "Breaking Up (Is Easy to Do)," a bitter breakup song and ode to sleazy sexual shenanigans at Cuffs, an infamous gay Los Angeles leather bar, which Jasmine says is a sonic take on a true story, proving that sometimes truth is stranger—and a lot sleazier—than fiction.

"I've been a sickening sleaze, just like you are.
At Cuffs, 3 A.M., down on my knees, just like you are."
—"Breaking Up (Is Easy to Do)," IAmLoved

"Our story songs are all true, especially 'Breaking Up,'" says Jasmine, who formed IAmLoved in 2001 with four buddies he met at the Faultline, a Silver Lake leather and cruise bar. "I broke up with my boyfriend and kept running into him everywhere! And one night I got drunk and later I ended up at Cuffs, and I was kind of fucking around with this guy, not like goin' down; I was just kinda justifying my love in a very in-your-crotch sorta way. And I look over across the room and my ex is giving some guy head. And the guy he was with was so fucking nasty. I was like, *ewwwww*—I won! And some how that all came out in a song."

IAmLoved may have never found any love at all if it wasn't for Los Angeles scenesters Eddie Hibbs and Steven Lozier's now-defunct but unforgettable homocore club Freak Show, which was hosted at the Gauntlet II bar in Silver Lake and served as the launching pad for IAmLoved—twice.

"Eddie Hibbs and Steven Lozier made it all happen at the first-year anniversary of Freak Show in 2001," says Jasmine, a refugee from the popular queertronic Los Angeles industrial band Drance. Jasmine had performed at the monthly Freak Show event earlier that year in a hardcore-electronic early incarnation of IAmLoved (then spelled I@mLov3d) that was made up of guitarist-vocalist Jasmine and bassist Chuck

Chugumlung, with a drum machine and sampler providing backup. Later, after hooking up with guitarist Johnny Alvarez, drummer Saul Acuna, and Marcus Cain (who replaced Chugumlung), Jasmine returned to Freak Show a few months later with a full band. After two weeks of rehearsals the queer quartet made its official debut as IAmLoved.

"We were in the right place at the right time," recalls the singer. "It was our first show and we played with like 13 bands—all gay or gay-friendly—and it snowballed after that. I was so nervous and had no idea how to be or what to say—and we only had like 10 minutes to play because there were so many great bands playing. The reaction was incredible; they really liked us. Before, in other bands, we never got the reaction IAmLoved gets.

"We reached a lot of people through the clubs and passed out like 150 million fliers to all of our closest friends, and as people saw that gay people were making music and kinda creating a 'scene,' they wanted to be involved and check it out," continues Jasmine. "I think anything different kinda catches people's attention and makes them wanna check it out. If you're good, they'll come back. If not...give blow jobs. It works!"

Of course. But what's a homocore band to do at straight gigs?

"We are consciously booking more and more gigs at straight venues," says Jasmine. "I would rather play more gay clubs, but the problem is that the sound is just so much better at regular rock clubs. But we try to play and act the same at all venues," he continues with a laugh. "However, I find myself fagging out more at straight shows. I love straight women; win over the women at a show and it's a success. The dudes will love you 'cause the chicks do. On tour we played straight venues, and when we played Vegas I spotted this group of hot indie-hip girls sitting on this pool table and checking us out. They totally got that we were gay, and they loved it 'cause this was a place where punks rule and usually straight guys play there. So they liked us 'cause we were different—and they danced to us too! That's way too cool!"

"But on the flip side, the straight girls might dance to us, but like they don't buy shit! We played to a full straight bar in Vegas and didn't even sell a pin," continues Jasmine. "But the next night we played to a crowd half the size at a gay place in Salt Lake City and sold *tons* of merchandise. Not that it's all about the 'gay dollar,' but support is support."

"Being in a band with all gay members is suicide if you want to play rock," adds Marcus Cain. "But then again, it depends on your goals as a band. I don't think any of us think we're going to sell a million records. We just want to take the band as far as we possibly can. Some people are going to dig us, and some people aren't. You can't beat yourself up as to why. We're satisfied with the basics: a good indie label, free booze, and a lot of male groupies."

One of the band's biggest supporters is Pansy Division's Chris Freeman, who put his bass down just long enough to produce IAmLoved's *Never Forget*. Freeman stumbled upon IAmLoved performing at a benefit show in Silver Lake.

"Chris came up and asked who our producer was," recalls Jasmine. "I was like, 'Um, you?' And he said, 'OK!' It was that easy."

"He made our ideas whole again—like a sculptor working with the finest Silly Putty. There is no way we could have done that record without him. Our first album was just us writing songs really quick and then having Chris Freeman, boy genius, make sense out of all of it and give us pointers on structures and producing it all."

"It just feels better working with fags because I've been in bands with straight guys and there's something cute about

hangin' out at the bar checking out guys after a great rehearsal or show, you know?"

"I think we can change things by not compromising ourselves, by just being who we are and trying to maintain quality material," continues Jasmine. "And if we stick to being true to our art, I think hetero rock circles will say, "Whoa, fags can rock!""

"But then again, we really aren't doing many 'gay' songs per se anymore," says Cain. "We've written a ton of new songs that are much more veiled lyrically. When you hear the new material we're working on for our next record, you won't hear any 'Look at us, we're fags!' songs. You definitely won't hear any tired 'Stand up against the forces that are trying to hold us down' crap either. I find that whole old-school punk rock 'conviction' thing really silly if you're over 25. Our main goal is not to 'open people's eyes' but to be the best rock band we can be. And everyone, straight or gay, can relate to a great band. Our audiences know we are gay. We don't have to sing about it. I mean, sucking cock is part of my everyday life. I don't need to express it in song."

CHAPTER 24

Live From New York, It's...Daniel Cartier

"You laugh, you smile.
You do it with such style.
No one would ever guess what you hide.
Way down deep underneath, with its rabid crazy teeth.
You're insecure, and it's ripping you up inside.
But we could all be beautiful."
—"Beautiful," Daniel Cartier

THE FIRST TIME YOU HEAR DANIEL CARTIER'S VOICE, IT'S LIKE A BEACON SHINING IN THE NIGHT. IT'S CLEAR AND PRECISE, WITH A CONFIDENT VULNERABILITY IN ITS UNWAVERING TIMBRE, AND NARY A TRACE OF IRONY TO BE FOUND. THE LYRICS ARE DARING IN THEIR OPENNESS, LIKE A WINDOW INTO THE SOUL. YOU CAN'T HELP BUT PAY ATTENTION. AS CARTIER SINGS HIS REVEALING SONGS OF LOVE—AND LOST LOVE—HE DRAWS YOU INTO HIS WORLD WITH HIS POWERFUL MIX OF WORDS, MUSIC, AND EMOTION.

Despite the power of his songs, however, the first thing most people mention when they write about Daniel Cartier is "the tattoo." It's on his head, a sunburst surrounded by roses, leaves, and odd squiggly lines and shapes, leading to a bright blue ankh on the back of his skull. Though he does get frustrated with having so much attention paid to what's on his head instead of what's coming out of his mouth, Cartier says it's a matter of convenience that he hasn't attempted to cover the tattoo up. "One of the reasons why I continue working this look is that I'm just so lazy!" he chuckles. "I *hate* growing my hair out. It's so much effort!"

It's hard to imagine an artist of Cartier's creativity being lazy. After all, he initially wrote 70 songs for his latest record, 2004's daring, uplifting *Revival*, and was faced with the daunting task of whittling the selections down to a mere 13. Then again, he's also the artist who basically gave up making music for five years after he was dropped from his deal with PolyGram-owned Rocket Records in 1997. "It was a really difficult thing for me to get back on my feet after that," Cartier says. But that's just what he did, picking himself up by his guitar straps and taking the initiative to learn how to produce and engineer his own albums and eventually put himself back out there.

"Well everyone's excited in the beginning.
Strung out on the city lights.
Expecting everything to happen so suddenly.
But then we find ourselves still down here, just wasting on these streets.
We pass all the things we've seen a thousand times before.
You know we'd walk on all night and all day.
We're gonna walk forever.
Maybe you'll find your way."
—"Avenue A," Daniel Cartier

New York City, 1991: A hodgepodge of creative energy was building, especially in the Village, where drag queens and poets put on shows together in venues like the Pyramid and Squeezebox, and a tattoo-headed singer-songwriter with a guitar could fit right in among all of them. "It was a really exciting time," Cartier remembers fondly. "It was this whole big mesh of rock bands and folksingers, and they were all really young, just doing random shows and plays." Cartier found comfort in the "wacky" East Village neighborhood along Avenue A, which would eventually come to factor into his music in a very big way. "It was symbolic of New York as a whole," he says fondly of his neighborhood. "All these young-at-heart people doing whatever they could to keep life interesting. Just very exciting."

Eventually Cartier fell in with drag performance artist Mistress Formica and started playing at her weekly club, Hippie Chicks, where he befriended a diverse group of fellow singer-songwriters. Then, seeing that other songwriters were eking out a living by playing in subway stations, Cartier picked up his guitar and went underground to play to the masses. The experience led Cartier to cultivate a solid stage presence. He explains, "It taught me that, as a performer, you're onstage the moment you open your guitar case until the moment you close it. I found out very quickly that in order to get a response—which down there was making money—you had to get people to stop what they were doing and pay attention. I had to constantly be engaging people and be myself, but kind of an exaggerated version of myself."

Before long, Cartier had literally become an "underground sensation," though he wasn't having the same luck above ground. He shopped his demo tape to major record labels, but to no avail. Eventually, he fell in with an unlikely admirer: '80s icon Daryl Hall of Hall and Oates, who decided to champion Cartier's journey to musical stardom. Hall produced several songs for Cartier and eventually asked him to record some albums to be released as part of Hall's

development deal with Sony Music. But Cartier wasn't ready for such a major commitment. "He wanted me to commit to doing seven albums, and at the time that was really frightening to me, so I said no," he recounts.

Later, Cartier recorded his debut, a live recording of himself performing on a subway platform that was fittingly titled *Live From New York—The Subway Session,* which he financed himself and released independently to immediate response. Gigs above ground at trendy New York music spots like Wetlands, the Mercury Lounge, Fez, Sin-é Café, and LaMaMa followed, as well as a tour to promote *The Subway Session,* which independent label Ignition Records re-released in 1995. "And," Cartier says, "that's when Elton John showed up."

Actually, it was John's vanity label, Rocket Records, that showed up first, having picked up on the word-of-mouth buzz surrounding Cartier. Rocket wasn't the only label who came calling at that point; Cartier was also approached by a few other companies—including A&M, which would later factor into his career in a not-so-positive light. A small bidding war began to secure a contract with Cartier, who in the end gave in to a little bit of star-fucking. "I went to meet with Elton, and, as a singer-songwriter, it doesn't get much bigger than meeting

Elton John," he says. John expressed admiration for Cartier's songwriting, so Daniel signed with Rocket, and was put on the fast track to releasing his first major-label album. Things were good.

"And if I walk down to Avenue A,
is it gonna change the way that I feel?
And if I walk down to Avenue A,
are you gonna take my dreams and
make them real?"
—"Avenue A," Daniel Cartier

In 1997, Cartier's dreams were indeed about to become reality. He had a major-label contract, a hot new record with A-list producers, and talent in the can—plus tons of positive press surrounding him. "There was a year in New York where you could not get away from me," he says. "You would open a magazine and I was in it; you turned a corner, and there was my flyer staring at you." Rocket put a lot of money into turning Cartier into "the next Chris Isaak," and it seemed as if Cartier was indeed about to break through to the mainstream. Reviews in the mainstream press were very favorable ("Here's proof that post-grunge rock can offer more flavor than the bland Verve Pipe and Matchbox Twenty," *Entertainment Weekly*'s Jeremy Hillagar wrote.

Then, suddenly…nothing happened. "My album got lost in the shuffle," Cartier says,

referring to a series of corporate moves that took place at Rocket. As it happened, Island Records, which was also owned by PolyGram, was to be the distributor for Cartier's disc. But when Elton John and Rocket decided they wanted A&M (also owned by PolyGram) to be their distributor, Cartier knew he was in some trouble. "The ironic thing was that A&M ended up being the distributor for Rocket, like, two months before my album came out," he says, referring to his decision to turn down A&M in favor of Rocket. "It wasn't a good thing."

Avenue A was released with a lot of fanfare in the press but little follow-up in the stores. As Cartier remembers, "My album had been out for six months, and because of all the moving back and forth between the labels, I had hardly sold any units. Half of the time you couldn't even find my album in the stores. They'd take out these big ads in *The Village Voice* and then you'd go to the stores and they wouldn't have any of my albums." Though Rocket had returned to Island Records for its distribution needs two months after *Avenue A* was released, Cartier's fate had already been sealed. A few weeks later, Cartier got a call from his manager, who told him he was being dropped from the label.

Cartier was understandably devastated. "I had gotten all this press, and then all of a sudden the rug was pulled out from under me," he says, his voice trailing off for a moment. "After working so hard for two and a half years and seeing the album so poorly mishandled, it was like I was being penalized.

"As cool as it was that Elton had signed me and taken a chance on me—and I appreciate that…but what I don't appreciate is that when I got dropped, to this day, I haven't heard anything from him, not even from an assistant to say, 'Sorry it didn't work out. Sorry we took two and half years of your life and left you stranded. Are you OK?'

"I say this with a lot of love, because I'm still a huge Elton John fan…and I think that everything happens for a reason, so obviously that situation wasn't meant to play itself out any other way or else it would have, but it was very hard."

"Are you always stumbling home,
just when the sun's about to rise?
With a headache in your pocket,
and sleep that hasn't graced your eyes?
Did the night pass by too quickly?
Too quick to feel them sympathize?
Are you always stumbling home, too tired to wipe off that disguise?"
—"Stumbling Home," Daniel Cartier

Depressed and unable to pick up his guitar following his departure from Rocket,

Cartier abandoned his music, started using drugs again, and barely managed to pay his bills by bartending and waiting tables. After a while of this, however, his musical instincts resurfaced and he began recording songs for what would become his next record, *Wide Outside,* which he released independently in 2001—then he promptly abandoned it. "I never really pushed that CD," he admits. "I just kind of recorded it as an experiment to see if I could record myself. It was wonderful for what it was, but in my opinion, it was wonderfully flawed."

Later, "the studio kept calling," says Cartier, and finally he had to heed its insistent holler. He wrote and wrote, then recorded, then wrote some more, carefully crafting a project that would eventually become the aptly titled disc *Revival,* which he released in March 2004. Cartier then started to play gigs to support the record. Calling on some of the industry players and music journalists he'd encountered during his days with Rocket, he began to work on creating a fresh buzz for himself. Soon after, he signed with the high-profile firm KSA Public Relations (whose clients include the likes of Lenny Kravitz and Sheryl Crow). In September, KSA relaunched *Revival* with a full-on media blitz, getting the album reviewed in major gay and lesbian publications and mainstream music magazines.

"Everybody wants to be loved by somebody.
Everybody wants to be someone's call.
Everybody wants to be loved by somebody.
But is anyone brave enough now to fall?
Everybody wants to be loved by somebody.
Everybody's wanting to feel that need.
Babe, I swear I just want to love somebody.
Cupid take that arrow and make me bleed."
—"Everybody Wants to Be Loved by Somebody," Daniel Cartier

Cartier says he doesn't worry that being labeled "a gay artist" might limit his chances of breaking through to the mainstream. "I kind of embrace [being categorized as gay] now, because it's one more thing to set me apart," he says. "America is ready to embrace a gay artist more wholeheartedly than it has up to this point. We still haven't had a breakout gay pop star who was open from the start. Rufus Wainwright has come close. It'd be great if I could be the one who did it."

Cartier's openness and acceptance of a publicly gay persona wasn't always a given. "I'm a lot more open now than I was a few years ago," he says, referring to his time with Rocket, where he recalls being told, " 'If [your sexuality] comes up in an interview,

fine, but don't bring it up and make a point of talking about it.'

"It was a different time," he says. "Reporters weren't eager to write stories about gay people, and it actually didn't come up as much in many interviews. But, like, please, I dated half of New York, so it's not like it was this big secret, so it was mentioned, particularly in the gay press."

Cartier says that while he has no problems being openly gay, he doesn't feel the need to limit his music by filling it with gender-specific pronouns. "I'm not against using them," he states. "I recorded 70 songs for *Revival,* and there are a few that have them ('Hey, Handsome Man,' 'Here He Comes,' 'Pretty Boy'). But I want my music to be universal. I am gay, but I want anybody to feel like they can relate to my music, because I'm also a human being.

"Do I feel like I need to be this big Pied Piper, like I need to run around draped by a rainbow flag? No, because, quite honestly, I think I'm doing a bigger service to the community by having all sorts of people embrace my music and then maybe find out after the fact, 'Oh, wow, he's gay? Well, I love that song.' I think in the long run, that does more good.

"I feel like my biggest responsibility is to create quality work, whether it's for the gays or the straights or just for humankind," he remarks, though he's quick to add, "But naturally, I always feel a soft spot in my heart for the gays, because I'm gay. And, I have to say, it's awesome to be up on the stage and sing a song like 'Lay It On' and have a cute boy in the audience that I can sing it to. That's a pretty cool perk of what I do."

"The weird thing about [the queercore scene] is that it is still a very small slice of life compared to when you think about gay culture in general," says Cartier. "That's what I've discovered from playing at gay pride events. Hearing about a band like the Butchies or the Bootlickers, and then realizing that the majority of gay people want to listen to heterosexual house divas. That's the sad truth." Like many other gay musicians struggling to make names for themselves, Cartier has experienced a frustrating lack of support from his own community when he has performed at various pride celebrations. He recounts an experience during his 2004 tour when he paid all his own expenses to play one particular pride event but was brushed aside so that pride officials could fawn over the event's headliner—a disco diva. "I figured it was a great opportunity to play in front of a bunch of gay people, and I wanted to be a part of it," he says. "They didn't pay, because all of their entertainment budget went to this house diva who warbled out three numbers to a prerecorded dance track. They pushed my performance back and pushed everybody else's performances around because she showed up and wanted to go on earlier than she was supposed to.

"The situation was insulting to me," he grumbles. "I'm like, 'I'm a gay artist. Shouldn't I be treated with respect too?' It sounds horrible, but gay pride makes me realize how much I sometimes hate gay [culture]. What am I proud of? Am I proud of the fact that sometimes we are so self-loathing that we need to look to heterosexual women to voice our feelings and we can't listen to another gay man sing a love song? I mean, I've noticed that a lot of straight men have an easier time listening to me than gay men. And I hope that's going to change. It's certainly not going to make me give up and not play to gay people, but I just thought that was really cheesy. It's like, why, for a gay pride celebration, wouldn't we give the extra-special treatment to the artists who are actually gay and out there struggling to get their voices heard? For me, it would have made a big difference."

Cartier says that such experiences prove that there is a need for something like the queercore music scene. "I think it's very important," he declares. "Like anything, it's very important for a community to have movements that get people together.

"Do I think of myself as a queercore

artist? Yeah, because I'm gay. But I also think of myself as just a musician, whether it's queercore or whether it's just great music that anyone can listen to.

"[The queercore scene] is obviously people who are there to listen to music," he says. "But do I think that queercore is just queer punk music? Not really. Queercore can mean a lot of different things. I think it means that it's very queer-identified, and it's also geared toward people who are still thinking outside the box.

"And in a way, going against the grain of what others think the movement is makes me even more a part of it, because it's a rebellion and an alternative. That's what homocore is all about."

"Life could be hate, spewing out of your face, towards everybody.
Life could be waste.
Life could be longing, but never daring to try.
Oh, life could just suck, and then we all die.
But I don't want to get all caught up in imagined misery.
Look again, there must be more to see."
—"Life Could Be," Daniel Cartier

"I don't know how I fit into rock music, to be honest with you," continues Cartier. "I guess I don't worry about that. I am who I am, and I've become much more comfortable with that over the years."

When asked what kind of a career he aspires to have, he is modestly ambitious. "I would love to have a career like Elton John's," he says. "He definitely put on a good show. I'm a singer-songwriter, and I write intelligent pop music, but I would love to turn on a classic rock station in 30 years from now and hear one of my songs. Do I want to be the biggest star of all time? No. I don't think what I'm doing would lend itself to that, but I do see myself as being able to build a following and maybe even have a hit at some point. I don't think that's out of the question."

Until then, he says, he is happy to merely provide his fans with music that speaks to them and gives them a sense of hope—not to mention helps him deal with his own demons. Recalling one traumatizing incident during his years in New York, he says he has learned that he can wield his guitar like a weapon against intolerance and bigotry. "I had seven big bad-ass guys beat the shit out of me when I was 19 just because I was gay," Cartier recounts. "They smashed a rock over my head, dragged me across the pavement, kicked me, and strangled me until I passed out. I guess, perhaps, they were trying to beat the gayness out of me.

Well…I hate to burst their bubbles, but guess what? It didn't work! I'm still here and I'm still really fucking gay.

"Oh! And one more thing," he says to those gay bashers with a mischievous twinkle in his eyes. "I have a microphone now, so watch out!"

CHAPTER 25

The Galaxy Is Gay

"I never wanted her like this.
I'm running out the door.
Gonna see a rock show now; gonna be so naive.
Smoking fags with fags with fags with fags."
—"17," the Butchies

ON A WINDY NIGHT IN HOLLYWOOD, INSIDE THE HIP MUSIC VENUE THE KNITTING FACTORY, THE BUTCHIES ARE PUTTING ON A SHOW ON THE MAINSTAGE. THE MODEST BUT ATTENTIVE CROWD IS MADE UP PREDOMINANTLY OF LESBIANS—BOTH FEMME AND BUTCH AND PEPPERED WITH A SMATTERING OF BABY BULLDYKES WHO DON'T YET HAVE QUITE ENOUGH CONFIDENCE TO REALLY PULL OFF THE FLATTOPS, DICKIES WORK JEANS, AND HIKING BOOTS THEY'RE SPORTING. THEY CLAP POLITELY AS THE BAND MEMBERS FINISH UP A KICKIN' RUN-THROUGH OF "SHE'S SO LOVELY," ONE OF THE SONGS FROM THEIR LATEST CD, *MAKE YR LIFE*, AS IF THEY'RE AFRAID TO EXPRESS THE OBVIOUS ADMIRATION THEY HAVE FOR THE THREE ENERGETIC ROCK AND ROLLERS ONSTAGE. THERE'S A SUBTLE JOY IN KNOWING THAT THESE YOUNG TEENAGE GIRLS ARE BEING AFFECTED IN BIG WAYS BY THE SHOW AT HAND.

There is also a handful of men in the audience—a few obviously gay, a few obviously straight. When the band's lead singer, Kaia Wilson, remarks on the preponderance of gay women in the audience, one of the hetero guys yells out, "Hey, I'm not a homosexual!"

"But we love you anyway!" drummer Melissa York quips as the crowd laughs along with her. Then, as if to drive her point home, she good-naturedly chides, "*You're* in the 10% tonight, buddy!"

The hetero dude laughs along with everyone else, cheering the band mates as they break into their next song, but a point has been made: *This is a queer music show, folks, and we're here to rock the house!*

"We've got sly moves, baby.
We are the numbers that knew.
Mark our words, we'll see you in the future.
Kiss your fashion goodbye.
We're for queer youth.
We're 'go union.'
We are pro-choice.
We are not scared by you."
—"More Rock, More Talk," the Butchies

Rewind to 1991, when the all-girl group called Team Dresch was part of the burgeoning "homocore" movement that began in San Francisco. Made up of bassist-guitarist Donna Dresch, singer-guitarist Jody Elizabeth Bleyle, singer-guitarist Kaia Wilson, and drummer Melissa York, the band quickly became established as the de facto riot grrrls of the queer rock scene with hard-rocking songs about girl-on-girl love and political outspokenness.

"It was a really cool time," Wilson recalls of the early homocore scene. "There was a lot of talk about feminism and queer activism, and it was all good. But I didn't understand how big it would become in some people's eyes."

Perhaps too big. "It kind of fucked us up in a way with starting the Butchies," York says, "because we had all these expectations of what it was going to be like."

Following the release of four well-received studio records, Team Dresch had run its course, and the band members decided to pursue other endeavors. Having bonded during the band's run, Wilson and York decided to stick together and form a new band, and they brought in Alison Martlew to sing and play bass. The Butchies were born in the spring of 1998. They wrote some songs, and immediately started looking to book shows. Their first gig was playing the birthday party of a friend's daughter. "It was really fun," Wilson recalls. "Then we just booked a tour that week."

Remembers York: "We got a van a week

before we left for that tour. An '84 Dodge Ram. We're still touring in the *same* van."

Within months, the girls had written enough for an album's worth of songs, and went into the studio to record 1998's *Are We Not Femme?* for North Carolina-based indie label Mr. Lady Records. Less anarchic and aggressive in tone than Team Dresch, the music was lighter, poppier, and more melodic, with little of the overtly lesbian themes that made Team Dresch so political. Not that the Butchies shied away from being out—the songs are still sung to or about other women, and with the band's punk-dyke look and song titles like "The Galaxy Is Gay," its members' sexual orientation was obvious.

As the band continued to tour and write new material, the Butchies began to establish a real presence—and 1999's *Population 1975* brought them even more acclaim and recognition. Building on the strengths of *Are We Not Femme?* the new CD rocked a little harder, sounded a little tighter, and brought politics back into the mix with "More Rock More Talk," a "protest song" (according to the lyrics) directed at other gay artists who attempt to "pass" as straight in order to achieve celebrity. ("Look at you with your straight lace / and your straight face and your Prada / Without feeling, you have no guts /You are empty.") 2001 brought the

release of *3*, on which the band recalled the alienation of growing up gay in a small town ("Junior High Lament") and rocked out in protest of violence against women ("For Kay"). The same year, the Butchies also appeared as the backup band for Indigo Girl Amy Ray on her solo debut, *Stag*. Yet, even with all the exposure and critical acclaim, the Butchies felt something was missing.

"We wanted to grow," York says of the period following the release of *3*. "We wanted to build a new audience. We definitely wanted to write some seriously fun songs and be happy."

The band members officially dropped "the" from the name, got serious about their career, changed record labels (they signed with fledging indie label YepRoc Records), and started writing new material. The resulting recording took three years to complete, but with the release of 2004's *Make Yr Life*, it became clear that Butchies had indeed grown up. The music is tighter and leaner than their previous efforts, with a much bigger nod to pop than punk—perhaps a reflection of Wilson's increasing fixation on seminal '70s rock band Cheap Trick. "We've gotten into Cheap Trick so much, it's kind of scary," Wilson jokes. (As a result of their manager's marketing savvy, the band received a special treat when they opened for Cheap Trick in the spring of 2004. "They wore our T-shirts onstage!" York exclaims with glee.)

"It took us a long time working on *Make Yr Life*," Wilson says. "A lot of the time when we go into recording, we feel rushed, and we're not able to weed out the weak songs, and we got to put in so much more time and thought and energy and pick the best songs we could do. I think we've all been able to stand back from a song and kind of analyze it and work on its arrangement. If something doesn't work, we figure out why. We're more able to craft a song."

"There was a lot of therapy and letting go," York adds. "There was no nurturing happening before, and I think we really nurtured this. And we got someone else [Greg Griffith] to produce us. We always wanted to be part of that, but this time we said, 'Produce us.' I'm really happy with the record."

Reviews of *Make Yr Life* were almost uniformly favorable, with most critics commenting on the band's improved technique and range. "The kind of versatility on which long, healthy careers are established," wrote *Billboard* magazine. Pansy Division front man Chris Freeman, in his review for *Frontiers,* said, "[The album] sounds great, and the mix is first-rate…Courtney [Love] can only wish to have a record this good, and somewhere, big sister Joan Jett is smiling." *Amplifier* touted the disc as a "damn fine rock and roll record," *Alternative Press* proclaimed it "as accessible as the Donnas, and just as sexy, regardless of your sexual preference," and *CMJ New Music Report* gushed, "If this is what punk rock sounds like when it grows up a little, more of those bands should trade in their training wheels."

And with that, Butchies officially arrived at the crossroads of Maturity and Validation.

"Come on, come on.
It's not like you enjoy it.
Don't wait for somebody to tell you that you don't know a thing about my life.
You don't know a fucking thing."
—"Ellen D.," the Butchies

The lyrics above—from *Are We Not Femme?*'s "Ellen D."—could easily be directed toward the review media. Though Butchies have received their share of glowing press and positive reviews like the ones above, there have been a few instances in which reviewers haven't been favorable toward them. "Luckily, we haven't had a whole lot of direct, overtly homophobic experiences. We've been very lucky," Wilson says. "It's been more on a wide level through reviews and certain people's attitudes toward us because we're queer and we're outspoken."

"And sometimes people just don't write about us," York adds. "They'll say there's no story there, and I'm saying, 'What are you talking about? We're three dykes, and we rock!'"

When journalists do come calling, it's sometimes with less than objective viewpoints. "There is a catch-22," says York when asked about the band's experience in dealing with the press. "I want people to write about us, but when all they do is focus on [our gender or sexual orientation] and they don't talk about the music, it's really annoying, like when the headline reads, 'Girls Who Can Rock.' *Of course* girls can fucking rock!"

Wilson has a slightly different take on the media. "On the one hand, I want the world to be there for the music," she says. "That's the reason why we're an out band and we're outspoken about it. It's because there's a lot of homophobia and hatred. So in terms of people writing about it, it sort of makes sense. Sometimes there's a positive to that, like 'Check out these dykes who rock!' It gives people more to grab onto."

Still, the band mates look forward to a day when rock writers find things to worry about other than who the band is sleeping with. "When the Vines get press, they don't get 'this straight band from Australia.' Why can't we just talk about the Butchies—that we rock?"

Wilson, for one, thinks the Butchies are perfectly suited for mainstream success—even if their visibility as lesbians makes that seem improbably. "Our music—pop/punk, it's melodic, it's catchy—is accessible; it's pretty good music, and I think it fits in with a lot of the stuff in the mainstream," she asserts. "But by the same token, we're definitely treated differently because we're out lesbians, and we definitely have a different perspective in relation to the world with music and with just the world as a whole because we're gay.

"Homophobia is just one of the things we deal with in our lives," she continues, "but it's an important thing. It ties us all together at one level. We definitely want to be in a queer band for a reason."

When asked how their music fits into the mainstream's seemingly limited appetite for outspokenly gay musicians in a hetero-defined genre, the girls are uniformly optimistic. "We're poised for a breakthrough," Wilson claims. "We're going to do it. We're trying to create a self-fulfilled prophecy by saying we want world domination in all our press and doing it our way, being exactly who we are and doing our thing and not changing anything." Citing gender-neutral hetero rock star Patti Smith as an example, Wilson adds, "There's always someone who changes the scope of things. That's going to be us."

"I don't care who defined rock music," adds York. "I'm ready to change that definition. It just takes four beats to rock."

"She's a rocker dressed like a killer.
She's got lips like wine, not sugar.
I'm running, running into timing.
Got a watch; it's stuck in shining.
She's so lovely, yeah, she's so lovely, yeah."
—"She's So Lovely," the Butchies

Unlike other queer bands, the Butchies say they don't feel a need to be politically oriented in their lyrics in order to portray themselves as activists for gays and lesbians. "I think activism can happen on so many different levels," Wilson says. "I think what we speak about and what we do and in the presentation of ourselves and how we reach out to the world in our shows is a form of activism."

The band's lyrics are more often focused on heartache and love than on politics and the culture wars—and that's the way the Butchies like it. "Most of the time I go very inside myself, into the ego," Wilson says of her writing. "It's not on purpose that I stay away from potently direct political topics.

"I want to be the Pat Benatar of queer rock," she goes on to say, "singing songs like 'Love Is a Battlefield,' but about a girl.

Singing love songs about girls is still considered to be pretty out there."

Indeed. As York adds, "We have a song called 'She's So Lovely,' and it's coming from a girl, so that in itself is pretty political."

Meanwhile, the group is happy to be included in the homocore movement, even if they're not sure what it is anymore. "I totally support the movement," York says. "I just don't know what it means."

"I like that there's an outspokenness about it, because people are still ashamed and embarrassed to talk about [being gay in music]," Wilson says. "I have a hard time with bands that don't want to be categorized as homocore, because I think that's internalized homophobia."

"Everyone has their own path," York counters. "And yeah, we could be taking the harder road by being out and outspoken, but this is something that is very important to us."

And important to their fans. As Wilson says, "We get a lot of letters from fans and kids coming up to us at shows and saying, 'Your music changed my life. I needed something queer.'"

Which leads to the topic of the responsibility openly queer musicians have to their audience. "What I hope for is different from what our responsibility actually is," Wilson says. "I don't think it's our responsibility to be outspoken rock and rollers, but that's what I want us to be. But I don't feel tied to that. If I wanted to become some New Age whale communicator, I wouldn't want the fans to tell me I couldn't do that."

"I want the queer people to support us, but when they shy away from us because we're so out, that hurts," York adds. "And with us being outspoken, there are certain things people expect from us. We're put into the role model category, and we have to be perfect. And perfect doesn't exist, so of course we're going to fail and fall on our face.

"Our last record is called *Make Yr Life,* and I feel that's what the Butchies are doing.

We're making our own lives to help others make theirs."

The band tries to temper the pressure that comes with the territory by simply concentrating on doing what they do best—rocking out with songs spun from the heart and giving them to their fans to enjoy and hopefully cherish. In fact, that ambition is what keeps the Butchies together.

"What drives us is the audience," York says. "When we have a really good show and the energy is crazy and some kid comes up to us and says we helped keep her from killing herself two years ago…that drives us."

CHAPTER 26

Homo on the Go: The Future of Queercore Rock

In rock music, one thing is certain: Nothing sticks around forever. Trends come and go, with newer, "hotter" things replacing what was once deemed hip. Over the years, "movements" such as disco and new wave reached soaring heights in their respective eras, but few had the legs to keep up their momentum. In the early '90s, the riot grrrl movement achieved a brilliant but brief apex, eventually giving way to more mainstream efforts when the movement's participants realized that performing with bands that actually made money wasn't necessarily "selling out." So where does that leave the homocore scene, a movement that arguably reached its pinnacle in the mid '90s with the almost-crossover success of Extra Fancy? Ask around, and it seems the future is unclear.

"Where is the queercore movement headed?" ponders Pansy Division's Chris Freeman. "I have no idea. I had no idea that there would even be a genre called 'queercore' when Pansy Division started, so thinking about a future for it at this point is folly. I think as long as there are infractions against our civil rights, then there will be something to rebel against, and queercore is a good forum for release and generating thoughts."

The last few years have seen many of the early homocore acts slowly die off. With Team Dresch, Tribe 8, Fifth Column, God Is My Co-Pilot, and Extra Fancy all long since disbanded, the torch has been passed to newer, more media-savvy youngsters who've been inspired by their predecessors—some who have stuck around, some who have not. While the Butchies are still going strong (and poised for a crossover of some kind with their increasingly muscular riffs and pop-punk melodies) and Pansy Division continues to evolve and grow musically in the band's 15th year together (the group's most recent CD— *Total Entertainment*—is by far its most accomplished record to date), incendiary bands like Los Angeles's Best Revenge and Slojack have already called it quits. It's nearly impossible to keep up with the revolving door of bands that come in and out of the scene.

Today, with new bands like Terazzo, Triple Creme, Boyskout, Sugarpuss, and the pansexual Scissor Sisters staking their claims in the movement and in the mainstream (the Sisters' self-titled debut was a number 1 hit in the United Kingdom and received a large heaping of favorable press in the States), it's

clear that queer musicians still have a need to share their experiences with other like-minded people. Perhaps the homocore scene hasn't worn out its welcome just yet. In fact, with our own Lollapalooza-esque touring venues like the Queercore Blitz Tour and our very own Woodstock (the biennial Homo a Go Go festival in Olympia, Wash.), it's obvious that the movement is here to stay—at least for a while.

Though many lament the glory days— when the idea of an underground community made up of creative types who shared a transgressive sexual orientation and political ideology was still fresh and the musicians were less jaded—some say that the movement is still just as important as ever. It's more urgently needed now, in fact, than it ever has been. "There comes a time in every queer man's and woman's life when they feel angry about the way that society and their families have handled their sexuality," says Los Angeles singer-songwriter Micah Barnes. "If they are rock and roll musicians speaking honestly about their experience, then that anger will find expression and could be considered queercore music no matter what form it may take in the future.

"Obviously," he continues, "there will always be the basic fact that growing up different sucks no matter which way you decide to personally triumph over it, and it's up to queer artists to claim their individuality as their own—and embrace its potential for informing the music that we create. Being different means we have to learn to love our own kind of noise. And that is indeed the stuff that great rock and roll in made of!"

Other queer musicians are very hopeful that the movement will, in fact, continue to grow and evolve so that it can keep inspiring even more new young artists to follow suit and create their own bands. "I think the queercore movement will continue to grow in America," says Boyskout's Leslie Satterfield. "There are a lot of great bands that are standing up and saying, 'Yes, I'm queer; yes, my band rocks; and yes, let's get together, make music, and have fun.' I think that the next generation of queer musicians will say, 'Yeah, we can do this too.'"

Brian Grillo, whose most recent musical venture eschews gay liberationist rhetoric in favor of more universal songwriting, says that he feels queercore can only survive if it is willing to break out of the homogeneous gay venues that have traditionally housed the movement's musical acts. "I think the movement is headed in a vital and healthy direction if bands like IAmLoved, Terazzo, and King Cheetah are any indication," he says. "I went to see Terazzo play at a hetero rock club and was blown away by how they totally won over the audience. I like the fact that these bands are breaking out of their comfort zone and playing to all kinds of audiences.

"I think gay venues have always been supportive of emerging queer artists," he adds, "but I think it is really important for those bands to get out and play in front of all kinds of diverse audiences to make their messages clear, and to continue to break down stereotypes and boundaries."

Other queercore artists feel that, until the gay population at large begins to treat its artists and musicians with respect, the movement will not be able to sustain itself. Says rocker Scott Free: "Along with many other queer musicians around the country, I'm pressuring gay pride festival organizers who book straight artists on the music stages to be more representative of our community. They are booking disco artists with the idea that disco somehow equals gay. I'm hoping that in challenging that concept, there will be more awareness in general of the LGBT community's need to support its musicians, no matter what genre of music it is." Citing Homo a Go Go and his own Queer Is Folk Festival in Chicago, Free notes that in the absence of validation from pride organizers, "members of the homocore community are taking it upon themselves to create scenes in their own cities."

While many people believe that the queercore scene has made great strides in its relatively short life, others feel that it is still experiencing a period of growing pains. "Musically, the core part of queercore is really dead to me," Chris Freeman says bluntly. "Punk as a genre is pretty tired. In its initial form, punk used to mean not sounding like anyone else. Now it means sounding as close to your idols as possible. That can only mean rehash."

Freeman does concede that there are a few new bands coming up in the scene that sound fresh, and it gives him hope for the future, though he still says, "They could easily use a bigger dose of individuality overall. As long as there are musicians willing to try on different styles of music to voice their opinions, then we have something to look forward to. Personally, I'm still hoping that queercore will have a place in history as a term for a type of music that was needed while getting our civil rights in line. Then, I want to be treated like the shamans were treated in Native American tribes, those who were outside the family-producing circle that were looked to for guidance and inspiration. We do have a lot to offer the rest of the population, and not just in fashion or hairstyles!"

Meanwhile, Kaia Wilson, who was a member of pioneering homocore band Team Dresch and now rocks with the Butchies, says that while she's not sure what kind of a "movement" still exists, she's still glad that there's an uprising of some kind out there. "I think it's important to have a community, something like queercore," she says. "I think being out about who you are, honest about who you are, and proud about who you are is important, and I think for queer people—as a group of people that is still struggling to gain equality—queercore is important in that respect. Some day, I hope it's not—or if it is, I hope it's not important for the same reasons."

When asked about the future of queercore, Wilson says that it's important for those involved in the community and those who are fans of it to look to the past for inspiration. "One thing that comes to me on a personal level is how there's this real serious line of inspiration," she says, "and how important it is for us to recognize that before us, there was somebody else that had a lot more obstacles upon them. And because they existed, it made it possible for us to do what we do."

By appreciating the pioneering men and women who blazed a trail for the queercore movement, Wilson says, we can find the inspiration to follow our own dreams and goals. "I always want to make sure to put the word out there into the world: Be really grateful for the people who made it better for you, even if those people made some mistakes too. Then just go for your fucking dream."

If gay rockers continue to shake, rattle, and roll over the archaic structure of rock music as aggressively as bands and musicians like Wilson and the Butchies, Pansy Division, Triple Creme, and Brian Grillo, homocore could become more than just a trendy catchphrase.

"The world wasn't ready for us then," Grillo says of Extra Fancy's time in the national spotlight in the mid '90s. "But look at how long the straight punk rock guys took to get into the mainstream. That didn't happen overnight. I do think that with this new [homocore] scene today and all these new bands coming up, it'll gradually happen. It'll happen naturally."

Will we one day be able to walk into Tower Records and ask, "Can you point me in the direction of the 'homocore' section?" Only time will tell. After all, just a few years ago, who would have thought that a misogynist, homophobic, blond-haired, blue-eyed, pasty-white kid from Detroit would become one of the most successful hip-hop artists in contemporary music?

THE SITES AND SOUNDS OF HOMOCORE

Fan Club: Lend an Ear to Hear Something Queer

LEARN MORE ABOUT THE BANDS IN THIS BOOK AND HEAR SAMPLES OF THEIR HARD-ROCKING HOMOCORE SONGS BY VISITING THEIR OFFICIAL WEB SITES.

BANDS AND MUSICIANS

Micah Barnes
www.micahbarnes.com

Boyskout
www.boyskout.com

Best Revenge
www.spitshinerecords.com

The Butchies
www.thebutchies.com

Bonfire Madigan
www.bonfiremadigan.com

Daniel Cartier
www.danielcartier.com

Vaginal Crème Davis
www.vaginaldavis.com

The Dead Betties
www.thedeadbetties.com

Evil Beaver
www.ridethebeaver.com

Fagatron
www.geocities.com/jo6512/
Fagatronpg.html

Scott Free
www.scottfree.net

Gina Young + the Bent
www.ginayoung.com
Brian Grillo
www.spitshinerecords.com

Human Hands
www.humanhands.com

IAmLoved
www.iamloved.00band.com

Alla Ivanchikova
www.allarocks.com

G.B. Jones/Fifth Column
www.queer-arts.org/archive/show3/
jones/jones.html

God Is My Co-Pilot
www.allan.hise.org/godco

Lip Kandy
www.lipkandy.com

Kelly Mantle
www.KellyMantle.com

Glen Meadmore
www.pervertidora.com/Bands/
GlenMeadmore/index.ph

Bob Mould
www.bobmould.com

Mutilated Mannequins
www.mutilatedmannequins.com

Nick Name and the Normals
www.nicknameandthenormals.com

Pansy Division
www.pansydivision.com

Linda Perry
www.lindaperry.com

Radio Berlin
www.radio-berlin.com

Amy Ray
www.daemonrecords.com/beta/
amy/amy.html

Sex With Lurch
www.saintthomasrecords.com/
SexWithLurch.htm

Skinjobs
www.agitproprecords.com/skinjobs

SöuR
www.sourweb.com

Sugarpuss
www.sugarpuss.net

Super 8 Cum Shot
www.supereightcumshot.com

Team Dresch
www.members.aol.com/ringard/team.htm

Terazzo
www.spitshinerecords.com

Three Dollar Bill
www.threedollar.net

Tom Robinson Band
www.tomrobinson.com
Tribe 8
www.tribe8.com

Triple Creme
www.triplecreme.com

Alicia Warrington
www.aliciawarrington.com

MUSIC FESTIVALS

Bent Festival
www.thetanknyc.com/bent

Homo a Go Go Festival
www.homoagogo.com

Ladyfest
www.ladyfest.org

Lesbopalooza
uoregon.edu/~women/lesbopalooza.htm

Queercore Blitz Tour
www.queercoreblitz.com

Scutterfest
www.spitshinerecords.com/scutterfest

Yoyo a Go Go
buyolympia.com/yoyo/sid=628387993

RECORD LABELS

Agitprop! Records
www.agitproprecords.com

Chainsaw Records
www.chainsaw.com

Daemon Records
www.daemonrecords.com

Dischord Records
www.dischord.com

Heartcore Records
www.heartcorerecords.net

K Records
www.kpunk.com

Kill Rock Stars Records
www.killrockstars.com

Lookout Records
www.lookoutrecords.com

Spitshine Records
www.spitshinerecords.com